The Go-To Guide for
ENGINEERING CURRICULA, Grades 6–8

Choosing and Using the Best Instructional
Materials for Your Students

EDITED BY
CARY I. SNEIDER

CORWIN
A SAGE Company

FOR INFORMATION:

Corwin

A SAGE Company

2455 Teller Road

Thousand Oaks, California 91320

(800) 233-9936

www.corwin.com

SAGE Publications Ltd.

1 Oliver's Yard

55 City Road

London EC1Y 1SP

United Kingdom

SAGE Publications India Pvt. Ltd.

B 1/I 1 Mohan Cooperative Industrial Area

Mathura Road, New Delhi 110 044

India

SAGE Publications Asia-Pacific Pte. Ltd.

3 Church Street

#10-04 Samsung Hub

Singapore 049483

Printed in the United States of America

ISBN 978-1-4833-0737-4

Acquisitions Editor: Robin Najar

Associate Editor: Julie Nemer

Editorial Assistant: Ariel Price

Production Editor: Amy Schroller

Copy Editor: Liann Lech

Typesetter: C&M Digitals (P) Ltd.

Proofreader: Dennis W. Webb

Indexer: Judy Hunt

Cover Designer: Gail Buschman

Marketing Manager   Amanda Boudria

This book is printed on acid-free paper.

14 15 16 17 18 10 9 8 7 6 5 4 3 2 1

The Go-To Guide for

ENGINEERING CURRICULA, Grades 6–8

Contents

Foreword

Janet L. Kolodner
Georgia Institute of Technology

I have a dream. Nearly all of our youngsters will graduate high school, and nearly all will be excellent readers, manipulate numbers and estimate easily, be able to argue a point using trustworthy evidence to back it up, make decisions informed by common knowledge, solve complex problems well, understand how scientists and engineers reason and be able to do some of that reasoning themselves, express themselves articulately, work well with others, recognize what they know and when they need to learn more, have passionate opinions backed by knowledge, and appreciate the roles they might take on (and love to engage in) as productive adults.

By middle school, students will begin to have some idea of the kinds of employment in which they might want to engage as adults, and as a result of the experiences they are having in school and at home, they will evolve their interests over time and develop mature passions as they move through high school and beyond, imagining what they might be or be doing as adults, working toward aligning themselves with some of these possibilities, deciding they are interested in some and not interested in others, and eventually identifying how they will live their lives and achieve their goals. Some will be scientists or engineers, some will be writers or expressive artists, some will provide services, some will be technicians, but all will be gainfully employed doing something they want to be doing.

Plenty of research on how people learn suggests that engaging learners in achieving engineering challenges that they are personally interested in and capable of solving successfully (with help) can go a long way toward fulfilling my dream, which I hope you share. You can play an essential role in your students' lives by engaging them in design challenges that are relevant to their personal interests and helping them to extract lessons from their work about how to define and solve problems and to imagine themselves as grownups who can solve important problems in the real world. A tall order, for sure, but not an impossible one. It won't happen tomorrow, and it won't happen at all if we don't seriously take on the challenge.

There are many reasons to be optimistic about the role design challenges can play in helping our youngsters grow and learn. First, it is not hard to make engineering design challenges fun, and it is not hard to help students see the value of math and science in their everyday lives if they are using disciplinary knowledge to address challenges they recognize as important. Achieving complex design challenges will not be easy fun for students, but if they are interested enough, they will put in the hard work. And if they see the value in what they are doing and learning and experience the success of learning and using science, more might enjoy science; more might see themselves as people who can engage well in thinking scientifically; more might understand the role science plays in our everyday world; more might become scientists, engineers, technicians, or policymakers who use science; and more might engage, during their adult lives, in thinking scientifically at times when that is appropriate.

Second, we know that developing deep understanding and masterful capabilities is hard and requires considerable time, but we also know that when people are really interested in what they are learning or in what they are attempting to do, and if the expectations are not so far beyond their capabilities that activities are overly frustrating, then they are willing to put in the time and effort. Learning something well, whether we are gaining understanding or learning how to do something, requires time and patience; it requires that we try our best to understand or achieve a challenge, that we pay attention to results and judge what is successful and not as successful, that we work on explaining when we don't understand something well or when we are not as successful as we want at solving a problem, that we develop new ideas and understandings, and that we have chances to try again (and fail again, and so on).

Achieving engineering design challenges provides opportunities for doing all of these things—trying and not quite getting it right, observing what happens, explaining, developing new understandings, and trying again. When a science class is achieving engineering challenges together, the teacher and class can work as a unit to provide the help everyone in the class needs to engage successfully in all of these processes. Not every student in the class will learn everything in depth or become masterfully adept at all skills and practices, but engaging together as a class in achieving engineering design challenges makes the classroom a place to help all students achieve as well as they can.

Third, engineering design challenges provide opportunities to use science, engage in carrying out disciplinary practices, engage in engineering design practices, and engage in 21st-century skills. When students get excited about achieving a challenge, they will want to develop the necessary skills well enough to be able to achieve the challenge; if they need each other's advice, they will want to learn how to give good advice and take advice well; and if they are working on a challenge that requires several kinds of expertise or perspective, they will want to learn to collaborate well. When a class engages in engineering design together, there are opportunities to reflect on and discuss how to carry out skills and practices well, and when students are eager to achieve the engineering design goal, they will also be eager to know how to do whatever is necessary to achieve that goal; they will take the time to reflect on what they are doing and work on refining the way they carry out processes if time is set aside for that and appropriate help is given.

Fourth, we know that learners become more engaged and interested and willing to work hard when they are able to take on agency, that is, when they are trusted to make choices. There are rarely optimal choices in achieving engineering goals; engineers are constantly involved in making trade-offs, and several engineers working on the same real-world problem might come up with very different designs. The context of achieving engineering design challenges is perfect for allowing learners agency. When different groups suggest different solutions, have a chance to present and justify their solutions for the class, and have a chance to argue with each other using evidence, learning opportunities are enhanced for everybody in the class, as each group gets to experience and think about not only its own ideas but also the ideas of others.

Finally, when learners are allowed to try on the shoes of scientists and engineers, they also can begin to imagine themselves in those shoes. Students who are helped to be successful student scientists and student engineers, as they are asked to do in achieving engineering design challenges, will also begin to develop understandings of the kinds of activities they enjoy and the kinds of work they might want to do later in life. If the set of challenges they attempt is large, encompassing a large variety of disciplines, life situations, and roles they might take on, they will have solid foundations on which to build in imagining their futures.

Everything we know about how people learn and how to promote learning suggests that engaging our young people in achieving engineering challenges and solving engineering problems has potential to promote deep science learning and mastery of important disciplinary and life skills. The Next Generation Science Standards (NGSS Lead States, 2013), in encouraging curriculum approaches that foster learning STEM skills and practices along with science content, give school systems and teachers permission to move in that direction.

* * *

This book documents 14 sets of curriculum materials that integrate engineering design as a part of science. Although these materials were developed before publication of the NGSS, the authors of these chapters explain ways that they can be used today to support the NGSS at the middle school level. And nearly all will be fine tuned in the years to come as developers gain further experience with the NGSS.

Each of the chapters illustrates different ways that engineering design can help achieve my dream, starting with *Chapter 1, Design Squad*, about hands-on activities by the creators of a television series that "aims to inspire its young viewers—to show that engineering is accessible, doable, and most of all, fun." Reruns of the series showing students solving engineering design challenges are available on the web, along with hands-on activities related to each of the episodes.

Chapter 2, Models in Technology and Science, engages students in a number of complex design challenges in which they build and refine windmills and water wheels, structures made of drinking straws, and tops and yo-yos made from plastic plates and rubber stoppers. Developing these working models takes time and considerable effort, so success is deeply satisfying. Like several of the curriculum materials in this book, *Models in Technology and Science* is appropriate for school or after school and for summer learning experiences.

In *Chapter 3, Everyday Engineering*, students can see that science and engineering are all around them, as they reverse-engineer everyday objects to see how they function. With topics such as "What Makes a Bic™ Click?" and "Times Up, Turkey: Pop-up Thermometers" students discover the science behind everyday items and imagine how they might be improved with a thoughtful redesign.

The *SLIDER* curriculum, described in Chapter 4, enables students to step into the shoes of scientists and engineers as they build and modify high-tech LEGO® robotic vehicles and then use their vehicles to solve important real-world challenges, such as investigating a dangerous intersection to figure out how to avert future accidents.

It's not only students that need support. Teachers also need encouragement and ideas, which are abundant in *Chapter 5, Teaching Engineering Made Easy*. The two books discussed in the chapter include activities that do not require a formal science lab and can be done with inexpensive materials that are easy to find.

The connections between forces and kinetic energy are brought into sharp focus in *Chapter 6, Fender Bender Physics,* in which students design and race model cars powered by mousetraps and carbon dioxide cartridges. The goal is not just to design cars that go fast, but to figure out how to design them so that they avoid rollovers and protect their "passengers" in case of accidents.

We know from research that learning is greatly enhanced when learners are encouraged to think beyond what might be obvious solutions, present and justify their solutions to their fellow students, and have a chance to argue with each other about the best possible solution. The purposes of such discussions are for students to learn to use evidence to critically evaluate their own ideas and listen critically and respectfully to the ideas of others. That is the kind of experience described in *Chapter 7, Technology in Practice: Applications and Innovations,* in which students design and debate alternative solutions to such real environmental problems as garbage dumps, oil spills, and air pollution.

Engineering in Investigating and Questioning our World through Science and Technology (IQWST), described in Chapter 8, engages students in design challenges inspired by driving questions that help them discover the scientific principles that underlie everyday technologies. For example, students design and build Rube Goldberg–like devices to explore the question "Why do some things stop and others keep going?" In another module, students make soap and improve the recipe as they consider the question "How can I make new stuff from old stuff?"

Chapter 9, Project-Based Inquiry Science (my own contribution to this book), describes a full three-year middle school science curriculum that engages students in both scientific investigations and engineering design challenges. In their roles as student engineers and scientists, learners move through the full cycles of reasoning in which engineers and scientists engage when they address pressing real-world challenges. Some challenges are local (e.g., improving the quality of the air in their own community), whereas others are more global (e.g., designing a new variety of rice that will grow under new climate conditions), and others are just fun (e.g., designing and building a small vehicle that can navigate a terrain). All are designed to appeal to the interests and passions of middle schoolers, and all engage learners in iterative cycles of asking questions, investigating, explaining, arguing, collaborating, reflecting, and more.

In *Chapter 10, Engineering Design in SEPUP's Middle School Issue-Oriented Science Program,* students learn science to help them design solutions to environmental issues. For example, they study the structure of the Earth in order to gain the knowledge they need to identify potential sites for the safe storage of radioactive waste over tens of thousands of years. In another unit, they investigate properties of rocks and minerals and consider the relative value of mined versus manufactured diamonds.

Chapter 11, Techbridge: Engaging Girls in STEM in Out-of-School Time, is aimed at expanding the representation of women and underrepresented minorities in STEM. Instructional guides and materials kits help Girl Scout volunteers and community leaders engage in design projects to make the world a better place. For example, in after-school clubs and summer camps, middle school-age youth design toys made from recycled waste materials.

In *Chapter 12, Waterbotics*®, students design and build robots that travel underwater. Building a successful robot is a very challenging task, but students are guided in developing their robots one step at a time so that they achieve success as they develop technological skills and learn how their robot functions.

Engineering Now, presented in Chapter 13, is a series of enrichment guides that introduces students to a wide variety of engineering careers. Each module focuses on a different kind of engineering, from mechanical and electrical engineers to transportation, agricultural, and pharmaceutical engineers. Students engage in activities that provide insight into the kinds of problems that these different sorts of engineers solve in the real world.

Engineering by Design, featured in Chapter 14, is part of a sequence of activities, kits, and courses for children starting in prekindergarten through Grade 12. In the three-course middle school sequence, students learn about the history of technology; the complex technological systems on which modern civilization depends; and how technology, innovation, design, and engineering are interrelated and interdependent. Students are challenged to improve technological systems in ways that not only solve a problem they have identified, but also are acceptable to society.

* * *

It will not be easy to make traditional classrooms into engineering design classrooms. Some students who are used to reading and answering questions will balk at having to work hard; other students for whom learning comes easy will balk at having to work collaboratively with their classmates. If you are new to engineering education, you will have to learn new ways of interacting with students and facilitating learning. It does not take long to draw students in if challenges are meaningful to them and if they are trusted with agency, but it will take a special effort to develop new ways of interacting with your students.

If this is your first time teaching engineering, you may not be as successful as you want immediately, but don't worry. As you learn to be a better facilitator of the engineering design process, your students will learn more deeply. If possible, work together with other teachers who are also learning to implement engineering or other project-based activities in their classrooms. And just as your students will be learning a new approach by attempting to solve a problem but not quite succeeding, getting help in understanding why their first approach didn't work, then redesigning and trying again, it is very likely that you will go through a similar sequence of stages in your teaching. It will take time and willingness to work through possibly frustrating attempts to enact very different kinds of activities than you are used to, but it will be worthy and worthwhile work.

* * *

The many chapters in this collection provide advice and resources for using design challenges and problems to promote science learning. I hope that the chapters help readers develop imagination about integrating engineering design and problem-solving experiences into science classes, passion for moving forward to implement engineering design activities in their classrooms, and understanding of the conditions under which integrating such activities into our classrooms will lead to deep learning.

Choosing which of these instructional materials are right for you and your students is, of course, a huge part of the challenge. But it should be possible to identify likely candidates by reading the first three or four pages of each chapter, then reading the complete chapter for those that are most likely to meet your needs. As you do that, you might keep in mind several thoughts:

- Good education is not about "covering the material." Developing deep understanding and masterful capabilities is hard and requires considerable time. It is more important that students spend significant time on a few projects than that they do a lot of brief activities that cover a wide variety of topics.

- In order to sustain your students' interests over time, it is essential for projects to be sufficiently interesting and diverse to maintain your students' attention. Resources will provide some advice about how to do that, but you know your students better than curriculum developers; use your judgment to help problems come alive for your students, and if you see interest waning, figure out how to bring interest back. It's not hard to keep youngsters excited about things that impact their world and that help them experience worlds they've become familiar with from TV or the movies, but sometimes they need to be reminded why they are doing what they are doing.

- Judging the difficulty of a task will require your best judgment as a teacher. The requirements of a task should not be so difficult that it becomes frustrating and students give up. Conversely, if what they are asked to do is too easy, students will not have opportunities to develop new skills or gain confidence in their abilities to tackle and solve really challenging problems. Some materials allow you to modify the level of the challenge to meet your students' needs.

- Opportunities for teamwork are evident in every one of these sets of materials. However, some are more explicit than others about how to manage teams and help students learn to work together effectively. What is important to remember is that working in teams should not be seen just as a way of managing the classroom, but rather, it is important for students to come to appreciate the benefits of collaboration and learn how to collaborate well. Help your students identify the understanding and capabilities they are gaining from teamwork and help them develop collaboration habits that they use and further develop across curriculum units and projects.

- Many of the materials described in this book expose students to the world of technology and a wide variety of career possibilities. Helping students recognize those possibilities provides a way of keeping them engaged and will aim students toward goals that are part of my dream (and I hope yours).

- In choosing materials to use in your classroom, remember that in addition to choosing particular curriculum units for the targeted content they address and the interests of your students, it is important that your students experience and appreciate the big ideas of science and technology. Curriculum materials used over a year or several years of school should build on each other in ways that allow learners to see the connections between topical areas and to exercise and develop their capabilities. Help your students see across curriculum units as well as digging deep into the content and skills targeted in each one.

I offer my best wishes and congratulations on all of your efforts! I will be cheering for all of you and looking forward to meeting your many learned and mature-thinking students and experiencing the success of your endeavors in the decades to come.

— Janet L. Kolodner, November 2, 2013

Reference

NGSS Lead States. (2013). *Next Generation Science Standards: For states, by states. Volume 1: The standards* and *Volume 2: Appendices.* Washington, DC: National Academies Press.

 **Janet L. Kolodner** is Regents' Professor at Georgia Institute of Technology, where she served as coordinator of the cognitive science program for many years. Dr. Kolodner was founding director of Georgia Tech's EduTech Institute, whose mission is to use what we know about cognition to inform the design of educational technology and learning environments. Dr. Kolodner is founding Editor in Chief of *The Journal of the Learning Sciences*, an interdisciplinary journal that focuses on learning and education. She is also a founder of the International Society for the Learning Sciences, and she served as its first Executive Officer. Her research has addressed issues in learning, memory, and problem solving, both in computers and in people. Dr. Kolodner's book, *Case-Based Reasoning*, synthesizes work across the field. Dr. Kolodner has focused most of her research on using the model of case-based reasoning to design science curricula for middle school, in which students learn science and scientific reasoning in the context of designing working artifacts. More recently, she and her students are applying what they've learned about design-based learning to informal education—after-school programs, museum programs, and museum exhibits. The goal of these projects is to identify ways of helping children and youth consider who they are as thinkers and to come to value informed decision making and informed production and consumption of evidence.

Acknowledgments

First and foremost, I wish to thank the authors of these chapters, not only for taking the time to craft a compelling description of their curricula, but also for the foresight and persistence that it took to develop instructional materials in engineering, long before there were standards to support their efforts.

Recalling my early education that technology and engineering are allied with science, but are also different in important ways, I want to acknowledge my early mentors—Robert Maybury, Harold Foecke, and Alan Friedman—as well as the leaders of the National Center for Technological Literacy at the Museum of Science in Boston, including especially Ioannis Miaoulis, Yvone Spicer, Peter Wong, and Christine Cunningham, and the many teachers and administrators in Massachusetts who were among the early adopters of what we now call Integrated STEM education.

I also appreciate the support of colleagues at Achieve, Inc., including the writers of the *Next Generation Science Standards*; Stephen Pruitt, who led the effort; the brilliant and supportive staff; and the members of the NGSS Lead State Teams, for their steadfast dedication to crafting standards that fully embrace engineering as an equal partner to science. The current leadership of Achieve, Inc. is commended for granting permission for us to quote extensively from the NGSS.

Thanks also to the extraordinary personnel at the National Research Council, including the committee members and staff who developed *A Framework for K–12 Science Education: Practices, Crosscutting Concepts, and Core Ideas* and members of the Board on Science Education, especially Helen Quinn, Linda Katehi, Heidi Schweingruber, Tom Keller, Martin Storksdiek, and Michael Feder, who played crucial roles in the development of new science education standards.

Senior staff of the National Academies Press have also contributed to this work and to science education more broadly by making available free of charge the Framework and Next Generation Science Standards, along with many other important science education reports. The Press has given its permission to quote freely from the *Framework* and has asked us to publicize the availability of both the free downloads and hardcopy versions of the Framework and NGSS at its website: http://www.nap.edu/catalog.php?record_id=13165.

Worthy of special thanks is the generosity of Jan Morrison, President and CEO of Teaching Institute for Excellence in STEM (TIES), whose major gift provided substantial support for this effort, and to the leadership of Corwin, who also provided financial support above and beyond the costs of publishing.

I also want to acknowledge Robin Najar, Julie Nemer, Amy Schroller, and Liann Lech, my editors at Corwin; editorial assistant, Ariel Price; and the many other people at Corwin who made this set of volumes possible, as well as David Vernot, a consultant at the Butler County Educational Service Center in Hamilton, OH, who volunteered to be an additional critical reader.

Although it is somewhat unusual for an editor to thank his readers, I also want to acknowledge your courage for being among the first to help bring the new world of STEM learning into being.

—Cary Sneider, Editor, August 1, 2014

Publisher's Acknowledgments

Corwin wishes to acknowledge the following peer reviewers for their editorial insight and guidance.

Joan Baltezore, Science Instructor
West Fargo High School
West Fargo, ND

Arthur H. Camins, Director
Stevens Institute of Technology/CIESE
Charles V. Schaefer School of Engineering
Hoboken, NJ

Kelly Cannon, K–12 Science Program Coordinator
Washoe County School District
Reno, NV

Mandy Frantti, Physics/Astronomy/Mathematics Teacher
NASA Astrophysics Educator Ambassador
Munising Middle-High School
Munising, MI

Loukea Kovanis-Wilson, Chemistry Instructor
Clarkston Community Schools
Clarkston, MI

Sara Stewart, Educational Technology Specialist
Washoe County School District
Reno, NV

About the Editor

 **Cary I. Sneider** is Associate Research Professor in the Center for Science Education at Portland State University in Portland, Oregon, where he teaches research methodology to teachers in a master's degree program. In recent years, he served the National Research Council as design lead for technology and engineering to help develop *A Framework for K–12 Science Education: Practices, Crosscutting Concepts, and Core Ideas*, which has provided the blueprint for Next Generation Science Standards (NGSS). He then played a similar role on the writing team to produce the NGSS, which was released in April 2013. The recognition that teachers would need access to instructional materials to help them meet the new standards led Cary to develop the current volume, *The Go-To Guide for Engineering Curricula*.

Cary was not always interested in engineering—or at least he didn't know that he was. For as long as he can remember, he was interested in astronomy. He read all he could find about it, and when he was in middle school, his father bought him a small telescope. In high school, Cary built his own telescopes, grinding mirrors and designing and building mountings. All this time, he thought he was doing *science*. Today, he recognizes that like many scientists, he especially enjoyed the *engineering* part of the work.

During his junior year at college, Cary had an opportunity to teach at an Upward Bound program and found that he enjoyed teaching even more than research in astronomy. In subsequent years, he taught science in Maine; Costa Rica; Coalinga, California; and the Federated States of Micronesia. He returned to college, this time to obtain a teaching credential and eventually a PhD degree in science education from the University of California at Berkeley. He spent nearly 30 years in Berkeley, developing instructional materials and running teacher institutes at the Lawrence Hall of Science. He spent another decade as Vice President at the Museum of Science in Boston, where he developed a high school curriculum called Engineering the Future, and finally moved to Portland, Oregon, to be closer to children and grandchildren.

Over his career, Cary directed more than 20 federal, state, and foundation grant projects, mostly involving curriculum development and teacher education. His research and development interests have focused on helping students and museum visitors unravel their misconceptions in science, finding new ways to link science centers and schools to promote student inquiry, and integrating engineering and technology education into the K–12 curriculum. In 1997, he received the Distinguished Informal Science Education award from NSTA and in 2003 was named National Associate of the National Academy of Sciences for his service on several National Research Council committees.

About the Contributors

Celeste Baine is the Director of the Engineering Education Service Center and the award-winning author of more than 20 books on engineering careers and education. She won the Norm Augustine Award from the National Academy of Engineering and the Engineering Dean Council's Award for the Promotion of Engineering Education and Careers from ASEE, and she is listed on the National Engineers Week website as one of 50 engineers you should meet. She has also been named one of the Nifty-Fifty individuals who have made a major impact on the field of engineering by the USA Science and Engineering Festival.

Roy Q. Beven is a Distinguished Alumnus of the School of Physical Sciences at UC Irvine. For more than 20 years, Roy taught physics, mathematics, and technology education in secondary schools. Roy received the Presidential Award for Excellence in Science and Mathematics Teaching for California. In addition to *Fender Bender Physics*, Roy has been on writing teams for many instructional materials, including *Move With Science* and *Seismic Sleuths*. Starting in 2001, Roy led the development of the science assessment system for Washington State based on scenarios about investigations, systems, and engineering design. Roy is working on assessment while maintaining his professional service with the Washington Science Teachers Association (WSTA).

Brooke N. Bourdélat-Parks, PhD, is a science educator at BSCS. In this role, she works on both curriculum development and professional development projects. As a curriculum developer, she has worked on projects for elementary, middle, and high school students in science and technology, including *Technology in Practice: Applications and Innovations, BSCS Middle School Science*, and *BSCS Biology: A Human Approach*. Brooke has conducted professional development on inquiry, specific curricula, leadership, practices of science and STEM, and curriculum development in a variety of schools and districts. She is the Academy Director for BSCS's STEM leadership academy. Brooke holds a PhD in biology/molecular genetics.

Barry N. Burke, DTE, is the Director of the International Technology and Engineering Educators Association's (ITEEA, formerly ITEA) STEM Center for Teaching and Learning. His work includes the development of standards-based professional development, curriculum, assessment, and research related to the Standards for Technological Literacy. Currently, he coordinates a consortium of 20 states that collaborate on the development and implementation of curriculum, instruction, and assessment through the Engineering byDesign™ (EbD™) K–12 standards-based model program. He was the founder of the EbD™ program in 2005. Prior to ITEEA, he was a curriculum director, supervisor, resource teacher, and teacher for the Montgomery County Public Schools (MD).

Arthur Camins is Director of the Center for Innovation in Engineering and Science Education (CIESE) at Stevens Institute of Technology. He was Executive Director of the Gheens Institute for Innovation in the Jefferson County public schools in Louisville, Kentucky. As Elementary Math and Science Director for the Hudson Public Schools in Massachusetts, he was Principal Investigator of two successful NSF projects, Formative Assessment in Science Through Technology and Critical MASS. In New York City, he was Associate Director of the New York City Urban Systemic Initiative and Principal Investigator for Science in the Seamless Day in CSD 16 in Bedford Stuyvesant.

Ruta Demery received her degree in science from the University of Toronto (U of T) and her degree in education from the Ontario Institute of Studies in Education at U of T. She has been involved in education as a middle school and high school teacher, a teacher's college associate, and a curriculum developer and writer of numerous middle school and high school science and mathematics programs. Recently, she has been the product development editor and contributing writer for many of It's About Time's middle school and high school science programs, including Project-Based Science Inquiry (PBIS) and the PBIS CyberPD website.

Susan Everett is Associate Professor of Science Education and Chair of the Department of Education in the College of Education, Health, and Human Services at the University of Michigan–Dearborn. Dr. Everett is the co-author of the featured column "Everyday Engineering" in the National Science Teachers Association middle-level journal, *Science Scope*. A compilation of the articles has been published by NSTA Press, *Everyday Engineering: Putting the E in STEM Teaching and Learning*. Dr. Everett regularly teaches science methods courses, graduate-level research courses, and inquiry-based earth science classes.

David Fortus develops learning environments that foster transferable learning. He investigates the factors that influence the motivation to engage with science both in and out of schools. He has received awards from the National Association for Research in Science Teaching and from the American Psychological Association for his research on Design-Based Science. His publications range from science education to theoretical physics to legal economics. He is an associate editor of the *Journal of Research in Science Teaching*. Before becoming a researcher, he was a high school physics teacher and a project director in the aerospace industry.

Linda Kekelis is Executive Director of Techbridge. She has a master's degree in linguistics from the University of Southern California and a doctorate in special education from the University of California, Berkeley. With more than 20 years of experience leading girls' programs, Dr. Kekelis participates in advisory boards, collaborates with girl-serving organizations, and works with professional groups and corporate partners to promote females' participation in science, technology, and engineering. She conducts research, participates in national conferences, and writes, translating research into practical applications for educators, professionals, and parents.

Janet L. Kolodner's research addresses learning, memory, and problem solving in computers and people. She pioneered the computer method called case-based reasoning and uses its cognitive model to design formal and informal science curricula. Learning by Design, her design-based, inquiry-oriented approach to science learning, is a foundation of Project-Based Inquiry Science (PBIS), a 3-year middle school science curriculum. In her informal science education endeavors, middle schoolers learn science through cooking and learn to explain while designing hovercraft. She is founding Editor in Chief of *Journal of the Learning Sciences* and a founder of the International Society for the Learning Sciences.

Joseph Krajcik is Director of the CREATE for STEM Institute and a faculty member in science education at Michigan State University. His research has focused on working with science teachers to reform science teaching practices to promote students' engagement in and learning of science. He served as lead writer for developing Physical Science Standards for the NGSS and the lead writer for the Physical Science Design team for *A Framework for K–12 Science Education*. He served as president of the National Association for Research in Science Teaching, from which he received the Distinguished Contributions to Science Education through Research Award.

Mercedes McKay is Deputy Director of the Center for Innovation in Engineering and Science Education (CIESE) at Stevens Institute of Technology. She has led several national and statewide K–12 teacher professional development and curriculum development programs in STEM education. Ms. McKay is Project Director and co-Principal Investigator for the National Science Foundation-sponsored *Build IT Scale Up* project to develop and disseminate an innovative underwater robotics curriculum for middle and high school students. She is a former practicing engineer and has taught high school science and mathematics.

Emily McLeod is the Director of Curriculum at Techbridge. She works with program coordinators, teachers, and youth to develop science, technology, and engineering activities that are engaging and fun. Prior to joining Techbridge, she worked for more than ten years as a curriculum developer at Education Development Center.

Richard Moyer is Emeritus Professor of Science Education and Natural Sciences at the University of Michigan–Dearborn. He coauthors a column for NSTA's *Science Scope* called "Everyday Engineering" that focuses on engineering and science concepts related to common items like ballpoint pens and popup turkey timers. NSTA Press has published a compilation of these columns as a book. Dr. Moyer is also the author of many publications and books, including a college text on inquiry, *Teaching Science as Investigations: Modeling Inquiry Through Learning Cycle Lessons,* and is one of the senior authors of McGraw-Hill's elementary textbook series *Science: A Closer Look.*

Barbara Nagle directs SEPUP at the University of California, Berkeley's Lawrence Hall of Science. She has developed many secondary science curricula and professional development programs. She has a PhD in cell biology from the University of Pennsylvania. Before joining SEPUP, she taught high school science in Oakland, CA.

Mike Ryan is on the research faculty at the Georgia Institute of Technology's Center for Education Integrating Science, Mathematics and Computing (CEISMC). Mike is a graduate of the Universities of Michigan and Kansas, with expertise in the design and use of project-based learning (PBL) to facilitate standards-based learning. Mike is the Co-Principal Investigator for the NSF-funded project Science Learning Integrating Design, Engineering and Robotics (SLIDER), overseeing curriculum design, teacher learning, and research strategy. The project investigates the integration of engineering in science classes to facilitate physics learning. Mike designs and facilitates online learning courses in PBL for educators, and he previously taught K–12 science.

Jason Sayres is a Senior Curriculum and Professional Development Specialist at the Center for Innovation in Engineering and Science Education at Stevens Institute of Technology in Hoboken, New Jersey. For the past several years, he has been working on the NSF-funded WaterBotics® project, which aims to help educators put together an underwater robotics program for middle and high school students that uses LEGO® kits and pieces as the building materials. Previously, he was a physics instructor at an advanced math and science high school. He is a strong believer in hands-on and project-based learning, especially when it comes to STEM education.

Marion Usselman is a Principal Research Scientist and Associate Director for Federal Outreach and Research at the Georgia Institute of Technology's Center for Education Integrating Science, Mathematics and Computing (CEISMC). She earned her PhD in biophysics from Johns Hopkins University and has been with CEISMC since 1996 developing and managing university–K–12 educational partnership programs. She currently leads a team of educators and educational researchers that is exploring how to integrate science, mathematics, and engineering within authentic school contexts and researching the nature of the resultant student learning.

Pamela Van Scotter is Acting Executive Director at BSCS, providing leadership across the organization. She previously served as Senior Associate Director and as Director of the Center for Curriculum Development, where she worked on curriculum development and professional development projects for 16 years. Pam was a curriculum developer for many projects, Grades K–12, including *BSCS Biology: A Human Approach* and *BSCS Science and Technology*. She has worked extensively with elementary, middle school, and high school science teachers in many professional development settings. Pam received an MA in anthropology with an emphasis in linguistics and physical anthropology from Washington State University.

Marisa Wolsky is Executive Producer at WGBH Educational Foundation for the NSF-funded series *Design Squad*, for which she oversees all aspects of the production, translating its engineering content across many platforms; *Peep and the Big Wide World*, responsible for managing its production and the implementation of its educationally rich preschool science curriculum; and *Plum Landing*, a multiplatform, environmental science project designed to help kids think green in a new way. She has worked on the development and production of many educational children's television series, including *Long Ago & Far Away, Where in the World Is Carmen Sandiego?, Arthur,* and *ZOOM*.

Peter Y. Wong is Director of University Relations at the Museum of Science, Boston, and supervises the Middle School Engineering Curriculum Development. Dr. Wong graduated with a BS, MS, and PhD in Mechanical Engineering from Tufts University (Medford, MA). His work supports STEM education in and out of classrooms.

Barbara Zahm received her PhD in anthropology in 1980. After teaching at City University of New York, Dr. Zahm became a full-time documentary film and video producer/director for public television and educational distribution, where she received multiple awards. Dr. Zahm is currently the Director of Product Development and Grants for It's About Time (IAT) and is responsible for all development, editing, and production of IAT products. In addition, she serves as Principal Investigator on the NSF-funded PBIS CyberPD project. She has also served as the PI on the Active Chemistry and Active Physics Revision curricula development projects.

Bernard Zubrowski is a developer of curriculum programs: Models in Technology and Science, Design-it, Explore-it, and Ponds and Trees. He is involved in various teacher education projects and has designed exhibits for the Boston Children's Museum such as Bubbles and Raceways. Zubrowski authored *Exploration and Meaning Making in the Learning of Science* which was published by Springer.

Introduction

Introduction to The Go-To Guide for Engineering Curricula, Grades 6–8

Cary I. Sneider
Portland State University

The Next Generation Science Standards (NGSS Lead States, 2013) have opened the door for engineering to join science as an equal partner in the classroom. What this will look like is still unfolding, but happily, we are not starting from scratch. Many talented educators have been developing instructional materials in engineering for a long time. That's what this book is all about.

The idea of integrating technology and engineering into science teaching is not new. More than 100 years ago, educators such as John Dewey advocated technology education for all students (Lewis, 2004, p. 22). The call for integrating technology and engineering into science standards began with publication of *Science for All Americans* (AAAS, 1989) and has been featured prominently in standards documents ever since. A case in point is the National Science Education Standards (NRC, 1996), which advocated that all students should learn about the relationship between technology and science, as well as develop the abilities of technological design.

Despite the many efforts to infuse science teaching with ideas and activities in technology and engineering, the call has been largely ignored. One of the reasons was simply momentum. Science education has traditionally included only the core disciplines of life science, physical science (including chemistry), and Earth and space sciences, so there has been little room for technology and engineering. A second reason is that although state standards were commonly derived from the *National Science Education Standards* (NRC, 1996) and *Benchmarks for Science Literacy* (AAAS, 1993/2008), which also called for engineering and technology, each state crafted its own standards, and most ignored engineering and technology. As of 2012, only 12 states included engineering in their science standards (Carr, Bennet, & Strobel, 2012, p. 552).

A third reason is confusion about the term *technology,* which most people apply only to computers, cell phones, or other modern gadgets (Rose, Gallup, Meade, & Dugger, 2004). There is even less understanding of the term *engineering.* If you've ever had difficulty with plumbing in a hotel room and reported the problem to the front desk, it is likely that they called "engineering" to fix the problem. It's not surprising that most people think of engineers as people who fix things (Lachapelle, Phadnis, Hertel, & Cunningham, 2012).

Today, the situation is entirely different. A blue-ribbon panel of the NRC, which included Nobel Prize–winning scientists, engineers, university professors, and educational researchers, has created a new blueprint for science—*A Framework for K–12 Science Education: Practices, Crosscutting Concepts, and Core Ideas* (NRC, 2012). The Framework calls for engineering to be included at the same level as Newton's laws and the theory of evolution. Furthermore, the *Framework* served as the blueprint for the NGSS, which are aimed at replacing the current patchwork of state science standards with a common core, as has already been done in mathematics and English language arts. To emphasize that these standards are not federal, but rather an initiative of the National Governor's Association, the full title of the new standards is *Next Generation Science Standards: For States, by States.*[1]

In the new world of science education that is being created by these two documents, engineering is a true partner to science. There are several good reasons why this change may pay off at the classroom level in a big way.

The Value of Engineering to Reduce Declining Interest in Science

Most children love science, but it doesn't last. The majority of research studies have found that interest in science remains strong for most boys and girls throughout the elementary grades, but begins to drop off in middle school (Osborne, Simon, & Collins, 2003; Sneider, 2011). A few studies, however, have shown some decline as early as elementary school, and a consistent finding is that at all ages, most girls exhibit less interest than boys, and students of most minority ethnic groups tend to be less interested in science than Caucasian and Asian American students.

The introduction of engineering as a continuous thread in the science curriculum has the potential to change that trend and maintain students' interests in science as they transition to high school. There are several reasons why (from Cunningham & Lachapelle, 2011):

- While many students who are competent in science view the subject as irrelevant for future careers or everyday life, some of these same students—and especially girls and underrepresented minorities—respond positively to subjects such as environmental and medical engineering because these topics have obvious relevance to people's lives.
- Engineering involves students working together in teams, so design challenges appeal to students who enjoy collaborative activities.
- Engineering design challenges have more than one answer, and creativity is a plus. So the activities themselves tend to be fun and engaging.
- There are many more jobs available for engineers than there are for scientists. NASA, for example, hires 10 engineers for every scientist (NASA Workforce, 2013). So students see engineering as offering real future job prospects, especially when they see role models of different genders and racial backgrounds who enjoy their work.

- Failure of a design to work as expected does not mean being "wrong." Failure is a natural part of the design process, leading to improved designs, so students are encouraged to try out their ideas without worry.

In the past, few children were exposed to engineering as a school subject. In rare cases, when children were given engineering activities at school, it was likely to have been called "science," and engineering skills were not made explicit. Even in those cases where children *were* given engineering opportunities, it is likely to have been in the physical sciences, such as robotics or building bridges and towers that boys tend to favor, rather than topics such as medical or environmental engineering that appeal equally to girls (Cunningham & Lachapelle, 2011).

So, now that we have science education standards that call for engineering to be deeply integrated into all science classes, how do we get from here to there? If you are reading this book, it is likely that you are interested in an answer to that question. And not surprisingly, there is more than one answer.

How to Get Started

First, you will need instructional materials. Such materials do exist, and many of them can be found on the Internet. A variety of websites with engineering activities are listed in Table 0.1. Each chapter in this book references additional websites associated with a particular engineering curriculum.

Second, it will be helpful to have at least one colleague, and hopefully several, who can work with you to comb through instructional materials, consider how your school's curriculum might change to implement the new standards, and perhaps establish a professional learning community to examine your first efforts as you try new approaches.

Third, you might be invited to spend a summer writing new curriculum materials that are fully aligned with the NGSS. Having spent a long career developing instructional materials in science and the related STEM fields, let me caution you to think carefully about how you might undertake such a project. Curriculum development is a labor-intensive process that often takes years, and the assistance of many other teachers, to develop an effective lesson that will engage your students' enthusiasm and that also has clear educational objectives and assessment tools. Nonetheless, I have found curriculum development to be a creative and rewarding experience, and you may too.

Fourth—and now we get to the reason this book has come into being—you will very likely find it to be a valuable and enriching experience to listen to the voices of the pioneers, the people who held the vision of "engineering as a partner to science" long before these documents were written and who have spent decades developing engineering curricula.

In the chapters that follow, you will see how engineering educators build on children's innate interests by presenting them with challenging problems, engaging them in designing creative solutions, and helping them understand how science and mathematics apply in their everyday lives. While many of the curricula do concern physical sciences, as a whole they span the entire spectrum of science disciplines.

How This Book Is Organized

Each chapter describes one set of instructional materials with vivid examples of what the curriculum looks like in the classroom, what learning goals it is intended to accomplish, and how it can help you address the vision of the Framework and the performance expectations in the NGSS.

Perhaps more importantly, the instructional materials described in these chapters do more than spark students' interests. They help students develop skills in defining and solving problems, and in working on collaborative teams to brainstorm creative ideas, build prototypes and use controlled experiments to compare different ideas, design an optimal solution, and learn about a wide variety of engineering professions.

All of the materials in the collection have been under development for several years, tested by teachers and their students from a wide range of communities, and revised based on feedback. In many cases, they are also supported by research studies of effectiveness. A listing of all the curriculum materials included in this three-volume sequence can be found in Table 0.2, which illustrates the full range of grade levels for which the curriculum can be used.

If you are looking for engineering curricula to try out, you will undoubtedly find something of interest on these pages. If you are part of a group of teachers interested in exploring engineering and science curricula, these chapters could provide stimulating topics for discussion. And if you are challenged with developing new instructional materials, these chapters will help you avoid the need to re-create the wheel.

As you read through these chapters, you may find that several strike you as top candidates for enriching your classroom or school science program. Although too many options is far better than too few, you may need some help in deciding among the top contenders. Happily, a new and very useful tool, with the acronym EQuIP, has popped up on the www.nextgenscience.org website. Educators Evaluating the Quality of Instructional Products (EQuIP) Rubric for Lessons & Units: Science is designed to help you review and select materials based on how well the lessons and units align with the NGSS, and provide instructional and assessment supports.

Before you can use the EQuIP rubric, you will need to have samples of the materials to examine. Contact information is provided at the beginning of each chapter to allow you to do that. You will also need to be familiar with the *Framework* and the NGSS. The next section of this book provides an overview of engineering in these two important documents; but of course, the documents themselves, which can be downloaded free of charge from the National Academies Press website (www. nap.edu), provide much more detail. If you are already familiar with these documents and want to move on to the main business of this book, which is to learn about existing engineering curricula as described by the people who created them, you can get started with Chapter 1, Design Squad: Inspiring a New Generation of Engineers.

The *Framework* and the NGSS have the potential to change the face of science education in the country, but only if educators like you embrace the opportunity and begin to imagine what it may mean for the students in your care.

Table 0.1 Selection of K–12 Engineering Education Websites

A Framework for K–12 Science Education—http://www.nap.edu/catalog.php?record_id=13165#

Building Big—http://www.pbs.org/wgbh/buildingbig/

Center for Innovation in Engineering and Science Education—http://www.ciese.org

Design Squad—http://pbskids.org/designsquad/

Discover Engineering—http://www.discovere.org/

Dragonfly TV—http://pbskids.org/dragonflytv/show/technologyinvention.html

Engineering Education Service Center—http://www.engineeringedu.com

Engineering Go For It (ASEE)—http://teachers.egfi-k12.org/

Engineering Our Future—https://sites.google.com/site/engineeringourfuture/

Engineering Pathways—http://www.ncengineeringpathways.org/

How to Smile: All the Best Science and Math Activities—http://www.howtosmile.org

Institute for (P–12) Engineering Research and Learning (INSPIRE)—http://www.inspire-purdue.org/

Intel Design and Discovery—http://educate.intel.com/en/DesignDiscovery/

International Technology and Engineering Education Association (ITEEA)—http://www.iteaconnect.org

Materials World Modules—http://www.materialsworldmodules.org/

Museum of Science, Boston (NCTL)—http://www.mos.org/nctl/

My NASA Data Lesson Plans—http://mynasadata.larc.nasa.gov/my-nasa-data-lesson-plans/

National Science Digital Library—http://nsdl.org/

Next Generation Science Standards—http://www.nap.edu/ngss

Oregon Pre-Engineering and Applied Sciences—http://opas.ous.edu/resourcesEngCurricular.php

Project Infinity—http://www.infinity-project.org/

Project Lead the Way—http://pltw.org

Sally Ride Science Academy—https://sallyridescience.com/

Science Buddies—http://sciencebuddies.org

Spark Plug into Science—http://www.gse.upenn.edu/spark/sparkkits.php

Stuff That Works (CCNY)—http://citytechnology.org/stuff-that-works/home

Teach Engineering—http://www.teachengineering.org/

Try Engineering—http://www.tryengineering.org/

Women in Engineering—http://www.wepan.org/displaycommon.cfm?an=1&subarticlenbr=39

Zoom—http://pbskids.org/zoom/activities/sci/

Table 0.2 Instructional Materials in *The Go-To Guide for Engineering Curricula* Series

Book Curricula	Elementary							Middle School			High School			
	P	K	1	2	3	4	5	6	7	8	9	10	11	12
E1 Seeds of Science/Roots of Reading				■	■	■	■							
E2 Physical Science Comes Alive!	■	■	■	■										
E3 Engineering by Design TEEMS, K–2		■	■	■										
E4 BSCS Science Tracks				■	■	■	■							
E5 A World in Motion		■	■	■	■	■	■	■	■	■				
E6 FOSS Full Option Science System		■	■	■	■	■	■	■	■	■				
E7 Engineering Is Elementary			■	■	■	■	■							
E8 Tangible Kindergarten	■	■	■											
E9 Engineering Adventures (OST)					■	■	■							
E10 Engineering by Design TEEMS, 3–5 & I³					■	■	■	■						
E11 Design It! (OST)								■	■	■				
E12 Junk Drawer Robotics					■	■	■	■	■	■				
E13 PictureSTEM		■	■	■	■	■	■							
E14 STEM in Action	■	■	■	■	■	■	■							
M1 Design Squad (OST)					■	■	■	■	■	■	■	■	■	■
M2 Models in Technology and Science							■	■	■	■				
M3 Everyday Engineering							■	■	■	■	■			
M4 SLIDER								■	■	■				
M5 Teaching Engineering Made Easy								■	■	■				

Book	Elementary							Middle School			High School			
Curricula	P	K	1	2	3	4	5	6	7	8	9	10	11	12
M6 Fender Bender Physics								X	X	X				
M7 Technology in Practice								X	X	X				
M8 IQWST								X	X	X				
M9 Project-Based Inquiry Science								X	X	X				
M10 Issue-Oriented Science								X	X	X				
M11 Techbridge (OST)								X	X	X	X	X	X	X
M12 Waterbotics (OST)								X	X	X	X	X	X	X
M13 Engineering Now								X	X	X	X	X	X	X
M14 Engineering by Design 6–8								X	X	X	X	X	X	X
H1 INSPIRES											X	X	X	X
H2 Active Physics											X	X	X	X
H3 Active Chemistry											X	X	X	X
H4 Engineering the Future											X	X	X	X
H5 Engineer Your World											X	X	X	X
H6 Global Systems Science											X	X	X	X
H7 Science and Global Issues											X	X	X	X
H8 Engineering by Design											X	X	X	X
H9 Science by Design											X	X	X	X
H10 Biology in a Box								X	X	X	X	X	X	X
H11 Voyage Through Time											X	X	X	X
H12 EPICS											X	X	X	X

Note

1. *Next Generation Science Standards* (NGSS), *For States, By States* is a registered trademark of Achieve, Inc. Neither Achieve, Inc. nor the lead states and partners that developed the Next Generation Science Standards were involved in the production of, and do not endorse, *The Go-To Guide for Engineering Curricula.* However, Achieve, Inc. has granted permission for the authors of this book to quote extensively from the NGSS.

References

American Association for the Advancement of Science (AAAS). (1989). *Science for all Americans.* Project 2061. New York: Oxford University Press.

American Association for the Advancement of Science (AAAS). (1993/2008). *Benchmarks for science literacy.* Project 2061. New York: Oxford University Press.

Carr, R. L., Bennet, L. D., & Strobel, J. (2012). Engineering in the K–12 STEM standards of the 50 U.S. states: An analysis of presence and extent. *Journal of Engineering Education, 101*(3), 539–564.

Cunningham, C., & Lachapelle, C. (2011). Designing engineering experiences to engage all students. Museum of Science, Boston. Retrieved from http://www.eie.org/sites/default/files/2012ip-Cunningham_Lachapelle_Eng4All.pdf

Lachapelle, C., Phadnis, P., Hertel, J., & Cunningham, C. (2012). What is engineering? A survey of elementary students. Retrieved from http://www.eie.org/sites/default/files/research_article/research_file/2012-03_we_paper_fo_p-12_engineering_conference.pdf

Li, J., Klahr, D., & Siler, S. (2006). What lies beneath the science achievement gap: The challenges of aligning science instruction with standards and tests. *Science Educator, 15*(1), 1–12.

Lewis, T. (2004). A turn to engineering: The continuing struggle of technology education for legitimization as a school subject. *Journal of Technology Education, 16*(1), 21–39.

NASA Workforce. (2013). Data on NASA workforce retrieved from http://nasapeople.nasa.gov/workforce/default.htm.

National Research Council (NRC). (1996). *National science education standards.* National Committee on Science Education Standards and Assessment, Board on Science Education, Division of Behavioral and Social Sciences and Education, National Research Council. Washington, DC: National Academies Press.

National Research Council (NRC). (2012). *A framework for K–12 science education: Practices, crosscutting concepts, and core ideas.* Committee on a Conceptual Framework for New K–12 Science Education Standards, Board on Science Education, Division of Behavioral and Social Sciences and Education, National Research Council. Washington, DC: National Academies Press.

NGSS Lead States. (2013). *Next generation science standards: For states, by states. Volume 1: The standards* and *Volume 2: Appendices.* Washington, DC: National Academies Press.

Osborne, J., Simon, S., & Collins, S. (2003). Attitudes towards science: A review of the literature and its implications. *International Journal of Science Education, 25*(9), 1049–1097.

Rose, L. C., Gallup, A. M., Meade, S., & Dugger, W. (2004, September). The second installment of the ITEA/Gallup Poll and what it reveals as to how Americans think about technology. *Technology Teacher.* Retrieved from http://www.iteaconnect.org/TAA/PDFs/GallupPoll2004.pdf

Sneider, C. (2011). Reversing the swing from science: Implications from a century of research. Presented at ITEST Convening on Advancing Research on Youth Motivation in STEM, September 9, 2011. Available online at http://itestlrc.edc.org/youth-motivation-convening-materials, and from the Noyce Foundation at http://www.noycefdn.org/news.php

Technology and Engineering in Middle School Standards

One of the most important contributions of the new standards documents has been to clear up the confusion among the terms *science, technology,* and *engineering.* According to the Framework,

> In the K–12 context, "science" is generally taken to mean the traditional natural sciences: physics, chemistry, biology, and (more recently) earth, space, and environmental sciences. . . . We use the term "engineering" in a very broad sense to mean any engagement in a systematic practice of design to achieve solutions to particular human problems. Likewise, we broadly use the term "technology" to include all types of human-made systems and processes—not in the limited sense often used in schools that equates technology with modern computational and communications devices. Technologies result when engineers apply their understanding of the natural world and of human behavior to design ways to satisfy human needs and wants. (NRC, 2012, pp. 11–12)

Definitions alone might not make a big difference, but combining these definitions with an entirely new approach to standards is very likely to be a game changer. Together, the Framework and the Next Generation Science Standards (NGSS Lead States, 2013a, 2013b) have the potential to change the way science is taught in this country.

The Three Dimensions of the NGSS

In order to explain how technology and engineering are integrated in the new standards, it is helpful to understand the three dimensions introduced in the Framework and how they appear in the NGSS.

Dimension 1: Science and Engineering Practices

In the *National Science Education Standards* (NRC, 1996), the set of abilities known collectively as "science inquiry"—what students should be *able to do*—was described separately from the list of what students should *know*. Although the *National Science Education Standards* (p. 20) advocated combining inquiry and content, it did not specify how to do so. In contrast, the Next Generation Science Standards merge specific practices and core ideas. But before we describe what that looks like, we first describe what has become of inquiry in the NGSS. In its new form, the term *inquiry* has been replaced with eight "practices of science and engineering." Each of the practices is described in some detail, and what is most important for this book, each practice refers to both science inquiry and engineering design. Following is a description of the eight practices for the middle school grades, with emphasis on engineering.

Practice 1: Ask questions and define problems. Just as science inquiry begins with a question, engineering design begins with the definition of a problem. With guidance from a knowledgeable teacher, students' interests in creating things can lead to the formulation of problems to be solved or goals to be met. With prompting, students in Grades 6–8 can define a design problem that can be solved through the development of an object, tool, process, or system. Their problem definitions may include multiple criteria and constraints, including scientific knowledge that may limit possible solutions.

Practice 2: Develop and use models. Whether they are doing science or engineering, students frequently use models. As an engineering practice, students construct models to help them design and test solutions to problems. In Grades 6–8, students can develop and/or use a model to generate data to test ideas about designed systems, including inputs and outputs, and systems at different scales, including scales that cannot be directly observed. They can also evaluate the limitations of a model for a proposed object or tool.

Practice 3: Plan and carry out investigations. There are many different kinds of investigations in science, ranging from controlled laboratory experiments to field biology investigations. In science, investigations are used to answer questions about the natural world. In engineering, students plan and carry out investigations to learn more about the problem they are trying to solve, or to test possible solutions. In Grades 6–8, students can plan and conduct an investigation to test one or more designs under a range of conditions, and determine how best to change the model based on the results of the tests. When planning tests, students should identify independent and dependent variables and controls, determine what tools are needed, and determine how data will be recorded.

Practice 4: Analyze and interpret data. Science and engineering both involve analyzing and interpreting data. Students in Grades 6–8 who are engaged in an engineering design project can construct, analyze, and interpret graphical displays of data and large data sets to provide evidence for design decisions. Data analysis may involve concepts of statistics and probability (including mean, median, mode, and variability) to analyze and characterize data, using digital tools when feasible. The students should also be able to consider the limitations of data analysis, such as measurement error, and seek to improve precision and accuracy of data with better technological tools and methods such as the use of multiple trials. Students of middle school age should also be able to analyze and interpret data so as to create the best possible (optimal) design.

Practice 5: Use mathematics and computational thinking. In addition to analyzing and interpreting data, mathematical thinking includes representing relationships between variables with equations; using computers and other digital tools for automatically collecting, analyzing, and graphing data; and using simulations to find out how a solution to a problem might function under different conditions. Middle school students should have opportunities to use mathematical representations and concepts—such as ratio, rate, percent, and simple algebra—to support their work in designing solutions to problems.

They should also use computers and other digital tools to analyze very large data sets to look for patterns and trends and to optimize the solution to an engineering problem.

Practice 6: Construct explanations and design solutions. In science, the end result is an explanation for a natural phenomenon. In engineering, the end result is a solution to a problem. Students in middle school can engage in the engineering design cycle by applying scientific principles to design, construct, and/or test a design of an object, tool, process, or system. They can also optimize the performance of a design by prioritizing criteria, making tradeoffs, testing, revising, and retesting.

Practice 7: Engage in argument from evidence. In science, students use evidence to argue for or against an explanation for a phenomenon, whereas in engineering, students use evidence and reasoning to determine the best possible solution to a problem, or to defend their choice of a given solution. In the middle school grades, students can make an oral or written argument that supports or refutes the advertised performance of a device, process, or system based on empirical evidence concerning whether or not the technology meets relevant criteria and constraints. They can also respectfully critique the arguments of others by citing relevant evidence and posing and responding to questions that elicit pertinent elaboration and detail.

Practice 8: Obtain, evaluate, and communicate information. Both science and engineering involve critical reading and the ability to communicate ideas in writing and speech. In the middle school grades, students should be able to critically read texts adapted for the classroom to gather information on problems to be solved and to find out how others have solved similar problems. They should also be able to develop visual displays and oral presentations to communicate the process and products of engineering design.

These eight practices of science and engineering are very important in the NGSS because they are woven into all of the performance expectations, which comprise the heart of the standards.

Dimension 2: Crosscutting Concepts

The second dimension is a set of seven crosscutting concepts. These concepts were also present in earlier standards documents; they were called "themes" in *Benchmarks for Science Literacy* and "unifying concepts and processes" in the *National Science Education Standards*. The purpose of this dimension is to illustrate that although the different disciplines of science concern different phenomena, they represent a unified way of understanding the world. For example, although "energy" may be treated somewhat differently when studying chemical reactions, ecosystems, and the Earth as a body in space, the concept of "energy" is the same in each case. The seven crosscutting concepts described in the Framework, and carried over into the NGSS, are as follows:

1. *Patterns.* Observed patterns of forms and events guide organization and classification, and they prompt questions about relationships and the factors that influence them.

2. *Cause and effect: Mechanism and explanation.* Events have causes, sometimes simple, sometimes multifaceted. A major activity of science is investigating and explaining causal relationships and the mechanisms by which they are mediated. Such

mechanisms can then be tested across given contexts and used to predict and explain events in new contexts.

3. *Scale, proportion, and quantity.* In considering phenomena, it is critical to recognize what is relevant at different measures of size, time, and energy and to recognize how changes in scale, proportion, or quantity affect a system's structure or performance.

4. *Systems and system models.* Defining the system under study—specifying its boundaries and making explicit a model of that system—provides tools for understanding and testing ideas that are applicable throughout science and engineering.

5. *Energy and matter: Flows, cycles, and conservation.* Tracking fluxes of energy and matter into, out of, and within systems helps one understand the systems' possibilities and limitations.

6. *Structure and function.* The way in which an object or living thing is shaped and its substructure determine many of its properties and functions.

7. *Stability and change.* For natural and built systems alike, conditions of stability and determinants of rates of change or evolution of a system are critical elements of study.

In addition to these seven crosscutting concepts, the writing team decided to add two other important ideas that were included in the Framework in a chapter on engineering, technology, and applications of science:

8. *The interdependence of science, engineering, and technology.* Without engineers to design the instruments that scientists use to investigate the world, modern science would be impossible. Conversely, new scientific discoveries enable engineers to invent and modify technologies. In a word, science and engineering drive each other forward.

9. *The influence of engineering, technology, and science on society and the environment.* Scientific discoveries and technological decisions profoundly affect human society and the natural environment.

Feedback from the public (and especially from science teachers) noted that ideas about the nature of science were missing from the Framework and the NGSS. Since concepts relating to the nature of science also cut across all of the science disciplines, these ideas were also included along with the other crosscutting concepts listed above.

Dimension 3: A Small Set of Disciplinary Core Ideas

One of the criticisms of today's science curriculum is that it's "a mile wide and an inch deep" (Schmidt, McKnight, & Raizen, 1996, p. 2). The problem of too much to cover in too little time is not new for those of us who have been in science teaching for decades, but the advent of high-stakes tests have brought the problem to the surface. One group of researchers (Li, Klahr, & Siler. 2006) that did its level best to help students in high-needs middle schools meet the state's standards claims that the achievement gap between racial and socioeconomic status groups (measured by differences in high-stakes test scores) cannot be bridged unless standards are fewer, and more specific, so that it is possible for teachers to spend more time helping students learn concepts in depth without penalizing them by failing to cover all subjects.

The Framework and NGSS are the first set of science standards to substantially reduce the amount that students are expected to learn. Furthermore, the content is more coherent than previous efforts. It is organized in just 12 core ideas that grow in sophistication and complexity across the grades. Eleven of the core ideas are in the traditional fields of life, physical, and Earth and space sciences. The twelfth core idea is engineering design. In other words, students are expected to learn the essential process used by engineers to solve problems and achieve goals, just as they are expected to learn about the concepts of energy and heredity. The 12 core ideas that thread through the standards from kindergarten to Grade 12 are listed in Table 0.3.

Table 0.3 Twelve Core Ideas in the Next Generation Science Standards

Physical Science	Life Science	Earth and Space Science	Engineering
• Matter and its interactions • Motion and stability: forces and interactions • Energy • Waves and their applications in technologies for information transfer	• From molecules to organisms: structures and processes • Ecosystems: interactions, energy, and dynamics • Heredity: inheritance and variation of traits • Biological evolution: unity and diversity	• Earth's place in the universe • Earth's systems • Earth and human activity	• Engineering design

Each of the core ideas above is further broken down into components, and each of those is integrated into the Next Generation Science Standards in ways that are grade-level appropriate. By organizing the content in this way, teachers can see how their contributions build on the work in prior grades and lay the foundation for further learning.

A Progression of Core Ideas for Engineering

Table 0.3 lists "Engineering Design" as the twelfth core idea for all students. Like the core ideas within the traditional science disciplines, these ideas grow in complexity and sophistication over time. Performance expectations for this core idea at all grade levels are shown in Table 0.4. Although this volume is concerned with the middle school level, it is important for teachers and administrators to be familiar with the entire span of the learning progression.

Table 0.4 Learning Progression for Engineering Design

K–2	3–5	6–8	9–12
Ask questions, make observations, and gather information about a situation people want to change to define a simple problem that can be solved through the development of a new or improved object or tool. Develop a simple sketch, drawing, or physical model to illustrate how the shape of an object helps it function as needed to solve a given problem. Analyze data from tests of two objects designed to solve the same problem to compare the strengths and weaknesses of how each performs.	Define a simple design problem reflecting a need or a want that includes specified criteria for success and constraints on materials, time, or cost. Generate and compare multiple possible solutions to a problem based on how well each is likely to meet the criteria and constraints of the problem. Plan and carry out fair tests in which variables are controlled and failure points are considered to identify aspects of a model or prototype that can be improved.	Define the criteria and constraints of a design problem with sufficient precision to ensure a successful solution, taking into account relevant scientific principles and potential impacts on people and the natural environment that may limit possible solutions. Evaluate competing design solutions using a systematic process to determine how well they meet the criteria and constraints of the problem. Analyze data from tests to determine similarities and differences among several design solutions to identify the best characteristics of each that can be combined into a new solution to better meet the criteria for success. Develop a model to generate data for iterative testing and modification of a proposed object, tool, or process such that an optimal design can be achieved.	Analyze a major global challenge to specify qualitative and quantitative criteria and constraints for solutions that account for societal needs and wants. Design a solution to a complex, real-world problem by breaking it down into smaller, more manageable problems that can be solved through engineering. Evaluate a solution to a complex, real-world problem based on prioritized criteria and trade-offs that account for a range of constraints, including cost, safety, reliability, and aesthetics, as well as possible social, cultural, and environmental impacts. Use a computer simulation to model the impact of proposed solutions to a complex, real-world problem with numerous criteria and constraints on interactions within and between systems relevant to the problem.

Combining the Three Dimensions

The Next Generation Science Standards combine disciplinary core ideas, practices, and crosscutting concepts in sentences called "performance expectations." These statements illustrate what students are expected to be able to do in order to demonstrate not only their understanding of the important ideas from the Framework, but also how they should be able to *use* what they've learned. Each performance expectation begins with one of the practices and explains how students are expected to use that practice in demonstrating their understanding of the disciplinary core idea. Crosscutting concepts are sometimes explicitly integrated into these sentences, and sometimes the crosscutting concept is simply clear from the context.

Unlike the vague statements from prior standards, which generally began with the phrase "students will know that . . .," performance expectations specify what students should be able to *do* in order to demonstrate their understanding. Although performance expectations are not so specific as to designate a given teaching activity or assessment item, they are sufficiently specific to provide the same clear learning goals for curriculum, instruction, and assessment.

Recall that each practice could be used for science or engineering. Keeping in mind that science involves the investigation of natural phenomena in the traditional disciplines, whereas engineering involves designing solutions to problems, it is possible to figure out which refer to science and which to engineering. Table 0.5 lists several performance expectations from the NGSS. See if you can determine which are science and which are engineering. The first two statements are classified for you. Fill in the rest of the blanks to test your ability to distinguish science from engineering practices.

| Table 0.5 Are These Performance Expectations Science or Engineering? | |

(The editor's preferred answers are below.*)

Middle school students who understand chemical reactions can	This is an example of
Develop and use a model to describe how the total number of atoms does not change in a chemical reaction and thus mass is conserved.	Science
Undertake a design project to construct, test, and modify a device that either releases or absorbs thermal energy by chemical processes.	Engineering
Middle school students who understand Earth and Human Activity can	**This is an example of**
1. Construct an argument supported by evidence for how increases in human population and per-capita consumption of natural resources impact Earth's systems.	
2. Apply scientific principles to design a method for monitoring and minimizing a human impact on the environment.	
Middle school students who understand ecosystems can	**This is an example of**
3. Evaluate competing design solutions for maintaining biodiversity and ecosystem services.	
4. Develop a model to describe the cycling of matter and flow of energy among living and nonliving parts of an ecosystem.	

(Continued)

Table 0.5 (Continued)

Middle school students who understand energy can	This is an example of
5. Apply scientific principles to design, construct, and test a device that either minimizes or maximizes thermal energy transfer.	
6. Construct, use, and present arguments to support the claim that when the motion energy of an object changes, energy is transferred to or from the object.	

*Answer Key: 1. Science, 2. Engineering, 3. Engineering, 4. Science, 5. Engineering, 6. Science.

The layout of the Next Generation Science Standards is shown in Figure 0.1. Each set of performance expectations has a title at the top of the page. Below the title is a box containing the performance expectations. Below that are three foundation boxes, which list (from left to right) the specific science and engineering practices, disciplinary core ideas (DCIs), and crosscutting concepts that were combined to produce the performance expectations above. The bottom section lists connections to performance expectations (PEs) in other science disciplines at the same grade level, to PEs of the same core idea for younger and older students, and to related Common Core State Standards in mathematics and English language arts.

Figure 0.1 Structure of the NGSS

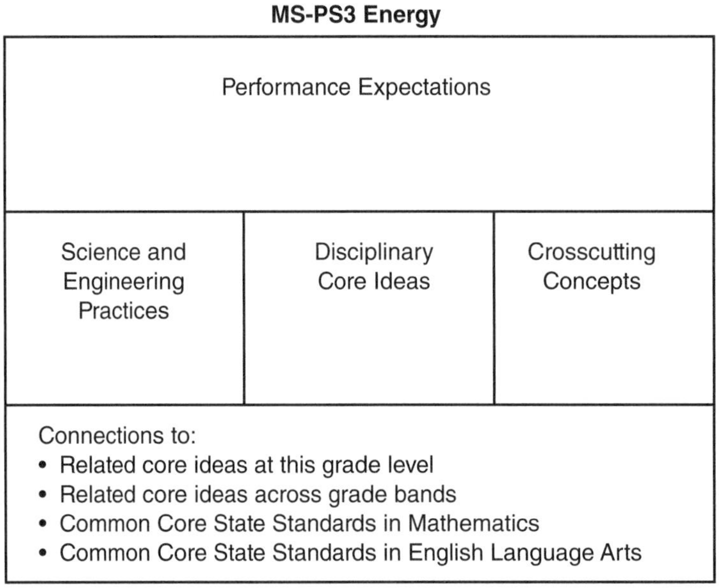

MS-PS3 Energy

Performance Expectations

Science and Engineering Practices	Disciplinary Core Ideas	Crosscutting Concepts

Connections to:
- Related core ideas at this grade level
- Related core ideas across grade bands
- Common Core State Standards in Mathematics
- Common Core State Standards in English Language Arts

Alternative Pathways for the Middle School Level

Although the NGSS specify which core ideas should be taught at each level in Grades 1–5, there is no such designation in middle school. The reason for this is that different states require different ways of organizing the science curriculum. Some states require that the disciplines be integrated, so that life, physical, and Earth and space science are taught every year. Other states require that one discipline be taught in a single year. The NGSS accommodate these differences by specifying what students should learn by the end of eighth grade, with no required schedule for instruction.

Nonetheless, some topics lay groundwork for learning in other subjects, so some sequences are better than others. Consequently, the state teams that developed the NGSS have published recommendations for alternative pathways to guide the development of a curriculum sequence that is compatible with a state's requirements, but that also enables students to learn in an optimal sequence. These recommendations are described in Appendix K of the Next Generation Science Standards (NGSS Lead States, 2013b).

Summary

The new standards are complex, so it's worth pausing for a moment to summarize the most important key ideas:

A Framework for K–12 Science Education (NRC, 2012)

- Was created by a blue ribbon panel of Nobel Prize–winning scientists, engineers, university professors, and educational researchers.
- Provides the blueprint for the Next Generation Science Standards (NGSS).
- Describes three dimensions to be included in the new standards: twelve disciplinary core ideas, practices of science and engineering, and crosscutting concepts.
- Calls for engineering to be included at the same level as Newton's laws and the theory of evolution.

Next Generation Science Standards: For States, by States (NGSS Lead States, 2013a, 2013b)

- Is organized by 12 core ideas in four disciplines: physical science, life science, Earth and space science, and engineering.
- Presents standards in the form of performance expectations, which combine disciplinary core ideas with practices and crosscutting concepts.
- Identifies which core ideas are to be taught at which grade in K–5, and by grade band in middle and high school.
- Provides clear and common targets for curriculum, instruction, and assessment.
- Offers alternative suggestions for sequencing the standards in Grades 6–8.

Engineering is woven throughout the Next Generation Science Standards, which means that students must be able to demonstrate that they can *use* a given core idea in science to solve a practical engineering problem. Secondly, engineering design is also a core idea that all students are expected to learn at successively higher levels as they mature and move through the grades. In other words, engineering design is both a practice (what students should be able to do) and a disciplinary core idea (what students should know and understand).

While existing instructional materials will need to be modified to meet the new standards—and there are several examples of such modifications in the chapters in this book—thanks to the NGSS, the problem to be solved is far more specific—and therefore more easily solved—than at any time in the past.

Cary Sneider
Portland State University

References

Li, J., Klahr, D., & Siler, S. (2006). What lies beneath the science achievement gap: The challenges of aligning science instruction with standards and tests. *Science Educator, 15*(1), 1–12.

National Research Council (NRC). (1996). *National science education standards.* National Committee on Science Education Standards and Assessment, Board on Science Education, Division of Behavioral and Social Sciences and Education, National Research Council (NRC). Washington, DC: National Academies Press.

National Research Council (NRC). (2012). *A framework for K–12 science education: Practices, crosscutting concepts, and core ideas.* Committee on a Conceptual Framework for New K–12 Science Education Standards, Board on Science Education, Division of Behavioral and Social Sciences and Education, National Research Council (NRC). Washington, DC: National Academies Press.

NGSS Lead States. (2013a). *Next generation science standards: For states, by states. Volume 1: The standards.* Washington, DC: National Academies Press.

NGSS Lead States. (2013b). *Next generation science standards: For states, by states. Volume 2: Appendices.* Washington, DC: National Academies Press.

Schmidt, W. H., McKnight, C. C., & Raizen, S. A. (Eds.). (1997). *A splintered vision: An investigation of U.S. science and mathematics education* [Executive Summary]. Boston/Dordrecht/London: Kluwer Academic Press.

1

Design Squad

Inspiring a New Generation of Engineers

Marisa Wolsky
WGBH Educational Foundation
Boston, Massachusetts

Figure 1.1 *Design Squad* TV Crew

Image courtesy of WGBH Educational Foundation.

In February 2007, the first kids' TV program dedicated to engineering premiered on PBS. Geared for upper elementary and middle school students, *Design Squad* pits two teams of teenagers against each other in high-energy, high-drama engineering competitions intended to solve real-world problems for real-world clients (see Figure 1.1). As a television series, *Design Squad* aims to inspire its young viewers—to show that engineering is accessible, doable, and most of all, fun. At the same time, *Design Squad* pushes the audience experience beyond passive viewing to include active, hands-on involvement in engineering activities. The television program is integrated into a powerful multiplatform initiative that reaches its young audience through a content-rich, highly interactive website and a wealth of educational materials. These materials are designed to deepen students' understanding of science concepts and the engineering design process, provide opportunities for teamwork and hands-on problem solving, and present engineers as creative problem solvers who design things that matter and improve people's lives.

Of course, to make the greatest impact on kids, we, the producers of *Design Squad*, need you, educators from across the country, to use these materials with your students—to introduce hands-on engineering activities in your classrooms, discuss with your students what engineers do in the real world, and grow your students' conceptions of what engineering is. In turn, we aim to make the process as easy as possible by providing materials that are geared to your needs, based on sound research, compatible with national standards, and easily accessible to teachers in all settings.

Educators know how powerfully hands-on exploration can impact young students' learning. This is why *Design Squad* has created a model for how to use open-ended, kid-driven, hands-on activities as a hook to get kids (and educators!) to engage in engineering (see Figure 1.2). We also know that teachers use resources in a variety of ways, depending on years of experience, teaching style, curriculum needs, time available, and students' learning needs. With this in mind, our goal is always to provide flexibility in our educational materials—offering not only self-contained lessons, but also units and activities that may be used separately or integrated into other lesson plans or curricula.

Negative stereotypes about engineering—that it's nerdy, tough, and for boys only—have discouraged many kids from considering engineering as a field of study or potential career choice. WGBH's research findings have shown that young people often hold such an opinion because they have no or little idea what engineering is or what engineers do. This conclusion is further supported by separate research conducted as part of the National Academy of Engineering's *Changing the Conversation* project. Through this research, we have learned that messages about engineering—which disproportionately emphasize the extraordinary math and science skills needed and the challenges inherent in these jobs—are off-putting to youth. Rather, *Design Squad* aims to emphasize the positive aspects of the field—that it's a collaborative, creative, and socially relevant endeavor.

The Parents and Educators section of *Design Squad*'s Emmy Award-winning website (http://pbskids.org/designsquad/) contains all the resources you need to bring engineering to life in your classroom. These include 8 educator guides, 46 half-hour TV episodes, 24 short career profiles of engineers, 62 animations of STEM concepts, 78 short videos, online training resources, and 63 hands-on activities. And it's all free!

Expanding Your Skills

Are you looking for ways to integrate the design process (also known as practices of engineering) into your lessons? Are you new to leading hands-on activities? Want to get kids excited about engineering? *Design Squad* offers a suite of free, online professional development resources. Check them out by clicking the "Training" link at http://pbskids.org/designsquad/parentseducators.

Leading Hands-On Engineering Activities Online Workshop. Use this free, 75-minute, self-paced tutorial to help you build skills and confidence in leading hands-on, open-ended engineering activities with kids. It will enable you to see what the design process looks like in the classroom, learn a host of implementation strategies, and experience the fun and relevance of engineering.

Training Others. Train volunteers, parents, and mentors how to lead engineering activities with kids. This 1-hour slide show comes with talking points, printable handouts, and preparation tips.

Training Video. Watch how an educator creates a rich, multifaceted learning experience for kids by integrating video resources into a hands-on activity from *Design Squad*'s Mission: Solar System educator's guide.

How-to Sheets. Find helpful how-to sheets in the front section of each guide. Topics covered include Introducing the Design Process, Talking to Kids About Engineering and Invention, Setting up an Engineering/Invention Club, Hosting an Event, and Working With Kids.

Introducing the Design Process

Engineers' initial ideas rarely solve a problem. Instead, they try different ideas, learn from their mistakes, and then try again. The steps engineers use to arrive at a solution are called the design process (see Figure 1.3). The design process is built into each *Design Squad* hands-on activity. As students work through an activity, they'll see that the steps of the design process encourage them to think creatively to solve a problem. The questions that follow will help you tie your students' work to specific steps of the design process.

Figure 1.2 Engineering Success!

Image courtesy of WGBH Educational Foundation.

Figure 1.3 Diagram of the Engineering Design Process

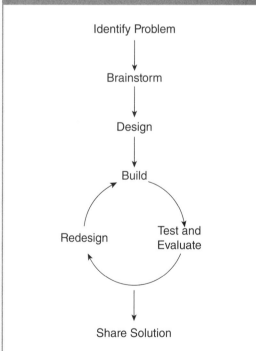

Image courtesy of WGBH Educational Foundation.

Brainstorm

- What are some different ways to tackle today's activity?
- Off-the-wall suggestions often spark *great* ideas. How creative can you be?

Design

- Which brainstormed ideas are really possible, given your time, tools, and materials?
- What are some problems you need to solve as you build your project?
- How can a sketch help clarify your design?

Build

- What materials will you need?
- What can you learn by looking at other students' projects?

Test, Evaluate, and Redesign

- Why is it a good idea to keep testing a design?
- What specific goal are you trying to achieve, and how will you know if you've been successful?
- How does the design meet the criteria for success?

Share Solutions

- What's the best feature of your design? Why?
- What were the different steps you did to get your project to work?
- What was the hardest problem to solve?
- Did you have to do something a few times to get it to work?
- If you had more time, how would you improve your project?

Using Video Clips of the Design Process in Action

A short video clip of each design process step can be found at www.pbslearningmedia.org/search/?q=design+process. By watching the *Design Squad* teams work through each step of the design process, students will learn to think creatively when solving a problem and strengthen their critical-thinking abilities. Also, if your class is struggling with any particular step or with group dynamics, these videos offer a convenient way to talk through an issue.

Identify the Problem (1½ minutes). Understanding the problem paves the way for solving it. This clip lets you emphasize to students the importance of defining the activity clearly before getting started. As a class, discuss how the *Design Squad* teams prepare to design and build furniture out of cardboard.

Brainstorm (1½ minutes). Coming up with many possible solutions is a powerful way to begin a project. This clip shows *Design Squad* teams generating lots of ideas for devices that a dancer can use in an underwater performance. As a class, discuss what made this brainstorm successful.

Design (1 minute). Now it's time to choose the best solution and plan how to build it. In this clip, the *Design Squad* teams squabble about when to stop designing and start building their specialized bikes. As a class, discuss possible solutions for moving a team forward when there is disagreement.

Build, Test, Evaluate, and Redesign (1 minute). Once kids settle on a design, it's time to build, test, and redesign it. This clip shows that things don't always work as planned. As a class, discuss how the *Design Squad* teams learn from their testing results and figure out how to redesign and make improvements.

Share Solutions (2 minutes). Presenting one's work to others is a constructive way to conclude a project. As a class, discuss how the *Design Squad* team's presentation validates the team's work, places it in a broader context, and lets the team members reflect on how effectively they communicated and collaborated.

Employing a Hands-On, Minds-On Approach to Engineering

Design Squad's hands-on activities

- use inexpensive, easy-to-find supplies;
- require minimal preparation time;
- allow for multiple solutions; and
- provide opportunities for adaptation or modification based on your students' interests and needs (see Figure 1.4).

Given the volume of *Design Squad* content available online, we want to ensure that teachers are able to quickly find what they are looking for. Thus, we have arranged all our resources on the website using the following topics: Force/Energy, Green, Health, Simple Machines, Sound/Music, Space and Transportation, Sports/Games, Structures, and Technology/Materials.

In addition, the matrix in Table 1.1, at the end of this chapter, can help you to align *Design Squad*'s hands-on activities to the science topics you are covering in your classroom.

Integrating Standards-Based, Hands-On Activities Into Your Science Curricula

Many of the activities described above are featured in *Design Squad*'s eight educator guides, which can be downloaded from the website. The educator guides contain simple pedagogical background, instructions, checklists, planning strategies, discussion tips, and reproducible handouts in English and Spanish. Through the use of the guides, you will be able to design units that can be integrated into other lesson plans or curricula to help support the Next Generation Science Standards (NGSS Lead States, 2013).

Educator's Guide. The Educator's Guide's 10 hands-on activities emphasize teamwork and creative problem solving. Kids build electronic dance pads, rubber-band cars, wind-powered sculptures, and ball launchers.

Figure 1.4 Hands-On Minds-On Activities

Image courtesy of WGBH Educational Foundation.

Figure 1.5 *Design Squad*'s design projects are very engaging

Image courtesy of WGBH Educational Foundation.

Event Guide. The Event Guide presents five activities especially suitable for use at lively, fun-filled events, such as a family night or science and engineering day. The Event Guide provides facilitators with an event checklist, reproducible activity sheets for five hands-on activities (also available in Spanish), and an evaluation form to help them plan and organize their event from beginning to end.

Activity Guide. The Activity Guide offers five hands-on activities for children ages 9–12 years (see Figure 1.5). In the activities, kids explore buoyancy by designing and building two kinds of boats, potential and kinetic energy by building a zip line and by using a rubber band to power a paddleboat, simple machines by building a mechanical arm, and tension and compression by building a paper table. The hands-on activity sheets are also available in Spanish.

Teacher's Guide. Written especially for middle school teachers of science, technology, engineering, and mathematics (STEM), the Teacher's Guide has 11 activities divided into three units—force, electricity, and sound—topics found in nearly every physical science curriculum.

On the Moon. NASA and *Design Squad* teamed up to produce a guide that offers kids in Grades 3–12 six hands-on activities that bring NASA's moon missions and engineering to life. Kids design and build projects related to living and working on the moon. For example, there are activities based on flying to and landing on the moon. Others focus on living and working on the moon, such as building a solar collector, a rover to traverse the moon's soft surface, and a crane to dig into it.

Mission: Solar System. NASA and *Design Squad* teamed up to provide six space-based hands-on activities for school and after-school programs serving children in Grades 4–8. They are designed to engage kids in engineering and in NASA's exploration of the solar system—and more broadly, to spark kids' interest in engineering and space science careers.

Invent It, Build It. *Design Squad* and Lemelson-MIT InvenTeams teamed up to develop a guide intended to spark the inventive spirit of kids ages 9–12 in school and after-school programs. Its six hands-on activities bring invention to life for kids, get them thinking like inventors and engineers, and show kids how invention improves people's lives. Kids use their ingenuity to invent solutions to real-world problems. For example, they invent games; green packaging; inexpensive shelters; and convenient, all-purpose carry-alls. The full guide is available in both English and Spanish.

Adaptive Technologies Special Collection. *Design Squad* materials, along with resources from another PBS project called *Medal Quest*, help students explore how science, technology, engineering, and math support athletes with physical disabilities as they compete at elite levels.

Going Beyond the Classroom Through *Design Squad*'s Video Resources

Four types of video resources can be found on the Parents and Educators section of *Design Squad*'s website (http://pbskids.org/designsquad/parentseducators/: TV episodes, animations, video profiles, and demos of activities.

TV Episodes. Televised *Design Squad* episodes feature two teams of kids using their problem-solving skills as they take raw materials and transform them into workable solutions. *Design Squad* cast members use basic technology in a wide range of activities that have a scale and complexity that excite an audience—constructing cardboard furniture for IKEA, building 20-foot bridges, and converting kiddie toys into dragsters are just three examples. Its spin-off series, *Design Squad Nation*, showcases engineer co-hosts Judy and Adam as they travel across the country, working side by side with teens to turn their dreams into reality through engineering. Tackling an array of engineering projects—including a water-saving toilet and a human-powered flying machine—the show aims to get kids thinking about the creativity and fun involved in engineering projects.

Animations. Dynamic animations elucidate science concepts such as "What is sound?" and "How does buoyancy float a boat?"; technology concepts like "How do servos work?" and "What is wireless transmission?"; and engineering concepts like "How do suspension and truss bridges differ?" and "What is a prototype?".

Video Profiles. Through these short videos, viewers meet engaging young engineers who demonstrate that engineering is a rewarding and creative career where you get to work with great people, solve interesting problems, and design things that matter. These segments air at the end of each episode and are available for download on the website. For instance, Debbie Theobald, mother of three, is part of a team developing BEAR, a robot that rescues people from dangerous situations. ("While science and math are very important, there's a lot that goes into it—teamwork, creativity, imagination, being able to see the opportunities from the future.") Another engineer, Evan Thomas, works on water recovery and purification systems for NASA and volunteers for Engineers Without Borders in Rwanda.

Demos of Activities. Many of the hands-on activities are accompanied by videos that demonstrate how to do them. Many teachers find it helpful to watch these videos by themselves to prepare for conducting the activity with their students. Other teachers have told us that they like to show the videos to their students after they have completed the activity so that students can compare their own results.

Sharing and Playing on the *Design Squad* Website

The *Design Squad* website (http://pbskids.org/designsquad) is an online destination for kids, tweens, and teens that promotes the following messages: *You are creative and can solve problems. You can make things that help people. You can dream big. Join* Design Squad *and let's build something together.* On the site, kids can post real-life solutions to real-world problems and respond to challenges by sketching and building their own prototypes. They can also play games that promote the design process and hands-on experiences with science concepts.

Fidgit. With this game, players employ their problem-solving and engineering skills to save small, cute creatures called Fidgits. The aim of the game is for players to use a variety of objects to design rooms through which they can bounce, flip, and roll their Fidgits to safety. Players who want to follow their own path can also build their own custom rooms from scratch. After logging in, they can then save and exchange their rooms with friends who are also playing the game. Fidgit's overarching goal is to help kids strengthen and build their engineering design process skills—observing, brainstorming, designing and building, testing and evaluating, and revising and testing again—while learning along the way that engineers rarely solve a problem on their first try.

Fidgit Factory. Fidgit Factory asks kids to help beloved Fidgit characters get ready for a dance party before the power runs out, while simultaneously giving kids an inside look at how circuits work. Players must first set up their factory by successfully building a circuit that will power its Fidgit-building machines, and then fulfill orders for different types of Fidgits. The game's primary audience is kids between second and fourth grade. It introduces them to fundamental concepts of circuits.

String Thing. String Thing is an interactive game in which students can change a virtual string's tension, length, and gauge to create different musical pitches. It is a great accompaniment to *Design Squad*'s hands-on Build-a-Band activity.

Deepening Your Students' Knowledge of Engineering

Evaluation has shown that *Design Squad* has had a significant positive impact on students' understanding of engineering and attitudes toward engineering.

Knowledge. Students exposed to *Design Squad* learned more about key science constructs (i.e., electrical circuits, sound, Newton's Laws, force, and air pressure) than students who were not exposed to *Design Squad* (Paulsen & Bransfield, 2010).

Design Process Skills. *Design Squad* increases children's design process skills. In a pre- and post-test, kids were asked to think about the steps they would take in designing and building a birdhouse. The number of design process steps that they correctly selected increased significantly from pre to post. Also at pre and post, in order to see if kids included any design process steps in their open-ended response, they were asked to write the best way to go about designing and building something. The number of kids who included *thinking of solutions/brainstorming* and *redesign* also increased significantly. Finally, after watching *Design Squad*, a significantly higher number of kids mentioned *brainstorming* and *redesign* when discussing how to design and build a paper bridge or a device to launch a ball (Vaughan, Bachrach, Tiedemann, & Goodman, 2008).

Attitudes. *Design Squad* significantly improved students' attitudes toward engineering, changing their stereotypes about engineering—for the better. After watching, middle school students, especially girls and minorities, viewed engineering as creative, rewarding, and socially relevant (see Figure 1.6). They were less likely to believe the stereotype that "engineering is boring" (Paulsen & Bransfield, 2010).

Behaviors. *Design Squad* increased students' interest in engineering programs. After watching *Design Squad*, nearly two-thirds of students were interested in participating in an engineering after-school program, compared to just below one-third prior to viewing (Vaughan et al., 2008).

Figure 1.6 Students engaged in *Design Squad* activities see engineering in a new light

Image courtesy of WGBH Educational Foundation.

Deepening Teachers' Knowledge of Engineering

Design Squad also provides educators with the tools they need to develop their own knowledge and attitudes about engineering.

Knowledge. *Design Squad* helps teachers learn how to use hands-on activities to teach students the design process. Teachers have reported back that the challenges helped them put ideas together, learn for themselves what works and what does not work, and formulate guided questions to help students come to their own understandings (Paulsen & Bransfield, 2010).

Design Process Skills. After using *Design Squad* resources, teachers reported that they better understood the engineering design process and increased their knowledge of engineering careers (Paulsen, Green, & Carroll, 2011).

Attitudes. Evaluation has shown that the *Design Squad Educator's Guide* increased teachers' comfort in talking to their students about engineering and using hands-on engineering activities in their classrooms (Paulsen, 2009; Paulsen & Bransfield, 2010).

Talking to Students About Engineering

Kids are influenced equally by what they see and what they don't see. Technical occupations, such as engineering, are much less obvious to young people than, for example, medicine or teaching. This is especially true for many girls and minorities, who, without role models, have little opportunity to imagine themselves in engineering. In fact, for those kids who have no contact with engineers, such careers often seem either unattainable or "not for them." According to one study of girls' attitudes toward engineering,

> High school girls believe engineering is for people who love both math and science. They do not have an understanding of what engineering is. They do not show an interest in the field, nor do they think it is "for them" (EWEP, 2005, p. 18)

Similarly, a study of public perception of engineers and engineering found widespread misunderstanding of what engineering is, what engineers do, and what it takes to become an engineer (NAE, 2008).

Design Squad goes a long way to address this issue by presenting viewers with diverse, positive role models who experience engineering as a fun and engaging process. Beyond using the *Design Squad* resources, you can also weave in the following talking points when discussing engineering with your students.

What's an Engineer?

Engineers dream up creative, practical solutions and work with other smart, inspiring people to invent, design, and build things that matter. They are changing the world all the time.

What Do Engineers Do at Work?

- Think creatively: Engineering is an ideal outlet for imagination and creative problem solving—the perfect field for independent thinkers.
- Work with great people: Engineering takes teamwork. As an engineer, you'll be surrounded by smart, creative, inspiring people.
- Solve problems and design things that matter: Engineers improve people's lives by tackling problems, improving current designs, and coming up with solutions no one else has thought of.
- Change the world and make a difference: Among many other pursuits, engineers develop systems that save lives, prevent disease, reduce poverty, and protect our planet.

How Do Engineers Make the World a Better Place?

Here are some things engineers do to help improve people's lives:

- Create a more fuel-efficient car
- Design a lighter bike frame
- Invent a more powerful superglue
- Create a satellite that detects drought around the world
- Develop a state-of-the-art cell phone
- Invent an artificial retina for the blind
- Develop a feather-light laptop
- Design clothing that repels mosquitoes

Hearing From Other Teachers

We're gratified to hear how our teachers have used these resources, and what features they find especially helpful. Here's what some of them have to say:

> "[Teamwork] creates a better learning experience for them and allows them to discuss designs as they work."

"I planned groups so that they could help each other. They also watched other groups. Several told me that they wish all our labs were on engineering design."

"One team was . . . so excited that they had been able to stack five books on top of the [paper] table they built—and they were still going!"

Conclusion

Design Squad does what television does best—it provides powerful images that show young people that engineering is a great way to solve real problems. In doing so, it demystifies engineering and reveals it as something that every kid can do. But that's not the end of the story. *Design Squad* also provides kids with a way to try out what they've seen on television through a robust education initiative that puts hands-on, standards-based activities into classrooms. In all of its endeavors, the project has incorporated messages that change kids' attitudes about engineering, emphasizing the teamwork, social benefits, and creativity of engineering. With your help in the classroom, *Design Squad* will be able to reach its ultimate goal: to smooth the pathway from a student's initial awareness of engineering to his or her career as a professional engineer.

Table 1.1 Topical Strands Through *Design Squad* Activities

Activity	Electricity	Force/Friction	Pot/Kin Energy	Simple Machines	Structures	Buoyancy	Heat	Open-Ended	Culminating
2 Wheel Balloon Car		X	X	X	X				
4 Wheel Balloon Car		X	X	X	X				
Air Cannon		X		X	X				
Balance Magic		X						X	
Balloon Joust		X	X						
Blimp Jet		X				X		X	X
Build a Band		X						X	
Build a Better Lunchbox					X		X	X	
Confetti Launcher		X	X	X	X			X	
Convenient Carrier					X			X	
Customized Car		X		X					X
Dance Off	X								X
Dance Pad Mania	X								

(Continued)

Table 1.1 (Continued)

Activity	Electricity	Force/Friction	Pot/Kin Energy	Simple Machines	Structures	Buoyancy	Heat	Open-Ended	Culminating
Down to the Core		X	X	X				X	
Electric Gamebox	X		X					X	X
Electric Highway	X							X	
Extreme Kicking Machine		X	X	X	X			X	X
Feel the Heat		X					X		
Four Corners				X	X				
Get-Moving Game		X		X	X			X	
Glow Sticks	X								
Harmless Holder					X			X	
Headphone Helper		X						X	X
Heavy Lifting		X		X	X				
Helping Hand		X		X	X				
Hidden Alarm	X								
High Rise		X			X				
Hovercraft		X	X					X	
Indoor Slingshot		X	X		X				
Inspector Detector		X							
Invent Better World								X	X
Invisible Force		X	X						
Kick Stick	X		X					X	
Kicking Machine		X	X	X					
Kinetic Sculpture		X			X				X
Launch It		X	X					X	
Marshmallow Blaster		X							
Motorized Car	X	X		X					
On Target		X	X					X	
Paddle Power			X	X	X	X		X	
Paper Table		X			X			X	
Pop Fly		X		X				X	

Activity	Electricity	Force/Friction	Pot/Kin Energy	Simple Machines	Structures	Buoyancy	Heat	Open-Ended	Culminating
Robo Arm		X		X					
Robo Wheel		X	X	X					
Roving on the Moon		X	X	X	X				
Rubber-Band Car		X	X	X	X				
Sky Floater		X				X		X	
Sky Glider		X				X		X	
Soft Landing		X	X					X	
Speedy Shelter					X			X	
String Puppet		X							
String Thing		X							
Touchdown		X	X		X			X	
Treasure Grab		X		X					
Unpoppable Balloon		X							
Watercraft						X		X	
Zip Line		X			X			X	

References

Extraordinary Women Engineers Project (EWEP). (2005). *Extraordinary women engineers—Final report.* Retrieved from http://www.aacei.org/wpc/library/ExtraordinaryWomen-FinalReport.pdf.

National Academy of Enginering (NAE). (2008). *Changing the conversation: Messages for improving public understanding of engineering.* Retrieved from http://www.nap.edu/catalog/12187.html.

NGSS Lead States. (2013). *Next generation science standards: For states, by states. Volume 1: The standards.* Washington, DC: National Academies Press.

Paulsen, C. (2009). Design Squad Season 2 *final evaluation report.* Concord, MA: Veridian inSight and American Institutes for Research.

Paulsen, C. A., & Bransfield, C. P. (2010). *Evaluation of* Design Squad, Season 3: *Final report.* Concord, MA: Concord Evaluation Group, LLC.

Paulsen, C. A., Green, S., & Carroll, S. (2011). Design Squad Nation: *Evaluation report.* In support of National Science Foundation Grant No. 0917495. Concord, MA: Concord Evaluation Group, LLC.

Vaughan, P., Bachrach, E., Tiedemann, M., & Goodman, I. F. (2008). Design Squad: *Final evaluation report.* Cambridge, MA: Goodman Research Group.

2

Models in Technology and Science

Bernard Zubrowski

The *Models in Technology and Science* series involves students in applying the engineering design process to building, modifying, and refining working models.

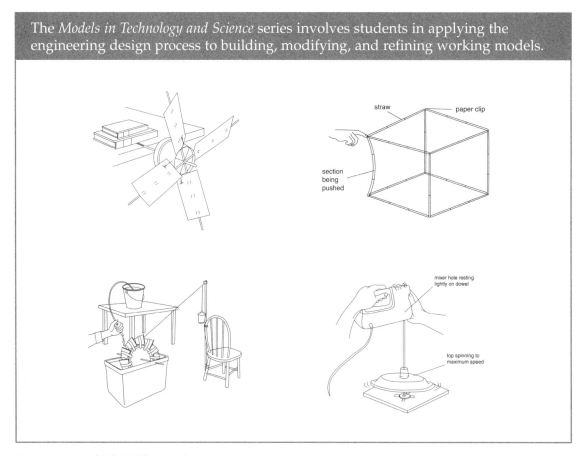

Image courtesy of Kelvin Educational.

Engaging in the practices of science helps students understand how scientific knowledge develops; such direct involvement gives them an appreciation of the wide range of approaches that are used to investigate, model, and explain the world. Engaging in the practices of engineering likewise helps students understand the work of engineers, as well as the links between engineering and science. Participation in these practices also helps students form an understanding of the crosscutting concepts and disciplinary ideas of science and engineering; moreover, it makes students' knowledge more meaningful and embeds it more deeply into their worldview.

The actual doing of science or engineering can also pique students' curiosity, capture their interest, and motivate their continued study; the insights thus gained help them recognize that the work of scientists and engineers is a creative endeavor—one that has deeply affected the world they live in. Students may then recognize that science and engineering can contribute to meeting many of the major challenges that confront society today, such as generating sufficient energy, preventing and treating disease, maintaining supplies of fresh water and food, and addressing climate change. (NGSS Lead States, 2013b, Appendix F, p. 6)

Models in Technology and Science (MITS) is a series of teacher's guides that provides directions for students in Grades 5–8 to carry out extended explorations of basic physical phenomena and technological systems and artifacts as advocated in *A Framework for K–12 Science Education* (NRC, 2012) and *Next Generation Science Standards* (NGSS Lead States, 2013a). Some of the projects in the series use an integrated design/inquiry approach, whereas other units focus on the exploration of basic physical phenomena. The overall approach is a combination of hands-on activities and careful follow-up discussions to help students make sense of their experiences. Information for how to obtain these guides is provided at the end of this chapter.

The physical context and team arrangements encourage the students to modify and refine their initial designs, reflect on the physical phenomena, and argue their ideas based on evidence so that their understanding of the phenomena comes to align more closely with scientific views as they develop scientific inquiry and engineering design skills.

In order for students to succeed at these activities, it is important that they have sufficient time—in most cases, four to six weeks of daily 40- or 50-minute class periods—to become thoroughly familiar with the materials, become deeply engaged in designing and refining solutions to the problem, and able to reflect on their experiences. For example, consider the Windmill unit. This is the first of several that we will describe in this chapter.

Windmills

In this project, students are challenged to design and build a model windmill using simple and inexpensive materials (index cards, thin dowels, a cup, a metal rod, string, and nails) and a small fan as a source of wind power (see Figure 2.1). The Windmills teacher's guide suggests a sequence of activities to move students along so that they are not completely overwhelmed with the initial challenge and are given enough time to be creative and exploratory. Thus, the first challenge is to design and construct a model windmill that will easily move when the fan is placed in front of it.

Figure 2.1 Student-Built Windmill

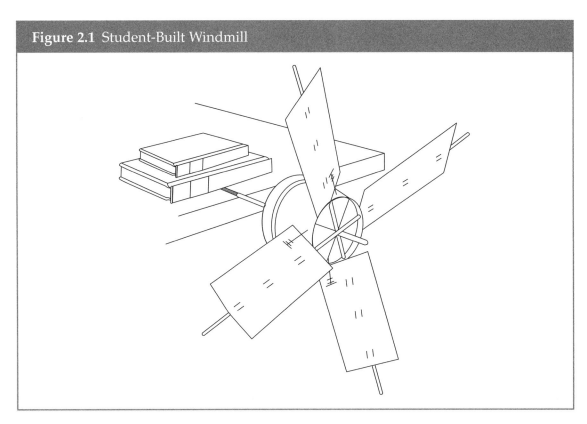

Image courtesy of Kelvin Educational.

Then, the students are challenged to add a cup with a string attached to the shaft of the windmill so that the model will be able to lift a specified number of nails. From there, they can try different arrangements of the arms of the windmill using more of the same materials or slightly different materials to see how they can increase the lifting capacity of their model.

It is at this point that guided inquiry can be introduced. Students can carry out systematic experiments by controlling variables. They can test to see whether a different number of arms, different size of arms, or arms further from the shaft make a difference in the lifting capacity of the windmill. These tests provide a context for the teacher to introduce the concept of turning moments and torque. The teacher can allow additional time for the students to work with these ideas and later introduce the concept of levers.

If there is sufficient time, the teacher can engage the students in a second set of activities using the model windmill in which the students focus on *how long* it takes to lift a graduated set of weights, rather than the *total weight* that their models can lift. This additional activity provides a context for the teacher to introduce the basic physical concepts of work and power.

If the teacher wishes to go further, a small electric motor and meter can be introduced. Students can be challenged to see how much electricity they can generate with their modified windmill.

Assessment. One type of assessment for this project is to have students examine several types of model windmills that have a problem in functioning or are not very effective. Can they isolate the problem or make recommendations for making each model more effective?

Another type of assessment is for students to draw upon all of their experiences during the project and build a model windmill that uses minimal materials but can lift a maximum number of nails. The teacher can observe each group during construction of the model and question the group members about why they have chosen specific design features. The importance of using models in engineering is explicitly called out in the NGSS.

> In science, models are used to represent a system (or parts of a system) under study, to aid in the development of questions and explanations, to generate data that can be used to make predictions, and to communicate ideas to others. Students can be expected to evaluate and refine models through an iterative cycle of comparing their predictions with the real world and then adjusting them to gain insights into the phenomenon being modeled. As such, models are based upon evidence. When new evidence is uncovered that the models can't explain, models are modified. (NGSS Lead States, 2013b, Appendix F, p. 6)

The Learning Approach

Embedded in the outline of activities is a well-founded pedagogical approach aligned with contemporary learning theory (embodied cognition), practical experiences of the author, and multiple field trials. This approach can be described as a developmental progression. Students naturally start out with an intuitive approach based on previous knowledge and experiences. Their initial designs are quick and barely functional. After some modifications, their designs perform better, but the changes tend to be more through trial and error rather than systematic testing. This situation provides a natural opportunity for the teacher to introduce inquiry as a means to help the students improve their designs.

At this point, groups of students may carry out systematic tests using their own designs, or the teacher can have the entire class conduct controlled experiments using a standard model, which is a composite of existing designs. As the students interpret the results of their experiments, they begin to formulate physical science concepts while improving their abilities to plan and carry out investigations, analyze data, and argue from evidence.

Next, the students can go back to redesigning their particular solution to the overall problem, drawing upon this newly gained knowledge to improve upon their initial designs. In this manner, scientific inquiry and engineering design go hand-in-hand with the development of conceptual understanding. This idea that science supports engineering and engineering supports science is also emphasized in the NGSS.

> Advances in science offer new capabilities, new materials, or new understanding of processes that can be applied through engineering to produce advances in technology. Advances in technology, in turn, provide scientists with new capabilities to probe the natural world at larger or smaller scales; to record, manage, and analyze data; and to model ever more complex systems with greater precision. In addition, engineers' efforts to develop or improve technologies often raise new questions for scientists' investigations. (NGSS Lead States, 2013b, Appendix J, p. 1)

These ideas are developed more thoroughly in *Exploration and Meaning Making in the Learning of Science* (Zubrowski, 2009). (See Zubrowski, 2002, for a more detailed development of this approach.)

Design challenges can vary greatly in their openness and structure. MITS takes the approach that students need to be challenged with highly engaging topics and given a situation that has manageable complexity. The teacher's guides provide a way for teachers to modify the problem and activities so that the challenge is neither too difficult nor too easy for a given group of students.

Also, design challenges need to be well defined and have associated with them carefully selected materials. The MITS projects utilize materials that are mostly familiar and relatively simple, so that students can quickly engage with them and develop a wide variety of possible designs that are creative and lead to consideration of physical science principles.

The MITS design challenges can also be used to lay the groundwork for students to engage in computer simulations that present similar design problems and also allow students to go further in the virtual world. For instance, the MITS project on bridge building can help students develop an intuitive grasp of engineering design principles before engaging in the Engineering Encounters Bridge Design Contest (http://engineeringencounters.org/programs/bridge-contest/).

Design challenges readily lend themselves to various types of embedded assessments. Students can be asked to keep a log to record changes that they make in their designs and results of systematic observations and experiments using tables and charts. They can also use digital photography to record the changes in their design, as well as take videos to show improvements in performance.

The MITS projects were field tested in urban and suburban classrooms with students representing a wide range of social and academic backgrounds. Many students who ordinarily do not do well academically became readily engaged and, in many cases, outperformed students who are considered advanced. We found that teamwork and a supportive classroom culture encouraged girls to become actively involved and sometimes outperform the boys.

The Teacher's Guide

Each teacher's guide in the MITS series includes the following sections:

Rationale explains the purpose of each activity and the unit as a whole.

Materials List specifies the supplies and equipment needed for each activity.

Preparation Ahead contains instructions for getting the right kinds of materials and what the teacher should try out before class.

Introducing the Activity includes suggestions for helping students understand the purpose of each activity.

Assisting Students During the Activity provides strategies for helping students as they attempt to construct their designs or carry out experiments. Sometimes, there are specific suggestions for student behaviors to watch for, both nonverbal behavior as well as spoken comments.

Interpreting the Results and Observations offers strategies for helping students report and interpret their observations and data, and for introducing terms and concepts and relating these ideas to the activities. It also suggests questions to probe student thinking. Some of these questions are related to the overall design challenge, while others are related to the specific activity.

Assessment provides ideas for what to watch for during the activities and discussions, including how students handle the materials, manipulate their designs, function as teams, and discuss their understanding of physical principles.

Homework includes ideas for further experiments and explorations for students to do at home.

Other MITS Teacher's Guides

Drinking Straw Structures

Students are challenged to design and build a house and a bridge using drinking straws as the materials of construction and paper clips as connectors (see Figure 2.2). The straws can be made longer and stronger by some simple techniques. The construction of a house or a bridge can happen within an extended single period or over two or three periods depending on students' prior experience with design challenges and their age level.

Students test their structures by hanging cups of nails on parts of the structure or by placing a flat piece of cardboard on the flat section of the house or bridge and placing weights on the cardboard. The Teacher's Guide recommends that the students discuss their initial designs and methods for conducting tests in order to learn about the design process.

In a series of guided inquiry activities, students test different kinds of construction materials (drinking straws, coffee stirrers, balsa wood) and build different truss frames. As students engage in these activities and discuss the results, the teacher has opportunities to introduce the concepts of tension and compression, and how engineers use trusses to strengthen structures without adding too much weight.

The use of drinking straws as a building material has advantages and disadvantages. Straws are cheap and available for purchase. They can be easily joined together to make

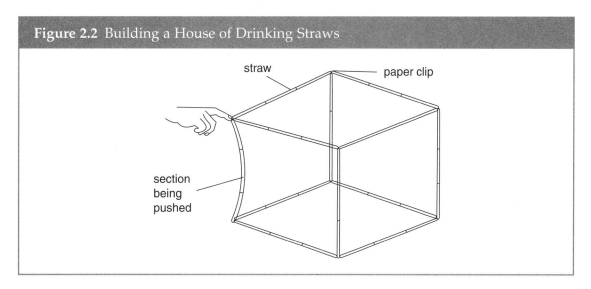

Figure 2.2 Building a House of Drinking Straws

Image courtesy of Kelvin Educational.

longer segments, and when structures are tested, failure points can be readily observed. Some sections will bend but not break when the cups of nails are hung on the structure. So, students can see where parts of a structure are undergoing compression. Or, sections of joined straws will be pulled apart when testing, showing that that section is undergoing tension. Likewise, at connecting points with paper clips, the straws may pull apart, indicating that this part is under tension.

Once students develop some skill in the handling of the drinking straws and paper clips, they can assemble their designs more quickly. This allows them to quickly modify their designs and carry out an iterative process, giving them the opportunity to learn from the problems and, with proper sense making, gain a deeper understanding of how these structures function. (This is in contrast to design projects using balsa wood, where much time is needed to carefully glue the wood together.) On the other hand, if students are not careful in the handling of the straws, they can end up building structures that have flawed sections due to bends in the straws.

The Teacher's Guide suggests that students start by building a house of a given dimension because students are familiar with houses and it allows them to have a personal imprint on the design. That experience will help them get started on a bridge design. As part of the bridge design project, the students research real bridges that have structures that the students can model and test using drinking straws and paper clips. This second project can act as a type of embedded assessment to see how the students have assimilated these experiences and to what extent they can apply their new understandings to the design and construction of a bridge. Students can also use online tools, such as the Engineering Encounters Bridge Design Contest, to construct and test virtual bridges.

Water Wheels

In this project, students are challenged to build model water wheels using simple materials (plastic plates and cups, a metal rod, string, weights, and a large container) (see Figure 2.3). The first challenge is to design and construct a water wheel from the plastic plates and cup. A string is added to the shaft of the wheel and a cup attached at the other end of the string, which is hanging from a pulley. Water from a soda bottle provides the means of power. Students test to determine the maximum lifting capacity of their model as they add nails to the cup.

The Teacher's Guide suggests a sequence of activities to move students from the simple construction and testing of one kind of water wheel to the construction of other kinds of water wheels using related materials. The overall challenge is to find out how to modify the dimensions or capacity of the water wheel so that it can lift more weight than the preliminary challenge. At this point, guided inquiry can be carried out. Students can systematically test to see whether different sizes of cups and different diameters of plates will make a difference in the lifting capacity of the model. These particular activities provide a context for the teacher to introduce the concepts of torque, turning moments, and the lever as one kind of simple machine.

An additional challenge is for students to design a model water wheel that spins at faster and faster speeds. Students can design ways of measuring the speed of the wheel or the teacher can provide a method for measuring speed. These activities provide a context for introducing the concepts of rotational momentum, as well as potential gravitational and kinetic energy.

Figure 2.3 Water Wheel Testing

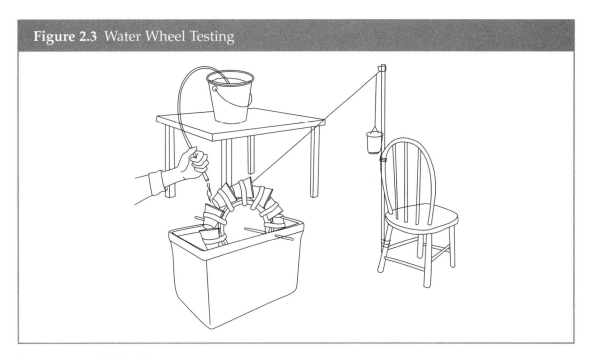

Image courtesy of Kelvin Educational.

Assessment. Once students seem to have a good understanding of the function of the model water wheel, they can be challenged to construct a water wheel that lifts a specified number of nails using the least amount of materials. The teacher can observe the type of designs each group constructs and question them about specific features of their design, noting the extent to which students draw upon their previous experiences to justify these features.

There are two other projects that are part of the Models in Technology and Science program. These are not explicitly design projects, but rather a type of guided design where more attention is given to inquiry and the development of physical science concepts.

Tops and Yo-Yos

In the Tops and Yo-Yos project, students are given simple materials (plastic plates, rubber stoppers, and a dowel). Also, they are given a device using a rubber band and a kitchen mixer, which can be used as power sources for spinning the assembled tops (see Figure 2.4). Students start off testing different circular materials to find out how long each can spin using the two different power sources. Then, they are given plastic plates and challenged to make up their own designs of tops modifying the designs such as trying different numbers and arrangements of plates. This is followed by guided inquiry, where students systematically test variables such as increasing weight (adding more plates), or using different diameters of plates and different positions of the plates on the shaft of the top. These experiments provide a context for the teachers to have students develop an understanding of the variables that affect rotational momentum.

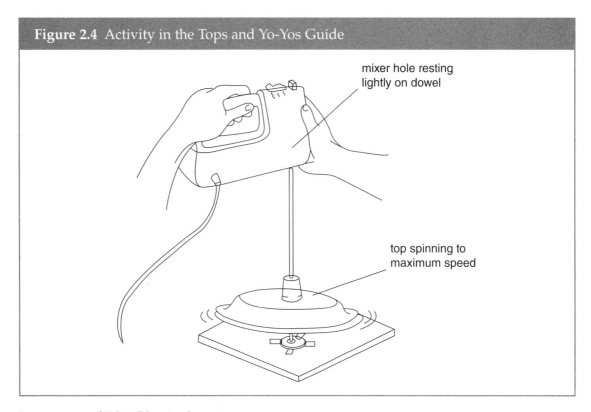

Figure 2.4 Activity in the Tops and Yo-Yos Guide

mixer hole resting lightly on dowel

top spinning to maximum speed

Image courtesy of Kelvin Educational.

Students can carry out a similar set of activities using the same materials to make yo-yos. Here also they can plan and conduct systematic experiments to see how these variables affect the running time of the yo-yos. Running time in this situation is how many ups and downs each yo-yo does while the end of the string is held stationary.

Ice Cream Making

Ice Cream Making is a project where students systematically test containers of different kinds of materials (metal, plastic, glass, paper) to determine which material will be the best conductor for moving heat out of a hot liquid in the containers when the different containers are placed in cold water; cold water and ice; and cold water, ice, and salt (see Figure 2.5). Based on these experimental results, students are given the opportunity to make a small amount of ice cream. Students need to decide what kind of container and what cooling environment will give them the quickest way of making ice cream.

Where to Get It

The following Models in Technology and Science (MITS) Teacher's Guides are available from Kelvin Educational (www.kelvin.com):

Mirrors: The Reflection of Light

Tops and Yo-Yos: Forces and Motion of Rotating Objects

Figure 2.5 Graph of the Thermal Conductivity of Metal, Paper, Plastic, and Glass, Showing Which Is Best for Making Ice Cream

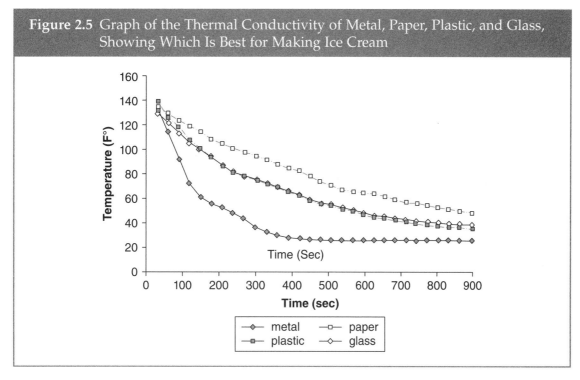

Image courtesy of Kelvin Educational.

Ice Cream Making and Cake Baking: Heat Transfer

Shadows and Images: How Images Are Formed

Structures: Houses, Bridges and Towers

Inks: Food Colors and Papers

Making Waves: Rhythmic Motion

Mobiles: Balancing Toys and Static Equilibrium

Water Wheels: How Work and Power Are Generated

Air and Water Movement: Patterns of Fluid Motion

Salad Dressing Physics: Density of Liquids and Solids

A Windmills Kit is available from Boreal Science Kit (www.boreal.com).

Conclusion

The key to each of the MITS units is that the practices of scientific inquiry and engineering design are carried out *together*. This helps students develop the core ideas of science in a meaningful and engaging context. The result is that they learn science in a way that makes sense and is useful, while they also learn how science and engineering complement each other in the real world, functioning very much like a team of professional scientists and engineers. This idea, that engineering must be included as a prominent part of science education, is a core value in the Framework and the Next Generation Science Standards.

> Any education that focuses predominantly on the detailed products of scientific labor—the facts of science—without developing an understanding of how those facts were established or that ignores the many important applications of science in the world misrepresents science and marginalizes the importance of engineering. (NGSS Lead States, 2013b, Appendix F, p. 2)

References

National Research Council (NRC). (2012). *A framework for K-12 science education: Practices, crosscutting concepts, and core ideas*. Committee on a Conceptual Framework for New K-12 Science Education Standards. Board on Science Education, Division of Behavioral and Social Sciences and Education, National Research Council. Washington, DC: National Academies Press.

NGSS Lead States. (2013a). *Next generation science standards: For states, by states. Volume 1: The standards*. Washington, DC: National Academies Press.

NGSS Lead States. (2013b). *Next generation science standards: For states, by states. Volume 2: Appendices*. Washington, DC: National Academies Press.

Zubrowski, B. (2002). Integrating science into design technology projects: Using a standard model in the design process. *Journal of Technology Education, 13*(2). Retrieved from http://scholar.lib.vt.edu/ejournals/JTE/v13n2/zubrowski.html.

Zubrowski, B. (2009). *Exploration and meaning making in the learning of science*. Dordrecht: Springer.

Everyday Engineering

Putting the E in STEM Teaching and Learning

Richard Moyer and Susan Everett
University of Michigan–Dearborn

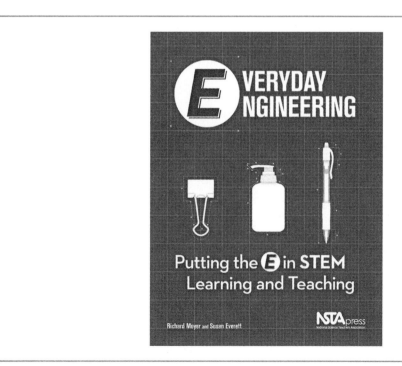

Reprinted from *Everyday Engineering: Putting the E in STEM* by Richard Moyer and Susan Everett, with permission of NSTA.

Everyday Engineering is a collection of 14 previously published hands-on engineering activities from a regularly featured column in the National Science Teachers Association's (NSTA) middle-level journal, *Science Scope*. Each activity examines a simple, everyday object looking at its design and function. Within each activity, science content and engineering practices are integrated as well as mathematics when appropriate. Each activity is illustrated with color photography by Robert L. Simpson III, reprinted courtesy of NSTA from *Everyday Engineering: Putting the E in STEM Teaching and Learning* by Richard Moyer and Susan Everett.

Introduction

In the summer of 2007, we were completing some curriculum materials for an elementary science methods book and began thinking about a new project. We became aware of a lack of engineering materials for teachers and students at the elementary and middle levels except for a few very popular activities like bridge building, egg drops, and paper airplane construction. We wanted to fill this gap, and at this level, since there were more engineering curricula available for high school students. It was our feeling that high school may be too late to interest students, especially girls, in engineering. That is, by that time, students have already made up their minds as to whether or not they wish to pursue the study of engineering.

This led us to begin tinkering with lots of things—taking them apart and looking at how they were made. We became fascinated with ballpoint pens, especially the retractable ones. A bit of research uncovered an interesting history of how they were developed and marketed. Quillpens were used for more than a thousand years and were ultimately replaced by fountain pens in the late 1800s. However, fountain pens were notorious for leaking, and since the ink took time to dry, writing with them often produced smeary results. Ballpoints were introduced in the 1940s as an improvement over fountain pens and were, at first, eagerly purchased. However, the initial ballpoints were not very successful due to poor quality. Inexpensive ballpoints became available in the 1950s and have led to the plethora of writing instruments available today—roller ball tips, felt tips and markers, highlighters, and so on. Looking at the history of technological development helped us see that invention is only the first step, and engineering can focus on the iterative process of innovation that may lead to many variations and successful solutions or products.

We presented a workshop at the 2007 NSTA Regional Conference in Detroit on the engineering of ballpoint pens. The response of the teachers was overwhelmingly positive. They, too, were taken with the elegance of the engineering required to make a 20-cent ballpoint pen that extends and retracts. At this point, we had a two-part realization—that very simple, everyday objects were amazingly interesting and they could be the key to engaging younger students in engineering. The positive response resulted in our writing an article for NSTA's journal for middle-level teachers about the pen activities. This quickly led to the proposal for the *Science Scope* column and subsequent book, *Everyday Engineering*, with each activity concentrating on one everyday object like sealable plastic baggies or toothbrushes. *Everyday Engineering* (Moyer & Everett, 2012a) is available from NSTA Press (www.nsta.org/publications/press/).

The book presents a slightly different focus from what many consider to be engineering. "Everyone recognizes that such things as computers, aircraft, and genetically engineered plants are examples of technology, but for most people, the understanding of technology goes no deeper" (ITEA, 2007, p. 22). We want students to appreciate that virtually every object that is not natural has been engineered—designed to solve a problem or meet a specific need. This includes all the simple objects we use every day.

Goals

Our overall goal for *Everyday Engineering* is to increase middle-level students' (Grades 5–9) awareness of the engineering that underlies the world around them. Specifically, we want these materials to

- **Attract a broader cross section of middle-level students to the study of engineering**. On one hand, we hope to encourage students who might not otherwise be interested in engineering to consider it as a possible career. On the other hand, we hope to help all students develop a basic level of literacy in engineering.
- **Increase students' curiosity about how the objects they encounter were designed and how they are used.** We provide many opportunities for students to "tinker" with objects by taking them apart and manipulating them to figure out how they work. We feel this process of reverse engineering helps students develop design abilities—the experience of seeing how things work is helpful when students are asked to design their own technology to solve a problem.
- **Engage students in science and engineering practices.** Since *Everyday Engineering* was published before the release of the Next Generation Science Standards (NGSS Lead States, 2013a, 2013b), each of the activities references content and process standards from the *National Science Education Standards* (NRC, 1996) and the ITEA *Standards for Technological Literacy* (ITEA, 2000, 2005, 2007). There is considerable congruency among these standards and the science and engineering practices in *A Framework for K–12 Science Education* (NRC, 2012) and the NGSS. All new *Everyday Engineering* columns published in *Science Scope* are related to the Framework and the NGSS.
- **Enable teachers to integrate science content with other STEM disciplines**. While we anticipate a variety of instructors (both in formal and informal settings) may utilize *Everyday Engineering*, the primary audience is the middle-level science teacher. For this reason, specific science content is emphasized in each of the activities as well as engineering and technology. When appropriate (such as the design of packaging), mathematics is integrated as well. This format provides an integrated experience with the STEM disciplines.

Instructional Model

Each lesson is driven by an inquiry investigation that follows the 5E Learning Cycle Model, which had its roots in the 1960s and has seen many variations. We have used this model extensively in our work, and we value the constructivist teaching/learning style it supports. In this pedagogy, students are asked to take an active part in their learning by exploring a question (or in engineering, a problem) that is developed at the onset of the lesson. This contrasts with more traditional didactic pedagogy, where students are asked to investigate after they have read or listened to an explanation of the topic. The particular Learning Cycle Model we use consists of five phases: engage, explore, explain, extend, and evaluate (Bybee, 1997; Bybee & Landes, 1990).

The purpose of the engage phase is to focus the students on the question (or problem) to be explored. In the exploration phase, students plan procedures using their ideas to seek solutions to their questions or problems. In the explain phase, the data and findings from the explore phase are used to develop conceptual understanding. During the extend phase, students make real-world applications related to the question or problem. The final phase is to assess the students' conceptual understanding.

This model is flexible enough to be used in engineering activities as well as science. While originally designed for students to use to answer science questions, the exploration phase can also be used to investigate engineering problems. These problems may consist of design activities, testing of different solutions, or taking things apart to find out how they work through reverse engineering. For example, in one activity, students are asked to design a life preserver (see Figure 3.1) that will keep an action figure afloat with its face out of the water. In another, students test different numbers of blades on a pinwheel. For reverse engineering, students take a squirt gun apart (see Figure 3.2) to see how the pump and valves facilitate the movement of water out of the reservoir (Moyer & Everett, 2009b).

Figure 3.1 Action Figure Life Preservers

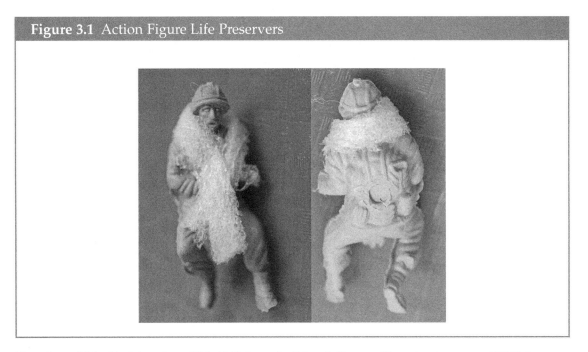

Photo first published in *Science Scope, 35*(6), 16–23. Image by Robert L. Simpson III, reprinted courtesy of NSTA from *Everyday Engineering: Putting the E in STEM Teaching and Learning* by Richard Moyer and Susan Everett.

Curricular Topics

Rather than the more traditional categories of engineering—mechanical, chemical, or biomedical—*Everyday Engineering* is divided into five areas—Office, Kitchen, Bathroom, Electrical, and Outdoor/Recreational Engineering—to emphasize the "everydayness" of our approach. Table 3.1 lists the unique topics found in each area. As noted earlier, our goal with *Everyday Engineering* is to provide unique activities that will be engaging to

Figure 3.2 Squirt Gun Cut-Away

Photo first published in *Science Scope, 33*(2), 10–14. Image by Robert L. Simpson III, reprinted courtesy of NSTA from *Everyday Engineering: Putting the E in STEM Teaching and Learning* by Richard Moyer and Susan Everett.

middle-level students and teachers. It is our hope that lessons related to the kitchen or recreation may reach students who otherwise might not be interested in engineering. Summaries of three different kinds of lessons are also provided below.

Table 3.1 *Everyday Engineering* Topics

Engineering Area	Topic
Office	What Makes a Bic™ Click? Clips and Clamps
Kitchen	Times Up, Turkey: Pop-Up Thermometers Charcoal—Can It Corral Chlorine? What Makes a Better Box? It's (Zipped) in the Bag
Bathroom	An Absorbing Look at Terrycloth Towels Toothbrush Design—Is There a Better Bristle?
Electrical	Holiday Blinkers Windmills Are Going Around Again A Little (Flash) of Light
Outdoor/Recreational	Life Preservers—Increase Your V to Lower Your D Ain't She Sweet—Bats, Rackets, Golf Clubs, and All What Makes a Squirt Gun Squirt?

Activity Format

Each of the investigations in *Everyday Engineering* is a complete lesson plan with all necessary information required for teaching to middle-level students. All of the activities are accompanied by high-quality color photographs (some magnified up to 40X) to help teachers understand the workings of the item being investigated. For example, the cutaway of a turkey timer (Figure 3.3) shows the alloy designed to melt at a predetermined temperature that releases the spring, which pushes up the red pop-up stem indicating the turkey is ready to eat (Moyer & Everett, 2009a).

Think about that for a minute—scientific understanding of metals enabled metallurgists to develop an alloy that would melt at just the right temperature so that engineers could create the pop-up timer. This relationship between science and engineering is one of the lessons identified in the Framework as important for all students to learn.

"Advances in science offer new capabilities, new materials, or new understanding of processes that can be applied through engineering to produce advances in technology." —A Framework for K–12 Science Education, NRC, 2012, p. 203

Figure 3.3 Turkey Timer Cut-Away

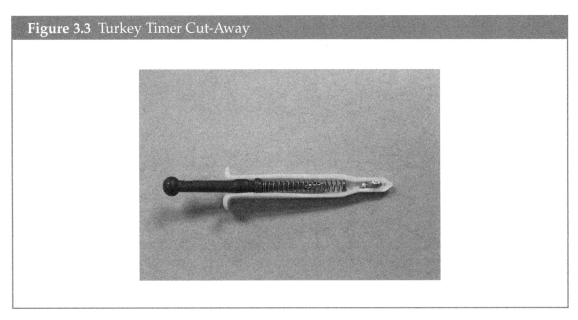

Photo first published in *Science Scope, 33*(3), 56–61. Image by Robert L. Simpson III, reprinted courtesy of NSTA from *Everyday Engineering: Putting the E in STEM Teaching and Learning* by Richard Moyer and Susan Everett.

In addition, each activity in the book includes a brief history of the topic, a discussion of all materials necessary for a class of 24 students, teacher background information, and a student activity guide following the 5E Learning Cycle Model.

Historical Information

Since one of our goals is to reach students who may be less inclined to gravitate toward engineering, we emphasize its human and social aspects by looking at a brief history of the everyday item being investigated. For example, flashlights got their name because the cells used at the time were weak and the bulbs dim, so they could be used for only short periods or "flashes." We have received positive feedback from our readers about the inclusion of the historical material. Some have related that they have their students do further research on the topic.

Materials

We realize that many schools do not have a large budget for engineering activities, which often can involve expensive equipment. One of the advantages of studying everyday phenomena is that the equipment required can be simple and inexpensive. As we noted, retractable ballpoint pens can be purchased for about 20 cents each. A one-dollar swim noodle provides more than enough foam for five classes of students in the life preserver activity (Moyer & Everett, 2012b). Patterns for construction materials—windmill blades or gears, for example—are provided when needed. In general, most supplies that are not available in a typical science classroom can be purchased at supermarkets or dollar stores.

Teacher Background Information

Our goal is to provide sufficient information so that teachers with limited background knowledge in science or engineering are comfortable teaching the lessons. Thus, we explain all of the science content information required. For example, in the binder clip activity, we include a side bar that discusses the mechanical advantage of levers. Safety requirements are also discussed in this section, and all activities follow NSTA safety guidelines. While some teachers may wish for their students to devise their own procedures for the investigation, we also provide one possible procedure for each activity, including sample data.

Complete teacher notes are provided for each phase of the 5E Learning Cycle as well. This includes suggested discussion items and questions. Detailed answers and explanations are included throughout each lesson phase. Ideas for extending the activities or additional resources are often provided.

Student Activity Guide

A reproducible guide is available with each lesson in the book for teachers who want to provide additional student scaffolding.

Sealable Plastic Bags. "It's (Zipped) in the Bag" has students look at mechanisms used to seal plastic storage bags. They then engage in their own engineering design challenge. Since it is not possible for them to engineer a new kind of plastic bag, they are challenged to plan and construct a system that will keep a file folder closed. An outline of the 5E Lesson follows.

Engage: Examine several different sealable baggies to note similarities and differences of the closing mechanisms.

Explore: Design, construct, and test a sealing mechanism for closing a file folder. Explain: Learn about the forces required to hold the sealing mechanisms in plastic bags together.

Extend: Investigate sliding sealing mechanisms as well as metal zippers.

Evaluate: Invent a new use for a sealing mechanism.

Towels. In "An Absorbing Look at Terrycloth Towels," students test different weaves, fibers, and densities of bath towels to assess their absorbency (Figure 3.4) (Moyer & Everett, 2010). This engineering challenge requires students to test existing designs and realize some of the costs and benefits of the various types of towels that are available.

Engage: Observe several different towel samples with a hand lens to note differences in the weaves.

Explore: Test the absorbency of three types of towels—microfiber, plush terry, and a flat weave tea towel.

Explain: Rank towels from least to most absorbent and calculate towel density using the industry standard GSM (grams per square meter).

Extend: Compare the dry mass of a given towel to the mass of water it can absorb.

Evaluate: Explain in writing the drying ability between an old worn-out towel and a new plush towel.

The towel investigation is a good example of a practice used in the service of engineering, rather than its usual use in science. This idea that an engineering investigation has a different goal than a science investigation is emphasized in the Framework and NGSS.

Figure 3.4 Close Up (10X Magnification) of Towel Weaves

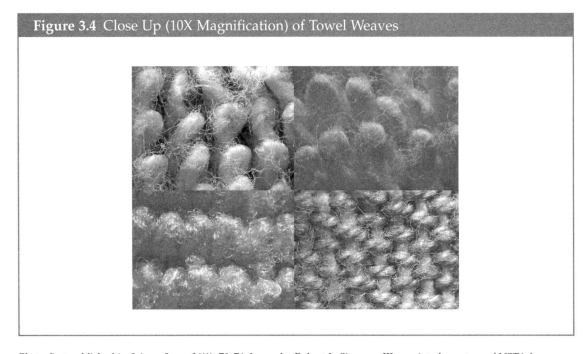

Photo first published in *Science Scope, 34*(1), 70–74. Image by Robert L. Simpson III, reprinted courtesy of NSTA from *Everyday Engineering: Putting the E in STEM Teaching and Learning* by Richard Moyer and Susan Everett.

"The purpose of engineering investigations might be to find out how to fix or improve the functioning of a technological system or to compare different solutions to see which best solves a problem." —NGSS Lead States, 2013b, Appendix F, p. 7

Sweet Spots. One of the NGSS practices for both science and engineering is to develop and use models. In "Ain't She Sweet—Bats, Rackets, Golf Clubs, and All," students test a model of a baseball bat to determine the location of the sweet spot (Moyer & Everett, 2011). In this activity, students use a meter stick as a model for the bat.

Engage: Tap different locations along the length of a bat with a hammer and note variations in sounds and vibrations of the bat.

Explore: Strike a coin at various points along a meter stick and record how far the coin moves at each location (Figure 3.5).

Explain: Determine the sweet spot of the meter stick.

Extend: Compare the location of the bat's sweet spot with that of the meter stick.

Evaluate: Determine the sweet spot of other types of sports equipment.

Developing and using models is another practice that can be used in engineering. Since engineering involves testing models, not just using them to explain phenomena as in science, engineering activities provide excellent opportunities for students to recognize the strengths and limitations of models. This too is pointed out in the NGSS.

"Although models do not correspond exactly to the real world, they bring certain features into focus while obscuring others." —NGSS Lead States, 2013b, Appendix F, p. 6

Figure 3.5 Determining Sweet Spot of Meter Stick

Photo first published in *Science Scope, 34*(5), 52–56. Image by Robert L. Simpson III, reprinted courtesy of NSTA from *Everyday Engineering: Putting the E in STEM Teaching and Learning* by Richard Moyer and Susan Everett.

Current and Future Endeavors

The main focus for *Everyday Engineering* is to engage middle-level students with engineering challenges that relate to daily living. However, the activities have also been adapted by elementary and high school teachers. And while we wrote these materials for use in schools, we have seen them used successfully by home school parents and in programs for children and families, after school science clubs, scouting programs, museums, and other settings.

We continue to author the *Science Scope* column and plan for the current activities to be published in a second *Everyday Engineering* book. Recent topics have included 3-D images and photography, Band-Aids™, ice cube trays, wind-up toys, and casein plastics. All of the newer activities are aligned with the NGSS and have a strong focus on the integration of all STEM disciplines.

Conclusion

Everyday Engineering focuses on many of the simple devices that we take for granted even though we use them every day. Many of these devices have a rich history and make use of elegant engineering designs. As we explain in our book, we hope that these activities will not only help you integrate engineering into your classroom, but will also encourage you to contemplate such questions as why the garlic press in your kitchen drawer is made the way it is, who first thought of the idea, and how you might improve on the design. That is a way of thinking that we have come to believe is an essential element of engineering literacy.

References

Bybee, R. W. (1997). *Achieving scientific literacy: From purposes to practices.* Portsmouth, NH: Heinemann.

Bybee, R. W., & Landes, N. M. (1990, February). Science for life & living: An elementary school science program from Biological Sciences Curriculum Study. *American Biology Teacher, 52*(2), 92–98.

International Technology Education Association (ITEA). (2000, 2005, 2007). *Standards for technological literacy: Content for the study of technology.* Reston, VA: Author.

Moyer, R., & Everett, S. (2009a). Time's up, turkey—pop-up thermometers. *Science Scope, 33*(3), 56–61.

Moyer, R., & Everett, S. (2009b). What makes a squirt gun squirt? *Science Scope, 33*(2), 10–14.

Moyer, R., & Everett, S. (2010). An absorbing look at terrycloth towels. *Science Scope, 34*(1), 70–74.

Moyer, R., & Everett, S. (2011). Ain't she sweet—bats, rackets, golf clubs, and all. *Science Scope, 34*(5), 52–56.

Moyer, R., & Everett, S. (2012a). *Everyday engineering: Putting the E in STEM teaching and learning.* Arlington, VA: NSTA Press.

Moyer, R., & Everett, S. (2012b). Increase your v to lower your d. *Science Scope, 35*(6), 16–23.

National Research Council (NRC). (1996). *National science education standards.* National Committee on Science Education Standards and Assessment, Board on Science Education, Division of Behavioral and Social Sciences and Education, National Research Council (NRC). Washington, DC: National Academies Press.

National Research Council (NRC). (2012). *A framework for K–12 science education: Practices, crosscutting concepts, and core ideas.* Committee on a Conceptual Framework for New K–12 Science Education Standards. Board on Science Education, Division of Behavioral and Social Sciences and Education, National Research Council (NRC). Washington, DC: National Academies Press.

NGSS Lead States. (2013a). *Next generation science standards: For states, by states. Volume 1: The standards.* Washington, DC: National Academies Press.

NGSS Lead States. (2013b). *Next generation science standards: For states, by states. Volume 2: Appendices.* Washington, DC: National Academies Press.

4

SLIDER

Science Learning Integrating Design, Engineering, and Robotics

Marion Usselman and Mike Ryan
Center for Education Integrating Science, Mathematics and Computing (CEISMC)
Georgia Institute of Technology

Figure 4.1 Assembled LEGO® MINDSTORMS® NXT Kit

Image courtesy of the authors.

Authors' Note: This material is based on work supported by the National Science Foundation under Grant Number 0918618. Any opinions, findings, and conclusions or recommendations expressed in this material are those of the authors and do not necessarily reflect the views of the National Science Foundation.

Science Learning Integrating Design, Engineering and Robotics (SLIDER) is an inquiry and project-based learning curriculum designed to teach middle school physical science disciplinary content, science and engineering practices, and crosscutting concepts within regular middle school physical science classrooms. SLIDER students use LEGO® MINDSTORMS® NXT kits to investigate and learn about force, motion, and energy (see Figure 4.1). During the two 3- to 4-week units, students organize, think about, and design solutions for engineering challenges, and, in the process, actively engage in investigations, data analysis, and scientific argumentation.

The SLIDER materials consist of (a) two comprehensive workbooks that introduce the challenges and guide students through the activities; (b) student handouts, data collection sheets, and so on; (c) videos that help frame the challenges; (d) LEGO® build instructions for students; (e) two-page, text-based teacher guides; (f) videos for teachers that include unit and section overviews, pedagogical support, LEGO® build instructions, and science content refreshers; (g) LEGO® management strategies; (h) practice problems; and (i) assessment rubrics.[1]

The SLIDER curriculum development and implementation research was supported by a grant from the National Science Foundation through the Discovery Learning K–12 program. Information about availability of the curriculum and associated teacher support materials is at www.slider.gatech.edu.

Goals and Philosophy

The SLIDER instructional materials are grounded in a project-based learning (PjBL) model of instruction. In this model, students work collaboratively to solve problems, and they learn within group settings as well as individually. They identify what they know and what they need to learn more about, plan how they will learn more, conduct research, and deliberate over the findings in an attempt to move through and solve the problem. Working together in groups allows students to share knowledge and build off the ideas and knowledge of others. Through the nature of this collaborative setting, students often are in the position where they need to articulate ideas, justify decisions, and construct scientific arguments. PjBL promotes content learning and skills development because it focuses on the exchange of ideas and provides motivation for students to seek content knowledge that helps them solve a problem or address a challenge.

There is a large amount of research extolling the benefits of curricula and learning experiences rooted in PjBL. These studies have found that PjBL promotes more active learning of content, the development of problem-solving skills, increased ownership of learning, greater understanding of the nature of science, more flexible thinking, improved collaboration skills, and opportunities for students to become STEM "experts." These advantages are also consistent with the science learning goals promoted in the *Framework for K–12 Science Education* (NRC, 2012).

SLIDER uses engineering design scenarios as the context for its PjBL challenges. Engineering design scenarios not only provide students with interesting contexts for learning, but also embody the content and skill knowledge of the Next Generation Science Standards (NGSS Lead States, 2013). Engineering challenges enable teachers to teach content in engaging ways and provide students with opportunities to innovate, create original solutions, and experience what engineers actually do. Perhaps for the first time, they come to see science, technology, and mathematics as subjects that exist beyond the classroom, as fields that can be integrated to create a final product, and as areas that they may pursue further in school or as a career.

SLIDER's curriculum design and instructional method grew out of, and is therefore pedagogically similar to, the approach and protocol developed by the Project-Based Inquiry Science (PBIS)™ curriculum, published by It's About Time (Kolodner, Krajcik, Edelson, Reser, & Starr, 2009). SLIDER has modified and streamlined the PBIS classroom protocols, and specifically incorporates LEGO® MINDSTORMS® NXT robotics as the instructional manipulative.

LEGO®s have been a part of children's learning through play for more than 50 years, are highly adaptive and accessible, and can serve as a motivational hook for many children. They are also widely available, relatively economical, reusable, and long lasting. The SLIDER curriculum was designed for classrooms where students work in teams of three students, with each team having its own dedicated LEGO® NXT robot that the team does not share with any other students (see Figure 4.2).

Most of the activities, however, can be accomplished in schools that have a class set of LEGO® NXT kits, defined here as one kit per every three children in the largest class implementing the program. The SLIDER teacher support materials include guidance on managing the LEGO® materials.

Instructional Materials

The SLIDER curriculum is comprised of two units that together develop standards from all three of the NGSS dimensions. The main science concept focus of Unit 1 is Energy (i.e., transfer of mechanical energy, kinetic and potential energy relationship, law of conservation of energy). Unit 2 focuses on Force and Motion (i.e., force, balance of forces, changes in motion, speed, acceleration, mass and inertia relationship).

The level of experiential learning in science curricula is generally conceptualized as "levels of inquiry" (Banchi & Bell, 2008; Bell, Smetana, & Binns, 2005). A common scale of inquiry is shown below:

> **Level 1. Confirmation Inquiry**—Students confirm a principle through an activity when the results are known in advance.
>
> **Level 2. Structured Inquiry**—Students investigate a teacher-presented question through a prescribed procedure.
>
> **Level 3. Guided Inquiry**—Students investigate a teacher-presented question using student designed/selected procedures.
>
> **Level 4. Open Inquiry**—Students investigate questions that are student formulated through student-designed/-selected procedures.

The SLIDER curriculum has been created to promote learning at the Guided Inquiry level—that is, the curriculum materials guide which

Figure 4.2 LEGO® NXT Robot

Image courtesy of the authors.

questions students ask, but the students develop their own experimental procedures, collect and analyze data, look for trends, and support design decisions using evidence and scientific reasoning. *A Framework for K–12 Science Education* (NRC, 2012) describes the similarities and differences between science and engineering practices. Whereas engineers ask questions and define problems that should lead to a concrete solution to a societal problem, scientists seek to understand *why* something is happening, and instead of designing solutions, they construct scientific explanations to explain the phenomenon. Within the science classroom, it is crucial that students spend ample time grappling with the underlying scientific concepts and puzzling over why, scientifically, something is happening, not just designing a solution to an engineering challenge. Every SLIDER engineering challenge (and its accompanying LEGO® design) must therefore predictably and explicitly lead students to a deeper understanding of a specific physical science concept.

At the same time, SLIDER also intentionally incorporates the engineering concepts articulated in the NGSS: defining problems, developing and testing solutions, and optimizing solutions. The engineering challenge plays a key role in the curriculum; it is the context that situates the learners, drives purpose and activity, and allows for science and engineering learning to occur in the same classroom.

Structure of the Curriculum

Each of the two units is divided into three phases.
In Phase 1, students

- Understand the specifications of the problem or challenge.
- Ask questions about phenomena involved.
- Identify possible investigations or models that would help answer questions.

In Phase 2, students

- Iteratively develop and conduct investigations that attempt to answer Phase 1 questions.
- Analyze and explain data to find causal effects.
- Explore science conceptual knowledge to make sense of investigation data and features of the challenge.
- Craft arguments to explain and justify possible components of a challenge solution.

In Phase 3, students

- Design and test multiple solutions to the challenge.
- Explore more science conceptual knowledge to make sense of investigation data and challenge features.
- Iterate on arguments crafted so far.
- Propose an end-of-unit solution to the challenge.

Students do not progress through all phases in a linear fashion. For example, in Phase 2, students might cycle through two or three iterations before they move on to Phase 3. Additionally, throughout each of the phases, students revisit the challenge to reflect on how what they are doing and learning impacts possible solutions to the challenge.

To facilitate students' learning in both science and engineering, SLIDER makes use of curricular structures that guide and assist teacher practice. These SLIDER Curriculum Structures (SCSs) move students back and forth from the engineering design process of defining problems and designing solutions, to the science skills of asking scientific questions, acquiring knowledge, and constructing explanations. The SCSs are intended to help students understand and participate in the Science & Engineering (S&E) Practices referenced in the *Framework for K–12 Science Education*, while providing a format that helps students see their usefulness in solving the challenge.

As students progress through the three phases of each unit, they engage in six distinct SCSs, each with its own action and protocol: Organize the Challenge, Explore, Share, Add to Your Understanding, Explain, and Reflect & Connect. These SCSs drive student collaboration, involving all members of the class, but each practice also has dimensions that require individual student work. These SCSs direct students to connect their more recent or smaller experiences to the challenge at large. They help students share information, reflect on what they have learned, and develop new ideas and connections to pursue during the challenge. For the teacher, the SCSs reveal student understanding and conceptions; that is, they serve as moments of formative assessment. As students iteratively engage in the SCSs over time within and across units, the nature of the assessment can be more summative.

So far, we have tried to provide a broad sense of the curriculum and its central components: challenge-situated learning; concurrent pursuit of science inquiry and engineering solutions; and a focus on the practices, cross-cutting concepts, and core ideas of NGSS.

Next, let's look more specifically at what happens in each of the units, and how students engage in each of the central components.

Unit 1: The Accident Challenge—Energy

Students learn about a serious issue affecting the Town of McFarland:

> The people of the Town of McFarland have an accident problem at the corner of Main Street and Park Street. During the past year, this heavily used intersection near downtown has been the site of a number of dangerous accidents involving large tractor-trailer trucks hitting smaller cars. Many of the accidents resulted in severe injuries and cars that had to be scrapped. That is, the cars could not be fixed and used again. There have even been fatalities as a result of these car accidents. Your challenge is to assist the Town of McFarland to
>
> - Understand why the accidents are causing so much damage and injury.
> - Investigate the factors that lead to such accidents.
> - Design possible solutions to decrease the accidents and injuries.

Through a mixed use of written text and video, the SLIDER curriculum provides students with a rich context that describes many dimensions of the problem and helps to scaffold possible solutions. Figure 4.3 shows the type of information provided as part of the student materials.

Phase 1 of Unit 1. After students have been introduced to the challenges and issues McFarland is facing, they are presented with several proposals from citizens and city council members about how to deal with these issues. These suggestions include reducing the

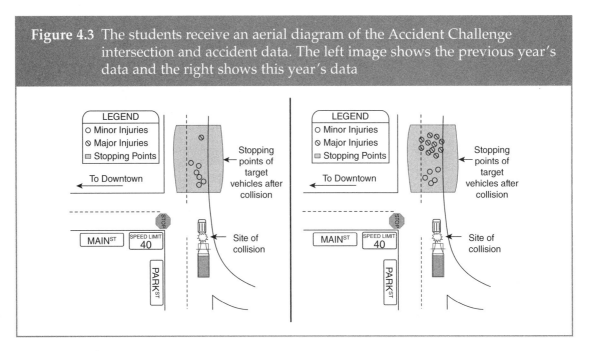

Figure 4.3 The students receive an aerial diagram of the Accident Challenge intersection and accident data. The left image shows the previous year's data and the right shows this year's data

Image courtesy of the authors.

maximum weight of the trucks, changing speed limits, and even redesigning the intersection. Students learn critical information about the traffic in the town; they review accident statistics and hear from various constituencies and experts about traffic accidents. They learn about traffic engineers and engineering, and are ultimately asked to play the role of a traffic engineer who must consider the proposals and test some possible solutions.

Phase 1 asks students to identify the problem's criteria and constraints, and then consider scientific questions that might help them gain knowledge to solve the problem. They create a model of the accident scene, test the validity of their model, and propose various investigations to run to see if changes in vehicles and/or driver behavior are contributing to the accidents (see Figure 4.4).

Phase 2 of Unit 1. Students use their model of the accident intersection to gather data about how various conditions might affect the damage and injuries suffered during accidents. In the model, the LEGO® truck does not have an engine so students, organized into groups, use ramps of varying heights to control the truck's initial velocity. Because some of the initial ideas involve limiting the maximum weight and/or speed of the truck, or creating lane restrictions, students investigate the effect of changes in mass, speed, and height of the truck rolling down a ramp and colliding with a LEGO® car at rest waiting at the intersection. As students change these variables and collect data, trends emerge about the transfer of energy. After each group has run five or six investigations that reveal some facts about energy, the groups present their model, the experiments they ran, and the experimental data to the rest of the class. It is after these investigations and presentations that the teacher engages in more traditional direct instruction on the concepts of energy transfer, potential and kinetic energy, and conservation of energy.

At this point, students, armed with science content knowledge, return to the questions asked in Phase 1 to identify more relevant investigations they would like to run.

Figure 4.4 Students create a model of the accident scene and use their model to collect data in order to understand the factors that have contributed to the increasing number of serious accidents

Image courtesy of the authors.

They gather data once again, share it with other groups, and the teacher again engages in more direct instruction about the science concepts at work. Throughout this cycling, students are developing scientific arguments for, or against, the ideas or opinions offered by the citizens and city council in Phase 1. Using a Claim-Evidence-Reason framework for argumentation (adapted from McNeill & Krajcik, 2012), students iteratively craft and edit arguments as they collect more data from their model and learn more through the direct instruction on science concepts.

Phase 3 of Unit 1. Students are now ready to return to the challenge and make recommendations on the ideas submitted by the citizens and city council during Phase 1. Using the Claim-Evidence-Reasoning format, students draft a final set of arguments for or against the ideas. Students are also provided the opportunity to design and share their own new set of traffic rules for the vehicles in the area of the intersection. Of course, they must heed all of the criteria and constraints identified in Phase 1. Here, the evidence and reasoning (science content knowledge) must be strong to either support or refute a claim (or citizen's idea).

The three phases of Unit 1 and the SLIDER Curriculum Structures (SCSs) in each phase are summarized in Table 4.1.

Unit 2: The Brake Challenge—Force and Motion

The second unit begins with a request from the factory whose trucks are involved in the accidents at the intersection.

The company has noticed that many of their trucks have been involved in severe accidents across the state and nation (not just in McFarland). Most of these car accidents

Table 4.1 Phases and Curriculum Structures in Unit 1

In Phase 1, students	
Organize the Challenge	• Record criteria and constraints from the challenge. • Determine the questions they wish to ask of a model that could simulate the accidents at the intersection.
Explore: *Modeling*	• Build the model to simulate trucks hitting cars at the intersection, develop a procedure to run the model consistently and usefully, and record and compare data from each set of tests. • Determine the type of investigations they would like to conduct with their model to isolate variables that might be contributing to the accidents.
In Phase 2, students	
Explore: *Investigating Accidents With Your Model*	• Design investigations and collect data on different variables that affect kinetic and potential energy in a system. • Use digital simulations to adjust variables similar to and beyond their test model.
Share: *Results of Your Investigations*	• Create poster presentations to share data collected and review trends. • Review the procedures and analysis of each other's work to identify errors and discuss sound scientific practice and measurement.
Add to Your Understanding: *Energy*	• Define and practice applying the concept of energy transformation. • Use simulations to identify variables that can affect the amount of energy in a system and how it transfers. • Define and practice applying the relationship between kinetic and potential energy in a system.
Explain: *Argument For or Against New Traffic Rules*	• Review claims made by citizens and search their data to find evidence in an argument for or against those claims. • Connect various claims and evidence to the science content knowledge learned so far.
In Phase 3, students	
Reflect and Connect: *Answer the Accident Challenge*	• Address and evaluate each citizen's idea as a traffic engineer might, using evidence from the model and science content knowledge to support or refute the proposed idea.

were similar to the accidents in McFarland and involved their trucks hitting the back of a car (rear end collisions). The company would like to examine the braking systems of its truck fleet to determine whether it should invest in an automatic braking and collision warning system. A system such as this would eliminate the reaction time of the truck driver in stopping the truck and potentially allow the stopping distance to be 40–100 feet shorter. Your challenge is to assist the company by

- Investigating how the automatic braking system might reduce stopping distance
- Investigating the factors that might improve the braking system
- Designing a new brake that improves upon current performance

Once again, students progress through the three phases in the unit, each with similar features and activities of Unit 1 (see Table 4.1). Of course, there are some differences and additions to this unit, including that students actually design a physical artifact (a truck with an automatic brake). This makes the engineering design focus more explicit, and those additions will be highlighted in our review of Phase 3 for this unit.

Phase 1 of Unit 2. Students begin this phase by watching videos of trucks braking hard or engaging emergency brakes. These videos and a series of iterative discussions inspire students to think about how a rolling vehicle or object actually comes to a stop and how braking distance varies depending on the situation. Students review the criteria and constraints of the new challenge, sharing any ideas they have about possible brake design. Then they complete a short investigation to see how different surfaces affect the time it takes the truck to coast to a stop once it has come off the end of the ramp. The teacher does not confirm or correct any conceptions or ideas the students might have. This is simply an exercise in understanding what students know about force and motion (formative assessment) and to have students generate some investigations they could conduct to better understand the factors that cause something to stop.

Phase 2 of Unit 2. Students quickly realize that in answering the challenge, modifying road surfaces to improve the brake performance isn't a likely option. But they know that they need to figure out how to change the forces acting on the truck. Students return to their Unit 1 truck design and modify it. They add the automatic emergency brake, which uses the LEGO® NXT computer, the kit's light sensor, a NXT motor, a brake arm assembly, and a simple computer program.

The NXT light sensor can detect when the surface it is scanning changes from light to dark. In Unit 2, the truck rolls off the ramp and crosses a strip of black tape to trigger the sensor. This models the automatic braking systems that use distance to detect that a possible collision is imminent. When the sensor is tripped, the brake arm assembly drops to the floor, and the brake pad drags behind the truck along the floor, causing the truck to slow to a stop. Students test initial performance of the basic brake design (see Figure 4.5). This provides a baseline braking distance the students know is too long. It also ensures that students know how to actually test the brake and become familiar with its operation.

Because some of the initial ideas involve changing the brake pad materials and pad design, students investigate how different brake pad materials affect the truck's stopping distance. As students change these variables and collect data, trends surrounding concepts like balance of forces, changes in motion, friction, speed, acceleration, mass, and inertia become apparent. Only after the investigation does the teacher engage students in more direct instruction about the relevant science concepts. Most notably, students learn to identify forces, draw simple force diagrams, and determine the balance of forces in an event. As in Unit 1, the students conduct multiple cycles of investigation/analysis/sense making, and they iteratively craft arguments about how the brake ought to be designed, supporting claims with evidence and scientific reasoning.

Figure 4.5 Students test their brake designs to see if the truck can stop before hitting the car

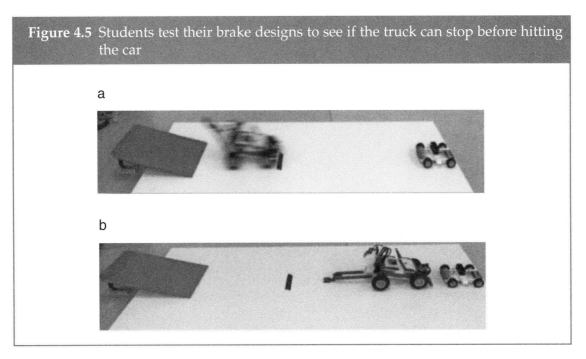

Images courtesy of the authors.

Figure 4.6 Students evaluate two different brake designs

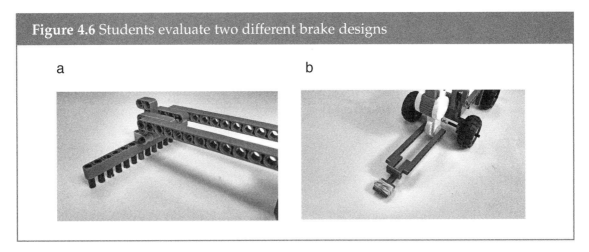

Images courtesy of the authors.

Phase 3 of Unit 2. Students are now equipped with data from multiple investigations and with an array of scientific disciplinary concepts about forces and motion. The challenge is then modified, and the students are told that for reasons of safety, the brake program and motor can only generate 50% of the downward push of its original design. However, the trucks must still meet the stopping distance challenge. Since none of the original materials or basic brake arm pads meets the challenge, students now move into more of an engineering design mode. They must create a new design, combining materials and brake pads to meet the challenge. In order to focus on optimization, each LEGO® piece and pad material has been assigned a cost. High-friction materials and large brake pads, both of which generate high friction and a large imbalance of forces, are the most expensive. Students attempt to design brakes that meet the product specifications and cost the least amount of money (see Figure 4.6). At the end of the unit, students present their final designs and test data, while supplying an argument for their design supported by evidence and reasoning. The three phases of Unit 2, and the SLIDER Curriculum Structures (SCSs) in each phase, are summarized in Table 4.2.

Table 4.2 Slider Curriculum Structures in Unit 2	
In Phase 1, students	
Organize the Challenge	• Record criteria and constraints from the challenge. • Determine the questions they wish to investigate that would help them determine how different brake designs make vehicles stop differently.
Explore: *Modeling*	• Briefly compare how various surfaces affect the motion of a coasting vehicle. • Generate (as a class) an operational definition of forces and how they affect moving objects.
In Phase 2, students	
Explore: *Investigating Accidents With Your Model*	• Design investigations and collect data on different variables that affect forces acting on the truck as it starts, accelerates, slows, and then stops. • Investigate the amount of friction generated by different materials attached to the brake pad.
Share: *Results of Your Investigations*	• Create presentations to share data and review trends, informing each other of the performance of different materials and brake assemblies tested. • Review the procedures and data analysis from different groups to identify errors and discuss sound scientific practice and measurement.
Add to Your Understanding: *Energy*	• Define and practice applying the concept of forces, net force, and balance of forces. • Define and practice applying the concept of net force and its effect on changes in motion.
Explain: *Argument For or Against New Traffic Rules*	• Draft arguments about various materials they've tested, supporting the claims with evidence collected during investigations and with reasoning discussed during class. • Review claims made by other groups about the performance of certain materials and search their data to find evidence for or against those claims.
In Phase 3, students	
Reflect and Connect: *Answer the Accident Challenge*	• Address and evaluate each brake design solution, using evidence from tests and science content knowledge to support the design.

Alignment With Next Generation Science Standards

As shown in Table 4.3, the core ideas and practices in which students engage during the SLIDER units can help them achieve several performance expectations from the Next Generation Science Standards, both in physical science and in engineering design.

Table 4.3 Performance Expectations From the NGSS Addressed in SLIDER Units

SLIDER Units	One			Two		
Phase	1	2	3	1	2	3
Physical Sciences						
MS-PS2–1. Apply Newton's Third Law to design a solution to a problem involving the motion of two colliding objects.					■	■
MS-PS2–2. Plan an investigation to provide evidence that the change in an object's motion depends on the sum of the forces on the object and the mass of the object.				■	■	■
MS-PS3–1. Construct and interpret graphical displays of data to describe the relationships of kinetic energy to the mass of an object and to the speed of an object.		■				
MS-PS3–2. Develop a model to describe that when the arrangement of objects interacting at a distance changes, different amounts of potential energy are stored in the system.		■				
MS-PS3–5. Construct, use, and present arguments to support the claim that when the kinetic energy of an object changes, energy is transferred to or from the object.	■					
Engineering Design						
MS-ETS1–1. Define the criteria and constraints of a design problem with sufficient precision to ensure a successful solution, taking into account relevant scientific principles and potential impacts on people and the natural environment that may limit possible solutions.	■			■	■	■
MS-ETS1–2. Evaluate competing design solutions using a systematic process to determine how well they meet the criteria and constraints of the problem.						■

SLIDER Units		One			Two		
Phase		1	2	3	1	2	3
MS-ETS1–3. Analyze data from tests to determine similarities and differences among several design solutions to identify the best characteristics of each that can be combined into a new solution to better meet the criteria for success.				▓			▓
MS-ETS1–4. Develop a model to generate data for iterative testing and modification of a proposed object, tool, or process such that an optimal design can be achieved.	▓			▓			

Future Modifications

The SLIDER staff is working to publish the curriculum materials and teacher support materials as interactive e-books. This will allow videos, simulations, and build instructions to be embedded directly in the text, greatly facilitating ease of use. These materials will be available on the SLIDER website.

Note

1. SLIDER, like all large curriculum development projects, is the result of huge amounts of work by a large and dedicated staff. The authors would like to gratefully thank Sabrina Grossman, Brian Gane, Anna Newsome, Beth Kostka, Jessica Gale, Julie Sonnenberg-Klein, Jayma Koval, Cher Hendricks, and Jeff Rosen for their enormous contributions to the SLIDER curriculum and project. And we owe a huge debt to the teachers in our SLIDER schools who piloted the materials over the past three years and provided invaluable feedback and insight. Thanks, all.

References

Banchi, H., & Bell, R. (2008). The many levels of inquiry. *Science and Children, 46*(2), 26–29.

Bell, R. L., Smetana, L., & Binns, I. (2005). Simplifying inquiry instruction. *Science Teacher, 72*(7), 30–33.

Kolodner, J., Krajcik, J., Edelson, D. C., Reiser, B. J., & Starr, M. L. (2009). *Project Based Inquiry Science (PBIS) middle school.* Mount Kisco, NY: It's About Time.

McNeill, K. L., & Krajcik, J. S. (2012). *Supporting grade 5–8 students in constructing explanations in science: The claim, evidence, and reasoning framework for talk and writing.* Boston: Pearson.

National Research Council (NRC). (2012). *A framework for K–12 science education: Practices, crosscutting concepts, and core ideas.* Committee on a Conceptual Framework for New K–12 Science Education Standards. Board on Science Education, Division of Behavioral and Social Sciences and Education, National Research Council (NRC). Washington, DC: National Academies Press.

NGSS Lead States. (2013). *Next generation science standards: For states, by states. Volume 1: The standards.* Washington, DC: National Academies Press.

5

Teaching Engineering Made Easy

Celeste Baine
Engineering Education Service Center, Springfield, Oregon

Teaching Engineering Made Easy: A Friendly Introduction to Engineering Activities for Middle School Teachers (Volumes 1 and 2) presents 20 engineering activities designed to introduce teachers to the world of technology and engineering teaching and to engage students in thinking like engineers.

Designed for middle school teachers with no engineering background, these easy and exciting, time- and work-saving books can be used in the classroom or informal science environments. They can be used to enhance an event or competition, at science and engineering summer camps, in after-school clubs, or in any other educational setting.

By engaging in these activities, students can see that engineering is not something to be afraid of but a realistic way to solve the problems of everyday life.

Teaching Engineering Made Easy is available at www.engineeringedu.com.

Overview

Teaching Engineering Made Easy gives classroom teachers an easy and dynamic way to meet curriculum standards and competencies. The lessons and activities actively engage students in learning about engineering and our technological world by applying creativity and innovation as they complete the projects. The activities do not require a formal science lab and can be done with materials that are inexpensive and easy to find.

Teaching Engineering Made Easy was developed and tested by a professional science teacher and an engineer who sought to expose students to engineering with enjoyable learning experiences (see Figure 5.1).

Feedback from teachers suggests that projects within the guides are being integrated in existing middle school curricula, and also used as fillers in Project Lead the Way courses, at Saturday engineering recruitment and celebration events, in summer camps, and in after-school programs.

Teaching Engineering

Engineering is problem solving. Many teachers enjoy teaching engineering because it combines math, science, language arts, social studies, team building, and creativity with a practical twist. Students learn to work together, increase their communication skills, and enhance their presentation abilities by demonstrating and discussing design strategies with the rest of the class.

Students enjoy using the skills and knowledge they gained previously during more abstract instruction. Engineering projects offer a great venue for students to show themselves and others that they can

- Manage time and projects
- Study a situation or problem critically
- Research relevant information
- Solve problems
- Use a logical process to plan solutions

Figure 5.1 Celeste Baine Talking to Teachers at a Professional Development Workshop

Image courtesy of the author.

Figure 5.2 Catapult Designed and Built During a Professional Development Workshop

Image courtesy of the author.

- Fail and learn from it
- Talk intelligently about what they've done and how they did it.

The projects in *Teaching Engineering Made Easy* are hands-on activities that are fun and effective ways to help students learn and retain more math and science concepts (see Figure 5.2). By choosing to teach engineering, teachers can help students make the links between classroom learning, their everyday lives, and the wider world. The projects can help students visualize abstract science and math concepts. Using hands-on activities, engineering design serves as the bridge to bring color to math and science concepts. This bridge makes our designed world more understandable, relevant, and fun.

By promoting engineering as a viable career option, teachers also

- Help provide a stronger workforce in all fields of science, technology, engineering, and math (STEM)
- Help create a technologically literate people and society
- Provide students with the skills they will need to thrive in a technological society

How engineering is presented to students can determine whether or not they develop an interest in the subject. In the old days, engineers were described as builders, operators, planners, and maintainers. Students today are more likely to respond well to a description of engineers as designers, creators, or inventors (NAE, 2008).

More exciting messages include the following:

- Aerospace engineers explore the galaxy!
- Biomedical engineers help people live longer and more comfortably!

- Environmental engineers protect the planet!
- Agricultural engineers feed the world!
- Telecommunications engineers connect the world!

Contents of the Volumes

Each of the two volumes begins with a section on teamwork and includes lessons from three different fields of engineering. Individual lessons include background information, alignments with the *Standards for Technological Literacy* (ITEA, 2000, 2005, 2007) and *National Science Education Standards* (NRC, 1996), a list of materials needed to complete the activity, an easy-to-follow procedure for presenting the lesson, teacher notes, reproducible student sheets, and safety notes. Activities range from 20-minute problem-solving exercises to engineering "challenge" activities that require several class periods. Each activity description includes reproducible student handouts, activity overviews, background information, teacher notes, safety notes, getting-started procedures, and materials lists. For easy use, the books have lay-flat formatting to enable 8.5" × 11" photocopying.

There are many types of challenge activities within the engineering discipline activity sections. The challenge activities integrate perfectly with the Disciplinary Core Ideas of the Next Generation Science Standards (NGSS Lead States, 2013). Engineering challenges are design problems that require students to identify needs, define problems (MS-ETS1.A), identify design criteria and constraints, develop solutions (ETS1.B), and evaluate their solutions (ETS1.C).

In these activities, there is more than one right answer (see Figure 5.3). In a class of 10 student teams, you will often see 10 different designs that all meet the design criteria. The right design is usually one that meets the engineering criteria and is built within the

Figure 5.3 In challenge activities, there is more than one right answer

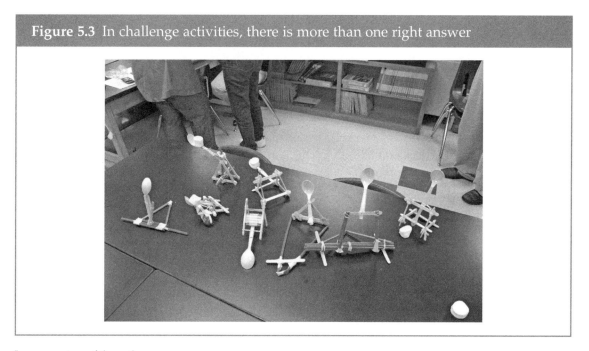

Image courtesy of the author.

materials budget. Students will design, construct, and test their engineering design solution and collect relevant data (if applicable). They will then evaluate the solution in terms of design and performance criteria, constraints, priorities, and trade-offs while also identifying possible design improvements.

The activities do not require a formal science lab and can be done with materials that are inexpensive and easy to find. However, as a time- and work-saving convenience, materials for all activities can also be ordered online at www.engineeringedu.com. Although not included, journals are highly recommended for most activities.

Many of the activities include "engineering design checklists" for students to evaluate their designs. Self-assessment encourages students to become lifelong learners. Teachers should encourage self-evaluation because self-assessment makes the students active participants in their education. Research suggests that the simplest tools to encourage student self-assessment are evaluative questions that force students to think about their work (Hart, 1999). Sample statements on the checklists include the following:

- The structure meets the stated challenge requirements.
- The project design team followed the challenge rules.
- The project team exhibited effective, cooperative group work with every member participating.
- The project prototype was carefully designed and built (if required).
- The project team showed perseverance and a willingness to try again if necessary.
- The project team was inventive in redesigning the original prototype.
- The final structure shows creativity and originality.
- The project meets the stated goals of the team.

Crossword and word search puzzle assessments are also included in each volume. Following is a brief overview of the two volumes.

Team-Building Activities

Each of the two volumes begins with team-building activities. Team-building activities include both large group and small group activities that stress problem solving and/or make career connections as students discuss possible solutions.

Teamwork is essential to engineering. If you have ever played a team sport, you understand that teamwork is integral to the success of the team. Each player brings different strengths to the team, without which the team can't function as efficiently. Engineering design works in the same way. Each member of the team contributes according to individual strengths, and the resultant learning and/or design produces a superior product. Jennifer Ocif, a performance footwear engineer at Reebok, says,

> Communication is a life skill that constantly needs attention and improvement. Unfortunately, it is not specifically taught in engineering classes but you can learn it by doing it anywhere. You just have to work at it because no matter how smart you are, if you can't communicate with the people you work with, your ideas will never go anywhere. (Baine, 2004, p. 19)

Suppose you have or know of a student that excels at communicating. Excellent communicators often become the most valued engineers. Those who have excellent verbal, written, and people skills, both for technical and nontechnical audiences; who can communicate using technology; and who are intuitive and receptive in understanding the social, cultural, and political motivations of people around the world are in great demand.

Students learn from each other, empower each other, and share the responsibility of finishing the project on time and on budget. Knowledgeable, effective teams can create extraordinary results by tapping into the strengths of each team member.

Teaching Engineering Made Easy, Volume 1

Chemical Engineering Activities

The chemical engineering section begins with career information that includes reproducible student handouts for reading material. Students will learn that chemical engineers may design products and systems such as agricultural systems, food packaging, athletic shoes, baseball and football equipment, bowling equipment, efficient transportation (cleaner fuels and energy systems), pharmaceutical advancements, Olympic training equipment, and much more.

Five chemical engineering activities that enable students to observe chemical reactions follow the career content. The activities are as follows:

1. Playful Polymers: Students learn to reverse engineer a diaper in an effort to manage moisture. Students extract superabsorbent polymers, make observations, conduct experiments, and then design the "best" system to contain moisture.

2. Colorful Concoctions: This activity allows students to practice observational skills and note the difference between observation and inference. It also provides the student with the opportunity to design and perform simple inquiry investigations in order to answer a question posed by the instructor. By combining specific amounts of sodium bicarbonate, calcium chloride, and phenol red in a closed resealable bag system, the learning experience focuses the student on the following concepts: physical properties of substances, evidence of chemical change, exothermic versus endothermic reactions, reactants, and products.

3. Writing With Style: In this activity, students act as chemical engineers to redesign various ink recipes for use in writing.

4. Reactionary Rockets: This learning experience incorporates scientific methods, chemistry, and physical science. Students must determine the best "recipe" for launching effervescing rockets the greatest distance. Exploring the possibilities gives the students opportunities to practice observing, communicating, measuring, inferring, predicting, controlling variables, and collecting and analyzing data.

5. Inflation Station: This activity allows students to engage in an exploration of a simple chemical reaction while developing a procedure designed to inflate a series of balloons at different rates.

The section ends with crossword and word search assessment puzzles to gauge how much career content the students retained. Puzzle questions come directly from the reading material. Answer sheets are provided.

Mechanical Engineering Activities

The mechanical engineering section begins with career information that includes reproducible student handouts for reading material. Students will learn that mechanical engineers usually create things that move; therefore, they have a hand in designing almost everything that contains a moving part or is created by a machine that has moving parts. This section covers trends, salary information, a career profile, and common applications.

Five mechanical engineering activities that enable students to create things that move follow the career content. The challenge activities presented can be extended from a one-day activity to two or more weeks in duration. Each failure of a design allows the students to evaluate and redesign until they have a vehicle or part that can pass a specific test assigned by the instructor.

We intentionally only provide a starting point for instruction. Instructors must evaluate their classrooms and student levels to determine if the activity levels are appropriate. Lessons are easily adaptable as materials can be added, budgets can change, and load requirements can be modified. The activities are as follows:

1. The Catapult (Challenge Activity): Using only the materials given, students design a catapult that can fling a large marshmallow into a bucket two meters away.

2. How Do I Hover? (Challenge Activity): This experience enables students to engage in an open inquiry where process skills and higher order thinking are needed in order to complete the challenge. Students work cooperatively to design a small, table-top hovercraft that behaves in the same manner as its real-world counterpart.

3. Totally Tops: Students move through three phases of inquiry as they learn about tops. Through initial learning experiences, students gain critical insight into how tops work in order to successfully design and test their own version of a top by the end of the exploration.

4. The Indy Card Car (Challenge Activity): Using only the materials provided, students work cooperatively while developing problem-solving and critical-thinking skills. A limited number of materials are made available, therefore providing a certain level of difficulty that the students must overcome in order to complete the challenge of constructing a functional car.

5. Hydraulic Crane (Challenge Activity): Using only the materials given, students design a hydraulic crane that can pick up a paper clip (see Figure 5.4).

The section ends with crossword and word search assessment puzzles to gauge the amount of career information the students retained. Puzzle questions come directly from the reading material. Answer sheets are provided.

Civil Engineering Activities

The civil engineering section begins with career information that includes reproducible student handouts for reading material. Students will learn that civil engineers usually create things that don't move (you don't want them to move) and therefore have a hand in designing almost all of our infrastructure such as buildings, bridges, roads, tunnels, and any other structure that needs to stay put and stay strong. This section covers trends, salary information, a career profile, and common applications.

Five civil engineering challenge activities that enable students to create structures that stay put and stay strong follow the career content. The challenge activities presented can be extended from a one-day activity to two or more weeks in duration. Each failure of a structure allows the students to evaluate and redesign until they have a structure that can pass a specific test assigned by the instructor.

We intentionally only provide a starting point for instruction. Instructors must evaluate their classrooms and student levels to determine if the activity levels are appropriate. Lessons are easily adaptable as materials can be added, budgets can change, and load requirements can be modified.

The activities are as follows:

Figure 5.4 Hydraulic Crane Designed During PD Workshop

Image courtesy of the author.

1. The Cantilever Challenge (Challenge Activity): Students work cooperatively to construct the longest cantilever that supports the most weight. Students will discover the relationship between joint strength and load.

2. Straw Bridges (Challenge Activity): Students work cooperatively to construct a straw bridge that can support the most weight.

3. Two Feet Feat (Challenge Activity): Students work cooperatively to construct a two-foot tower from straws and paper clips that supports the most weight.

4. Careening Coaster (Challenge Activity): Students work cooperatively to construct a roller coaster with one 360-degree loop or spiral, one hill, and one 45- to 90-degree turn. Students will discover the relationship between gravity, mass, and potential and kinetic energy.

5. Wrecking Ball (Challenge Activity): Students work cooperatively to construct a one-foot tall building out of balsa wood that can survive the impact of a wrecking ball. Students will discover the relationship between gravity, mass, and potential and kinetic energy.

The section ends with crossword and word search assessment puzzles to gauge the amount of career content retention. Puzzle questions come directly from the reading material. Answer sheets are provided.

Teaching Engineering Made Easy, Volume 2

Engineering Principles Activities

The engineering principles section is very broad and builds on the career content provided in the previous team-building activities section. Students learn about many different types of engineers and some of the applications within each field. The team-building section includes reproducible student handouts for reading material. Students will learn about 20 different types of engineers and some of the foundational building blocks of engineering such as measuring, forces (compression and tension), and Newton's 1st Law of Motion.

The activities are as follows:

1. Measure It! In this activity, students compare independent systems designed to measure the same object.

2. Born to Rock (Challenge Activity): Students work cooperatively to verify Newton's 1st Law of Motion and create a rocker that rocks longer than any other in the class (i.e., balance an object and find its equilibrium).

3. Forces—Compression and Tension: Students learn the difference between compression and tension and identify which members in a structure are in tension and which are in compression.

4. Tsunami Shelter Platform (Challenge Activity): Students work cooperatively to construct a model solution to a real-world, interdisciplinary problem. The activity ties in natural disasters and engineers as problem solvers.

5. Flight Time: Students work cooperatively to build a paper airplane that stays in the air the longest or travels the furthest distance.

The section ends with crossword and word search assessment puzzles to gauge the amount of career content retention. Puzzle questions come directly from the Top 20 Engineering Disciplines reading material and the team-building activities. Answer sheets are provided.

Biomedical Engineering Activities

The biomedical engineering section begins with career information that includes reproducible student handouts for reading material. Students will learn that biomedical engineers usually create things that protect the human body and therefore have a hand in designing hospital equipment, pharmaceuticals, prosthetics, athletic equipment to protect against sports injury, and systems to help us better model the internal workings of the body. This section covers trends, salary information, and common applications.

Five biomedical engineering activities that enable students to model the human body follow the career content. The prosthetic hand design challenge activity follows the same model as the other challenge activities in the mechanical and civil engineering sections.

The activities are as follows:

1. Boning Up on Bones: In this activity, students learn about bone strength by building models with different hard outer layers and testing them to failure.

2. Keep It Moving: In this activity, students explore various methods to open blocked arteries.

3. Prosthetic Hand (Challenge Activity): Students work cooperatively to construct a three-fingered hand that can pick up a wad of paper using only the materials given.

4. Gut Reaction: In this activity, students explore different aspects of swallowed medicine delivery, one of the engineering aspects of developing new medications.

5. Protect Your Melon: In this activity, students learn about protecting their melon "head" from damage in a fall through a challenge to design a cost-effective helmet. Students design a helmet to protect a melon when it is dropped vertically (see Figure 5.5). The winning design is the one that best protects the melon at the lowest cost.

Figure 5.5 Protective helmets were designed by students. "Egg people" often have personalities and names

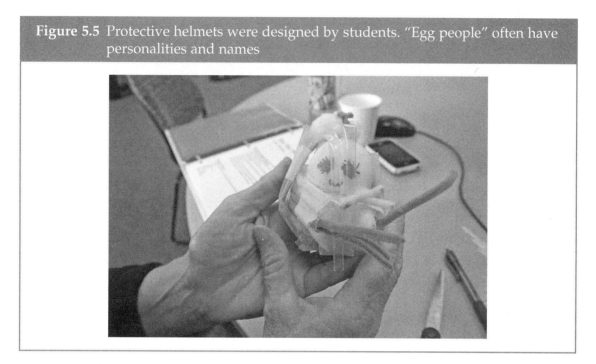

Image courtesy of the author.

The section ends with crossword and word search assessment puzzles to gauge the amount of career content retention. Puzzle questions come directly from the reading material. Answer sheets are provided.

Electrical Engineering Activities

The electrical engineering section begins with career information that includes reproducible student handouts for reading material. Students learn that electrical engineers design everything that has an on/off switch, anything with electronics and energy systems. They make sure our schools, buildings, and homes have electricity as well as conduct research on future technologies such as wind, wave, and solar energy. This section covers trends, salary information, a career profile, and common applications.

Five electrical engineering activities that enable students to learn about the basics of electricity, conductivity, and engineering design follow the career content.

The activities are as follows:

1. Bright Light: Using a simple circuit and LED (light emitting diode) bulbs, students build a flashlight.

2. Putting It to the Test: Students determine which materials conduct electricity.

3. Spider Circuits: Students learn that electricity will flow to light up a bulb only if the circuit is complete. With broken circuits, the bulb will not light.

4. Amplifies Kazoo: Students convert mechanical energy (analog sounds) into electrical energy (digital sounds) and thereby amplify a kazoo through a set of computer speakers.

5. Lunar Treasures: In this project, students build their own "Lunar Treasures" game from foam core, wire, and basic electronic components, including a buzzer and an LED. In Challenge 1, they set up the game board. In Challenge 2, they make the electrical connections and try their hand at extracting the jewels without any damage! This game is very similar to the game called Operation sold in toy stores.

The section ends with crossword and word search assessment puzzles to gauge how much career content the students retained. Puzzle questions come directly from the reading material. Answer sheets are provided.

Connections to the NGSS

The NGSS specifies the core ideas and practices of engineering design in middle school as defining the problem, developing and testing possible solutions and optimizing the solution.

At the middle school level, students learn to sharpen the focus of problems by precisely specifying criteria and constraints of successful solutions, taking into account not only what needs the problem is intended to meet, but also the larger context within which the problem is defined, including limits to possible solutions. Students can identify elements of different solutions and combine them to create new solutions. Students at this level are expected to use systematic methods to compare different solutions to see which best meet criteria and constraints, and to test and revise solutions a number of times in order to arrive at an optimal design. (NGSS Lead States, 2013, Vol. 2, Appendix I, p. 106)

Table 5.1 shows how the activities in *Teaching Engineering Made Easy* Volume 1 are related to the performance expectations in the NGSS for engineering design. Connections for the activities in Volume 2 are similar.

Conclusion

The activities in *Teaching Engineering Made Easy* are a good fit to the NGSS's Discipline Core Ideas. The activities build communication and teamwork skills, increase student engagement, and serve as a launching pad to engineering design in a formal or informal learning environment. Teachers can determine the length of the activities and adapt them to meet the needs of their students or situation. The materials are easily accessible, and no formal science lab is needed.

Table 5.1 Correlations of Activities With Middle School Performance Expectations in the NGSS

	Section	Learning Experiences	MS-ETS1-1 Define the Problem	MS-ETS1-2 Develop Possible Solutions	MS-ETS1–3 Analyze Data From Tests	MS-ETS1–4 Optimize the Design
1	Team Building	The Whale Band-Aid	x	x	x	
2	Team Building	Carbon Copy Creations	x			
3	Team Building	What's in the Bag?	x			
4	Problem Solving	Hampered by Height	x	x	x	
5	Problem Solving	The Puzzle of Nine	x	x	x	
6	Chemical Engineering	Playful Polymers	x	x	x	
7	Chemical Engineering	Colorful Concoctions	x	x	x	
8	Chemical Engineering	Writing With Style	x	x	x	x
9	Chemical Engineering	Reactionary Rockets	x	x	x	x
10	Chemical Engineering	Inflation Station	x	x		
11	Mechanical Engineering	Catapult	x	x	x	x
12	Mechanical Engineering	How Do I Hover?	x	x	x	x
13	Mechanical Engineering	Totally Tops	x	x	x	x
14	Mechanical Engineering	The Indy Card Car	x	x	x	x
15	Mechanical Engineering	Hydraulic Crane	x	x	x	x
16	Civil Engineering	Cantilever Challenge	x	x	x	x
17	Civil Engineering	Straw Bridges	x	x	x	x
18	Civil Engineering	Careening Coasters	x	x	x	x
19	Civil Engineering	The Two Feet Feat	x	x	x	x
20	Civil Engineering	Wrecking Ball	x	x	x	x

As the NGSS takes hold around the country and engineering becomes more integrated into classrooms and programs, *Teaching Engineering Made Easy* will be updated and improved to fit even more tightly to the new standards.

References

Baine, C. (2004). *High tech hot shots: Careers in sports engineering.* Alexandria, VA: National Society of Professional Engineers.

Hart, D. (1999). Opening assessment to our students. *Social Education, 63*(6), 343–436.

International Technology Education Association (ITEA). (2000, 2005, 2007). *Standards for technological literacy: Content for the study of technology.* Reston, VA: Author.

National Academy of Engineering (NAE). (2008). *Changing the conversation: Messages for improving public understanding of engineering.* Washington, DC: National Academies Press.

National Research Council (NRC). (1996). *National science education standards.* National Committee on Science Education Standards and Assessment, Board on Science Education, Division of Behavioral and Social Sciences and Education, National Research Council (NRC). Washington, DC: National Academies Press.

National Research Council (NRC). (2012). *A framework for K–12 science education: Practices, crosscutting concepts, and core ideas.* Committee on a Conceptual Framework for New K–12 Science Education Standards. Board on Science Education, Division of Behavioral and Social Sciences and Education, National Research Council (NRC). Washington, DC: National Academies Press.

NGSS Lead States. (2013). *Next generation science standards: For states, by states. Volume 1: The standards and Volume 2: Appendices.* Washington, DC: National Academies Press.

6

Fender Bender Physics

Roy Q. Beven
Science and Engineering Educator, Bellingham, Washington

Author's Note: Images in this chapter courtesy of NSTA.

*F*ender Bender Physics is an integrated science and engineering curriculum built on the theme of transportation safety. It was developed through a partnership between the National Highway Traffic Safety Administration and NSTA. An engineering design process is used as the curriculum design for each of the three units. These units can be used together, individually, or as enrichments to middle school physical science or technology education programs. Instructional activities are focused on the practices of science and engineering while building understanding of core ideas in physics, engineering design, and important attributes of vehicles.

Fender Bender Physics was published by NSTA Press in 2001. A PDF of it can be found at www.wsanford.com/~wsanford/gr8ps/zz_old-files/red/mpv/Curricula/Fender-Bender-Physics.pdf.

Goals

In *Fender Bender Physics*, students learn the practices and core ideas of both science and engineering while engaged in a design challenge. For each design challenge, students engage in a seven-phase design process, ending with team presentations of their work. As illustrated in Figure 6.1, these seven phases (bullets) are well-aligned to the three-phase design process (shown in the circles) of the Next Generation Science Standards (NGSS Lead States, 2013). A later section of this chapter shows how the three units map to performance expectations in the NGSS and the Common Core State Standards (NGA and CCSSO, 2010).

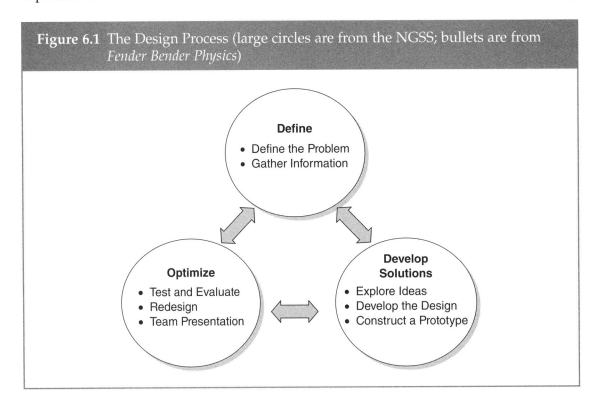

Figure 6.1 The Design Process (large circles are from the NGSS; bullets are from *Fender Bender Physics*)

The Units

The Mousetrap Car

After the students are hooked by an introductory activity, they investigate the force of a mousetrap's lever arm. They measure the relationship between the distance a mousetrap is opened and the force it exerts, as well as the effect of the snapper-arm length on that force. Then students apply their finding to the design of a mousetrap car. To evaluate their designs, students measure, graph, and describe the motions of their prototype cars. Students read background information on force and motion and communicate their results to others.

This project relies on the accumulation of accurate data. Students make their own database of definitions, concepts, and experimental results. They establish design requirements and specifications and learn how to incorporate sufficient detail in order to get a design approved. Students also develop sketching skills as a tool for designing and communicating ideas.

Finally, students gain the satisfaction of seeing their designs take shape from a prototype. Prototyping is a standard engineering process that involves testing a variety of materials to determine which ones best meet the requirements of a project. A design portfolio is the authentic assessment of the inquiry process.

Working in teams, students evaluate data by comparing car designs and communicating their progress through reports and expository writing. The unit culminates in a Great Race, in which students race their vehicles and display pride in their achievements. The unit should be fun, ending with friendly, cooperative team presentations of design portfolios and completed mousetrap vehicles.

This unit on the mousetrap car illustrates the dynamic relationship between scientific investigations and engineering design. Students use experimentation, testing, and evaluation at each step of the process. They learn that their progress must be measurable and must be communicated in operational terms. When questions arise, controlled investigations provide answers.

Fender Bender Physics was developed to meet the Standards for Technological Literacy (ITEA, 2000, 2005, 2007) and the National Science Education Standards (NRC, 1996).

However, the units also meet many of the goals in the NGSS, such as the following:

> By the time students reach middle school they should have had numerous experiences in engineering design. The goal for middle school students is to define problems more precisely, to conduct a more thorough process of choosing the best solution, and to optimize the final design. (NGSS Lead States, 2013, p. 85)

The units can also be adapted to more closely meet the NGSS goals. One way to do this is to modify the objectives to emphasize the close connections between practices of science and engineering, and core ideas, such as, "Plan and conduct an investigation to determine how the distance a mousetrap is open affects the force it exerts."

The CO₂ Car

The CO_2 Car unit provides background for extending lessons on automobile safety into new areas. The high speed of the CO_2 car introduces the issue of control into the design process. Students examine wheel alignment to reduce the potential of rollover in model trucks. The unit also introduces the concept of center of gravity. Using force diagrams, students can examine the differences among vehicle designs and compare the stability of various kinds of vehicles under high-speed conditions in a structured laboratory situation.

One of the significant core ideas developed in the unit is the use of force diagrams (a.k.a. free body diagrams). Middle school students can easily see how in-line force arrows can add or subtract without the use of vector mathematics. Figure 6.2 shows the expected student force diagram for Activities 2 and 3.

Figure 6.2 Force Diagrams

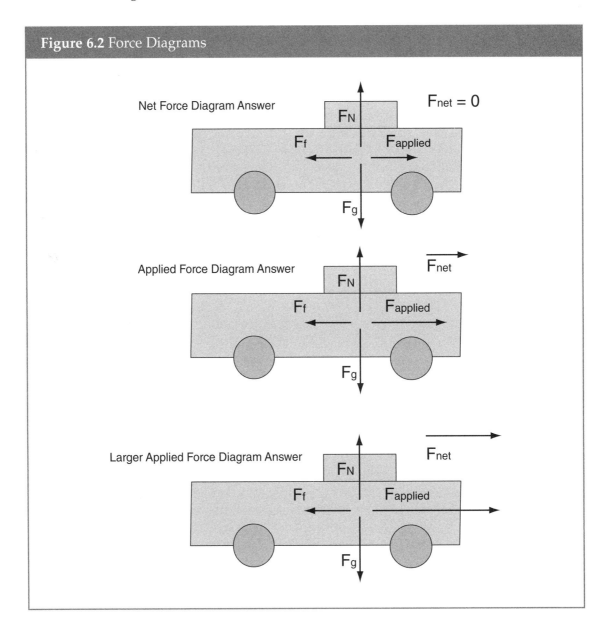

To use this unit without first presenting the Mousetrap Car unit, the activity titled Writing a Design Process Paper needs to be added to the unit plan and customized for CO_2 cars.

The materials for making CO_2 cars can be purchased as kits with partially shaped wooden blanks. There are instructions for making these wooden blanks if so desired. Shaping the cars requires the use of more tools and much more stringent safety precautions, which can be facilitated with a serious review of Reading 5: Student Safety Guide of the Supplemental Materials (p. 88). The lessons on mass, velocity, and friction can be achieved with either commercial or student-built car bodies.

If teachers are unable to obtain the materials needed for all of their students to build, test, and run CO_2 cars, the unit can still be done using computer simulations. Simulations are available from sources such as WhiteBox Learning at www.whiteboxlearning.com that enable students to virtually research, design, perform wind tunnel tests on their designs, and run their virtual CO_2 cars on a track.

The Spaceframe Vehicle

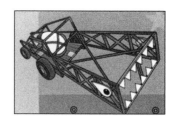

Students begin their engineering design process by exploring how passenger safety can be engineered in a vehicle. Next, students construct force-path diagrams that describe crashes. With these graphic models, students see that energy-absorbing structures in vehicles can protect passengers.

Next, students investigate the amount of energy/work needed to roll their spaceframe vehicles to the top of a ramp, and they use their results to predict the stopping force on the vehicle during a crash. They compare materials as they plan their designs.

Students design and build their prototype vehicles from wood for a passenger egg. The three sections of the space frame are the front end, passenger compartment, and luggage compartment, and all have size criteria. The style and size of the passenger seat and seatbelt are identical on all the student vehicles. Because the passenger seat is attached to a solid wood base, the vehicle must absorb the energy while directing force around the passenger or the egg will crack. Impact-absorbing material may be added if the agreed-upon constraints allow for it. The final testing is both spectacular and fun.

Students record and analyze the collisions with the help of video technology. They analyze the force paths and energy transfers of the destroyed spaceframe by observing the performance of the vehicle and the condition of the passenger egg. Then they document their design process and present their design portfolio to the class.

As mentioned above, it is easy to adapt *Fender Bender Physics* units to more closely match the goals in the NGSS. For example, one of the crosscutting concepts in the NGSS is *structure and function*. This concept is clearly demonstrated as the students modify their vehicles and see how changes in the structure of their inventions enable them to function differently during an accident, and why that is important in saving lives.

This unit can be enhanced with today's easy, inexpensive computer-aided design (CAD) applications. An example of this is shown in Figure 6.3 from the Spaceframe Vehicle unit.

The whole notion of a spaceframe and of force paths can be applied to many structures. Future application could be buildings, trains, bridges, spaceships, or anything of interest to students.

Connections to the NGSS

Fender Bender Physics is a curriculum in which science ideas and engineering ideas are taught simultaneously in a natural, not forced manner. The syntax of the activities is a design process so that students can build understanding and the skills needed for the practices of science and engineering. The context of the curriculum is on designing and testing vehicles with an emphasis on safety, which is a very engaging topic for adolescents. This marriage of core ideas, practices, and context makes for an engaging focus and meets the goals of the NGSS.

As shown in Table 6.1, each of the three units involves students in the engineering design process. As in professional engineering, the order of the phases varies from project to project.

As students engage in these activities, they have opportunities to achieve all four engineering design performance expectations while building understanding of force, motion,

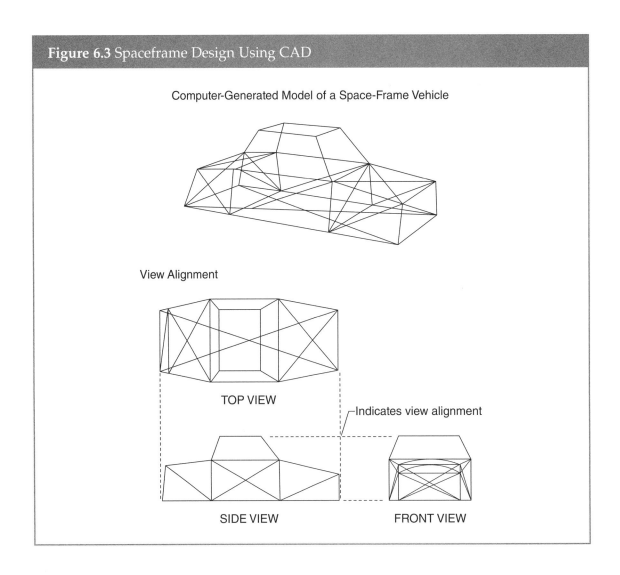

Figure 6.3 Spaceframe Design Using CAD

Computer-Generated Model of a Space-Frame Vehicle

View Alignment

TOP VIEW

Indicates view alignment

SIDE VIEW

FRONT VIEW

and energy. These activities embody the goals of the NGSS as described in the *Middle School Engineering Design Storyline:*

> By the end of 8th grade students are expected to achieve all four performance expectations (MS-ETS1–1, MS-ETS1–2, MS-ETS1–3, and MS-ETS1–4) related to a single problem in order to understand the interrelated processes of engineering design. These include defining a problem by precisely specifying criteria and constraints for solutions as well as potential impacts on society and the natural environment, systematically evaluating alternative solutions, analyzing data from tests of different solutions and combining the best ideas into an improved solution, and developing a model and iteratively testing and improving it to reach an optimal solution. While the performance expectations shown in Middle School Engineering Design couple particular practices with specific disciplinary core ideas, instructional decisions should include use of many practices that lead to the performance expectations. (NGSS Lead States, 2013, p. 85)

The three *Fender Bender Physics* units also help students meet specific performance expectations in the NGSS as shown in Table 6.2.

Table 6.1 Engineering Design Process in *Fender Bender Physics* Activities

Engineering Design Process	Unit 1 Mousetrap Car	Unit 2 CO$_2$ Car	Unit 2 Spaceframe Vehicle
Define the Problem	1. Writing Design Briefs	1. Requirements and Constraints	1. Passenger Safety
Gather Information	2. Measuring Force 5. Measuring Lever-Arm Effects	2. Mass and Motion 3. Force Diagrams 4. Frictional Force	2. Force-Path Diagrams I 3. Force-Path Diagrams II
Explore Ideas	4. Testing Wheels and Axles	5. Writing Design Briefs	4. Testing Material Properties
Develop the Design	3. Writing a Design Process Paper 6. Developing a Design	5. Writing Design Briefs	5. Design Documentation
Construct a Prototype	7. Constructing a Prototype	6. Prototype Development	5. Design Documentation
Test and Evaluate	8. Measuring Motion	8. Time and Velocity	6. Work and Energy
Redesign	3. Writing a Design Process Paper	7. Performance Testing	7. Destructive Testing 8. Energy Transfer
Team Presentations	9. Team Presentation	9. Team Presentation	9. Team Presentation

Table 6.2 Connections to NGSS Performance Expectations

	Unit 1 Mousetrap Car	Unit 2 CO$_2$ Car	Unit 3 Spaceframe Vehicle
MS-ETS1–1. Define the criteria and constraints of a design problem with sufficient precision to ensure a successful solution, taking into account relevant scientific principles and potential impacts on people and the natural environment that may limit possible solutions.	✓	✓	✓
MS-ETS1–2. Evaluate competing design solutions using a systematic process to determine how well they meet the criteria and constraints of the problem.	✓	✓	✓
MS-ETS1–3. Analyze data from tests to determine similarities and differences among several design solutions to identify the best characteristics of each that can be combined into a new solution to better meet the criteria for success.	✓	✓	✓
MS-ETS1–4. Develop a model to generate data for iterative testing and modification of a proposed object, tool, or process such that an optimal design can be achieved.	✓	✓	✓
MS-PS2–1. Apply Newton's Third Law to design a solution to a problem involving the motion of two colliding objects.			✓
MS-PS2–2. Plan an investigation to provide evidence that the change in an object's motion depends on the sum of the forces on the object and the mass of the object.	✓	✓	✓
MS-PS3–5. Construct, use, and present arguments to support the claim that when the kinetic energy of an object changes, energy is transferred to or from the object.		✓	

Connections to the Common Core State Standards

With the emphasis on writing design briefs and building a design portfolio, *Fender Bender Physics* is a fine science curriculum to support the Common Core State Standards (CCSS). The middle school CCSS about writing informative/explanatory text in science and technical subjects are well aligned to the task of writing a design brief.

Additionally, the supplemental readings described below can be used to support the CCSS reading standards for literacy in science and technical subjects, such as the following:

Grade 7: 2. Determine two or more central ideas in a text and analyze their development over the course of the text; provide an objective summary of the text.

Grade 8: 1. Cite the textual evidence that most strongly supports an analysis of what the text says explicitly as well as inferences drawn from the text. (NGA and CCSSO, 2010, p. 39)

Instructional Materials

Fender Bender Physics is designed to help students develop ideas and skills while engaged in fun, interesting design challenges guided by instructional activities. These activities include many scientific investigations whose results can be applied in student designs. Students investigate lever-arm effects to design a mousetrap car, in contrast to the standard physics lab where students hang objects on a balance beam as a model of a lever. Students investigate air friction to optimize their CO_2 cars, which is never done in traditional middle school science classrooms. And in the spaceframe challenge, a project to design structural support for a car or truck, students use an intuitive mathematical analysis of how forces move through structures to simulate a crash test of their prototype, before the actual crash test. When parents ask students what they did in school today, they should hear something intriguing, such as, "We engineered the frame of a car to protect the car's passenger egg."

Each unit of *Fender Bender Physics* includes a Teacher's Guide that provides an overview of the unit and gives tips for making the unit work, including a list of materials. There is a physics background section as well as sections for time management, assessment criteria, keeping a notebook and a design portfolio, and preparing an oral presentation. The first activity of the unit is a student handout describing the design challenge and a chart of the student products.

Each instructional activity includes a student handout that can be used as written or customized by the teacher to meet the needs of a particular class. Each activity also includes instructions for the teacher that describe how the activities tie into the practices of scientists and engineers, the intended conceptual learning goals, and suggestions for extensions for individual students.

Fender Bender Physics is written for students and for teachers. The student handouts and supplemental materials are written for students to read and use, while the Teacher's Guides are written for teachers to explain the science, engineering, and pedagogy of each unit and activity.

Where Does This Course Fit in the Curriculum?

Fender Bender Physics can be used as guide for a year of science-technology in middle school as written. It can be adapted to be the basis for just a trimester or quarter by selecting just Unit 1, 2, or 3. If Unit 2 or 3 is selected, appropriate activities from Unit 1 can be easily added. For example, the Unit 1 activity about writing design briefs for mousetrap cars should be added to Units 2 or 3 and adapted to writing design briefs for CO_2 cars or spaceframe vehicles.

Fender Bender Physics can also be used in a high school physical science course. In one application, Unit 3: Spaceframe Vehicles made for a fine force-energy unit. The core ideas of how force is related to energy are challenging for middle school students but less challenging for high school students.

Who Should Teach This Course?

Any physical science or tech-ed teacher can use *Fender Bender Physics* if he or she is interested and motivated. The curriculum guide gives some background information and instructional resources to enable a science teacher to facilitate students in engineering design. In addition, by reading and discussing *A Framework for K–12 Science Education* (NRC, 2012), teachers can build conceptual understanding. The same may be true for tech-ed teachers; they can build understanding of science along with their students, while reading and discussing the *Framework* and other supplementary materials.

Perhaps a partnership between physical science teachers and tech-ed teachers is ideal for teaching *Fender Bender Physics*. The organization of middle schools into departments is not necessarily an obstacle. The middle school administration should welcome collaboration for the benefit of students.

Supplemental Materials

Reading 1: Brainstorming. This reading is a brief listing of ways for a small group of students to work together followed by a list of brainstorming techniques.

Reading 2: The Design Process. This reading is a description of the seven-phase engineering design process used as the curriculum model for *Fender Bender Physics*. As suggested in the unit activities, it can be used to deepen student understanding of writing a design brief and design process paper.

Reading 3: Mind Mapping. This reading is a brief description of how to build a mind map that includes a sample for the term *vehicle*.

Reading 4: Motion and Force. This reading is an explanation of the physical science core ideas of constant motion, increasing speed, the connection between increasing speed and net force, and how forces move through structures. These ideas are all in the context of the activities of *Fender Bender Physics*. This reading can also be used as informational text for students to develop the ability to meet CCSS Grade 6–12 reading standards.

Reading 5: Student Safety Guide. This reading is a brief description of safety guidelines and how to implement them while involved in the units of *Fender Bender Physics*.

Reading 6: Work as Mechanical Energy. This reading is focused on energy as work and on how that idea is connected to the activities of Units 2 and 3. Like Reading 4, this reading is also an explanation of physical science core ideas and can be used to support the CCSS for Literacy in Science and Technical Subjects.

Reading 7: The Manufacturing Process. This brief reading helps students understand the difference between engineering design and manufacturing, including quality control.

Sketching Guide. Students have found this unique guide to be invaluable in developing and expressing their design ideas. The guide begins with the basics of lines and shapes before asking students to sketch objects. Using examples from *Fender Bender Physics*, the guide also explains how to illustrate details in a design and how to make scale drawings.

These paper-and-pencil activities not only help students illustrate their ideas, they also help students improve their spatial reasoning skills and prepare them for using CAD or other software for drawing images on a computer.

Conclusion

Everyone in the modern world rides in cars, buses, trucks, trains, and planes as a part of daily life, yet we give these amazing technologies scant attention. Through highly motivating activities that help students achieve science education standards, *Fender Bender Physics* is designed to help students recognize the intense effort by engineers, scientists, technicians, and many others to bring these inventions to life and modify them as needed to meet people's needs for transporting themselves and their goods economically and safely. Like the developers of the Framework and the NGSS, we believe that it is important for everyone in modern society to have this awareness, and that by recognizing and enjoying the process of engineering, many of our students may wish to continue their education along pathways that will enable them to eventually participate in the community of professionals who make such inventions possible.

References

International Technology Education Association (ITEA). (2000, 2005, 2007). *Standards for technological literacy: Content for the study of technology*. Reston, VA: Author.

National Governors Association and Council of Chief State School Officers (NGA and CCSSO). (2010). *Common core state standards: English language arts*. Washington, DC: Author.

National Research Council (NRC). (1996). *National science education standards*. National Committee on Science Education Standards and Assessment, Board on Science Education, Division of Behavioral and Social Sciences and Education, National Research Council (NRC). Washington, DC: National Academies Press.

NGSS Lead States. (2013). *Next generation science standards: For states, by states. Volume 1: The standards*. Washington, DC: National Academies Press.

7

Technology in Practice

Applications and Innovations

Brooke N. Bourdélat-Parks and Pamela Van Scotter
BSCS, Colorado Springs, Colorado

Figure 7.1 Having students work collaboratively prepares them for doing so in the future workforce

Image courtesy of BSCS.

Technology in Practice: Applications and Innovations is an innovative technology and engineering program for middle school students and teachers designed to help students meet the engineering standards and practices articulated in the Next Generation Science Standards (NGSS Lead States, 2013). We developed this program to help all middle school students understand what technology is and why it is relevant in their daily lives.

In Technology in Practice, students explore many ideas related to technology and engineering—the design process, costs, benefits, criteria, constraints, and decision making. These concepts help students learn and practice critical-thinking and problem-solving skills that are important as today's students work toward the NGSS and move into the 21st-century workforce (see Figure 7.1). Even if students do not choose a career in engineering, the skills they learn in this program will be valuable in all walks of life.

The program is made up of three modules, plus an introductory chapter called Doing Technology. Each module is composed of four chapters that allow students to explore different aspects of technology and engineering in different and interesting contexts. The modules are Technology and the Diversity of Limits, Responding to Patterns of Change, and Designing Environmental Solutions. Taken together, the entire program provides students with a rich exploration of the principles of technology and engineering design. On the other hand, the program offers flexibility in that each module is able to stand alone. This flexibility allows teachers to tailor the program to meet their own classroom needs.

Learning Goals

We designed and developed Technology in Practice to engage all students in working on collaborative teams to design and test creative solutions. Specifically, Technology in Practice is designed to help educators accomplish the following goals:

1. Develop students' understanding of basic concepts and skills related to technology and engineering within a science context.

2. Improve students' understanding of how technology relates to their lives.

3. Develop students' critical-thinking and problem-solving abilities.

4. Increase the participation and success of all students, particularly in populations underrepresented in STEM fields.

Organizing Principles

Technology in Practice is designed with two underlying principles.

1. Teaching about technology and engineering should be situated in real-world contexts.

2. All students across the range of cognitive styles and abilities should have opportunities to learn.

When people think of technology, they often think of electronics. This program helps students understand that technology is something that helps people like themselves solve a range of problems (see Figure 7.2). Throughout the modules, students examine real-world situations such as designing technology to help disabled people, using technology to predict weather patterns, and solving environmental problems using technology. Using these real-world contexts not only helps students understand why technology is important in their own lives, but it also serves as motivation for students to become interested and explore further.

It is also the case that all students should have opportunities to learn in ways that meet their needs and acknowledge and make use of their own strengths. To address this principle, we designed the program with a range of different types of strategies that allow students to represent their understanding through multiple means and different modalities, such as through the use of simulations, debates, role playing, research projects, and creative writing. These multiple opportunities, aligned with principles of Universal Design for Learning, help all students succeed (CAST, 2008).

Figure 7.2 Each of these objects is a technology that helps people solve a problem

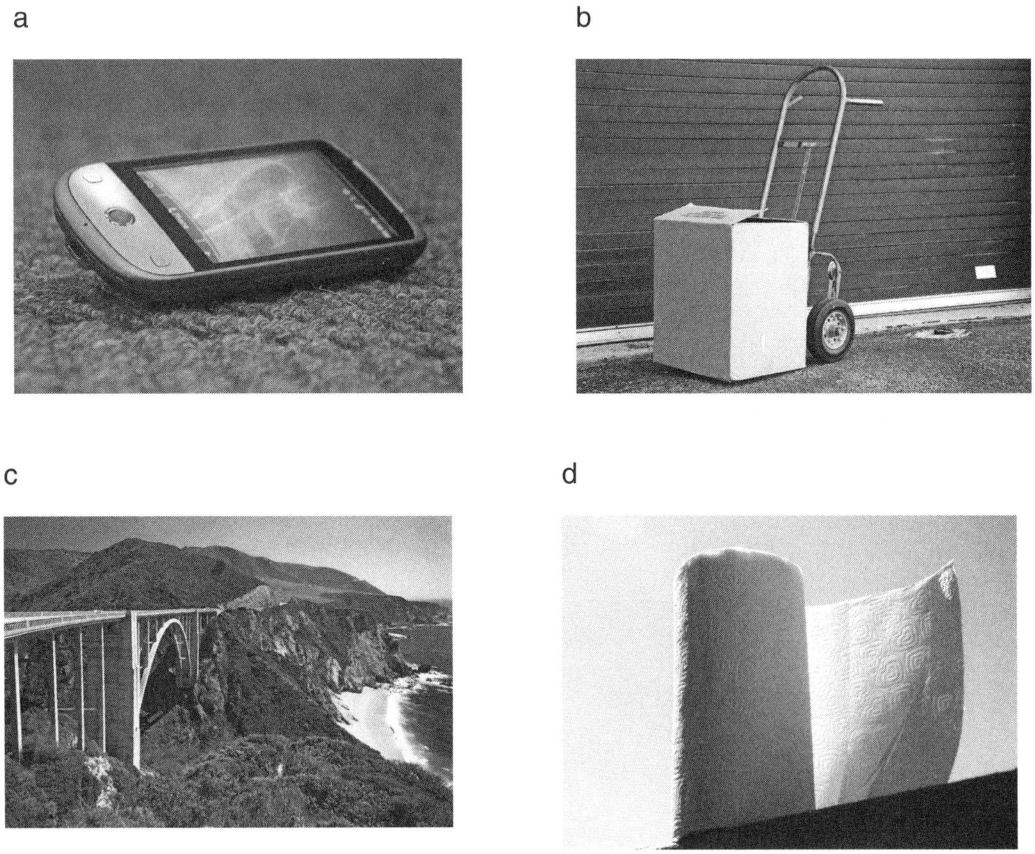

a

b

c

d

Copyright Laura Ciapponi/ Design Pics

Online Dissemination With Hands-On Activities

The program is distributed by Kendall Hunt Publishing (www.kendallhunt.com) through their online portal Flourish. This online dissemination provides easy access anytime and anywhere; the digital design, navigation, and interactions are engaging for students; and the interface uses the best affordances of technology with respect to learning. An interactive chapter organizer allows students to see the overall flow of each chapter, the major ideas they will be exploring, and the linking questions that tie one activity to the next. Within each chapter, students have easy access to digital features that allow them to take notes, highlight sections of the page, and use bookmarks at places they choose. There is also an online glossary available to the students. In addition, the digital simulations that are included enable the students to interact with phenomena that might be difficult or too time consuming to conduct in the classroom.

Although the dissemination of the program is online, in each chapter, students spend a significant amount of time doing hands-on activities in the classroom in collaborative teams as they grapple with problems and materials firsthand and learn by doing.

Modules in the Program

In each of the three modules, students work in collaborative teams. When students work in teams, they are able to share and exchange information with other students instead of having to rely on information provided solely by the teacher. Following is a brief description of the modules.

Doing Technology: An Introduction to Technology Design

Each module begins with a chapter called Doing Technology in which students are introduced to the nature of technology and engineering. In this chapter, students begin by identifying items that they think are and are not technology. They have an opportunity to read a scenario and design a tool to help the character in the story solve a problem. They are then introduced to a female engineer to learn more about her job and to analyze how her work involves the process of technology (also called the engineering design process) (see Figure 7.3). Students then have an opportunity to develop their own solution by following the phases in the process of technology design. Throughout the chapter, students are able to refine their ideas about what technology is.

Technology and the Diversity of Limits

The first module in the program is Technology and the Diversity of Limits. As the title suggests, the module explores the need to attend to both diversity and limits when solving problems and creating solutions. The content of this module helps students understand how technology affects and can benefit people in society. Students continue to learn about the process of technological design as they solve problems. The students learn about the nature of technological problem solving by exploring concepts such as criteria, constraints, the design process, and the idea that "form follows function." This last idea helps students understand that criteria and constraints limit the diversity of a design.

Figure 7.3 The Process of Technology

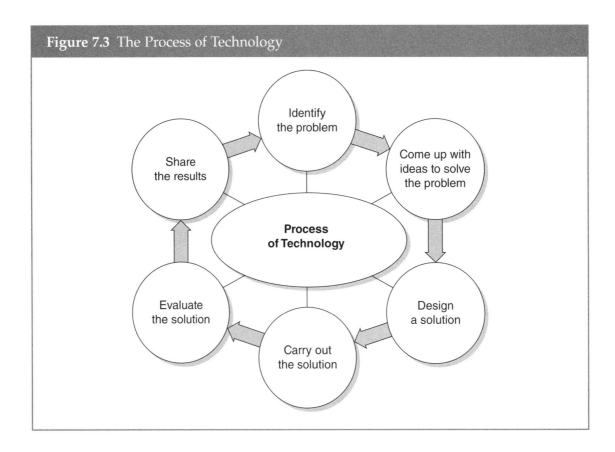

In this module, students perform activities to further develop the skills they learned in the Doing Technology chapter. They continue to develop their understanding of the process of technological design, learn to create and understand data tables, solve problems, develop procedures for testing designs, and consider how technology affects society.

By the end of the module, students should understand and be able to explain the following:

- The processes involved in designing and implementing a product, including accounting for human factors associated with individuals with disabilities
- The differences between design criteria and design constraints

The students should also be able to do the following:

- Explain that people work with a variety of criteria and constraints
- Design a product that accounts for constraints, including human factors, available materials, cost, and time
- Plan and conduct fair scientific tests, including creating operational definitions, deciding on variables in a test, and presenting results

The module consists of four chapters. In Chapter 1, Consumer Concerns, the students are introduced to two fundamental engineering design concepts—criteria and constraints. Students learn about these concepts as they explore and test paper towels and breakfast cereals. As they complete the activities, they learn about the importance of operational definitions, think about variables to include in a test, and learn how to construct and organize data in tables in ways that are useful.

In Chapter 2, Diversity in Technology, students focus on how criteria and constraints affect the end product as they explore furniture and airplanes. They think about why products with the same goal might have different designs (see Figure 7.4). They also think about why there might be diversity among the designs for a similar product.

In Chapter 3, Testing Your Way to a Solution, students focus on why testing is important and learn how to conduct a fair test. They imagine themselves working for a fictitious company to test boats and rockets and then help the company come up with a rocket design.

Chapter 4, Masters of Design, is the capstone chapter for this module. During this chapter, students complete an entire cycle of the process of engineering design. They use the information they have learned in Chapters 1–3 to design a product for a person with a disability. Each activity is devoted to one or two stages of the process of engineering design.

Figure 7.4 Students consider how products with the same goal might have different designs

Copyright © vadimmmus.

Responding to Patterns of Change

In the module Responding to Patterns of Change, students learn about different weather events and how they can be explained by science. They also learn about the technologies that have been developed to help scientists study storms and natural disasters.

The theme of this module is the science of weather patterns. Students learn fundamental science concepts that enable people to understand weather, such as evaporation, condensation, and patterns of air movement in the atmosphere. They apply these concepts to learning about how people use them to make predictions about weather events, including those that become natural disasters. Students also learn about how scientists use a variety of technologies to monitor, record, and study weather data.

As part of the module, students also use the skills they developed as part of the Doing Technology chapter. They consider materials and other criteria that could help a house withstand a natural weather event. They also have an opportunity to use the process of technology design to develop a technology that would be helpful during a weather event.

By the end of the module, students should understand and be able to explain the following:

- Evaporation and condensation as part of the water cycle
- How temperature, air pressure, and density influence air movements in the atmosphere
- How a variety of factors can interact to make a natural event more severe

The students should also be able to do the following:

- Describe how patterns help scientists make predictions about future weather events
- Give examples of benefits and costs associated with choices
- Use probability to inform decisions

Chapter 1, What Causes Weather Patterns?, introduces students to some of the important science concepts that influence the weather. The activities in this chapter help students understand how the sun, water, and wind interact to cause various weather patterns. They use several models to help them visualize and understand the patterns.

In Chapter 2, Extraordinary Events, students use models to study some of the events and then learn more about events that become natural disasters (see Figure 7.5). They use tornado data sets to make predictions about weather events (see Figure 7.6).

In Chapter 3, Chance Affects Decision Making, students learn about the idea of probability. Probability relates to technological problem solving because people use probability when making decisions. The activities in this chapter help students to see how understanding the chances of different events occurring can help people decide what action they should take.

In Chapter 4, Making Decisions to Solve Problems, students use the process of technology design to design an object that helps in a weather event. They first design a house,

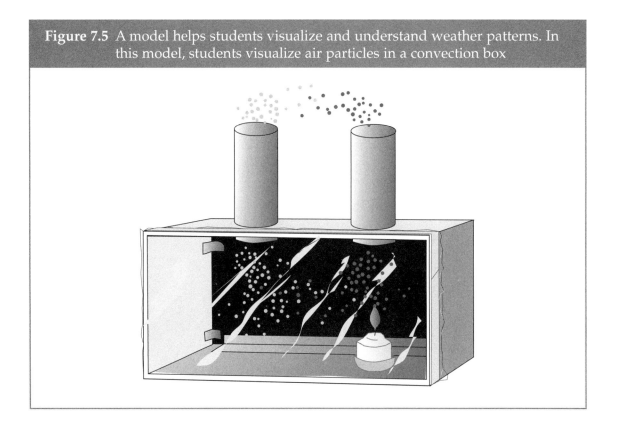

Figure 7.5 A model helps students visualize and understand weather patterns. In this model, students visualize air particles in a convection box

considering the costs and benefits of different aspects of the house. Students then design their own technology to solve a problem and come up with a plan to communicate the features of the technology in order to sell it.

Designing Environmental Solutions

In the Designing Environmental Solutions module, students learn about environmental issues and how we can use technology to solve some of those issues. They use the contexts of garbage, air pollution, and oil spills to explore how humans use technology to deal with environmental issues. Students use models and computer-based simulations to test different technologies. They learn about some of the costs and benefits associated with each technology.

Students also further develop their skills with engineering and the process of technology design by researching and choosing a local environmental issue and designing a solution that would help solve it or reduce its severity.

By the end of the module, students should understand and be able to explain the following:

Figure 7.6 Students explore natural weather events, such as hurricanes, shown in this satellite image of a hurricane along the Gulf Coast

Copyright Stocktrek Images.

- The processes involved in designing and implementing a product, including accounting for human factors associated with individuals with disabilities
- The differences between design criteria and design constraints

The students should also be able to do the following:

- Explain that people work with a variety of criteria and constraints
- Design a product that accounts for constraints, including human factors, available materials, cost, and time
- Plan and conduct fair scientific tests, including creating operational definitions, deciding on variables in a test, and presenting results

In Chapter 1, Garbage In, Garbage Out, students focus on an environmental issue with which many communities struggle—garbage. Many students may not know what happens to garbage once they put the container out at the curb by their house or drop bags off at the local dump. Although many schools now have recycling programs, students may not realize why recycling is beneficial for the environment. In this chapter, students learn about some of the challenges associated with the disposal of waste (see Figure 7.7).

Figure 7.7 Students study landfills as they consider garbage as an environmental issue

Copyright hroe.

In Chapter 2, Air Pollution Solutions, students take part in activities to learn about why air pollution is a serious issue in some communities. They use models and an investigation to collect data about the effects of air pollution. They also consider the costs and benefits of some technologies that relate to pollution.

Chapter 3, Clean Up Your Spills!, involves students in activities that help them understand oil spills. They take part in an investigation and a computer-based simulation to learn about the technologies to clean up oil spills (see Figure 7.8). They calculate the efficiencies of different technologies and share their findings with other teams.

Students choose a local environmental issue in Chapter 4, Taking Action. They develop a technology to help solve the problem. Each activity in this chapter is dedicated to one or two phases in the process of technology design to allow students to fully engage in designing their solution.

Chapter Organizers

To better understand how chapters in Technology in Practice are written and what students do in activities, we have created a chapter organizer (Figure 7.9) that helps you see the key ideas and activities for Clean Up Your Spills! This organizer also shows the linking questions that help students develop the storyline of the chapter and understand how the activities connect to one another. Each chapter in each of the modules has a chapter organizer to help teachers and students understand the storyline and concepts in the chapter.

Figure 7.8 Oil booms that keep the oil from spreading are one of the technologies that students study as they consider how to clean oil spills

Copyright Brain Scantlebury.

Connections With the Next Generation Science Standards

The Technology and the Diversity of Limits module helps students accomplish the MS-ETS1 Engineering Design standards from the NGSS. It also helps students develop the practices of science as described in the Doing Technology section of this chapter.

The Responding to Patterns of Change module helps students accomplish some of the performance

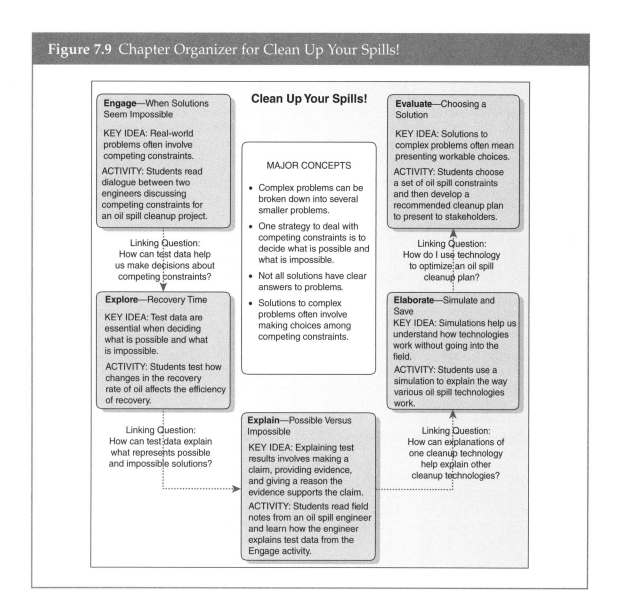

Figure 7.9 Chapter Organizer for Clean Up Your Spills!

Clean Up Your Spills!

Engage—When Solutions Seem Impossible

KEY IDEA: Real-world problems often involve competing constraints.

ACTIVITY: Students read dialogue between two engineers discussing competing constraints for an oil spill cleanup project.

Linking Question: How can test data help us make decisions about competing constraints?

Explore—Recovery Time

KEY IDEA: Test data are essential when deciding what is possible and what is impossible.

ACTIVITY: Students test how changes in the recovery rate of oil affects the efficiency of recovery.

Linking Question: How can test data explain what represents possible and impossible solutions?

MAJOR CONCEPTS

- Complex problems can be broken down into several smaller problems.
- One strategy to deal with competing constraints is to decide what is possible and what is impossible.
- Not all solutions have clear answers to problems.
- Solutions to complex problems often involve making choices among competing constraints.

Explain—Possible Versus Impossible

KEY IDEA: Explaining test results involves making a claim, providing evidence, and giving a reason the evidence supports the claim.

ACTIVITY: Students read field notes from an oil spill engineer and learn how the engineer explains test data from the Engage activity.

Evaluate—Choosing a Solution

KEY IDEA: Solutions to complex problems often mean presenting workable choices.

ACTIVITY: Students choose a set of oil spill constraints and then develop a recommended cleanup plan to present to stakeholders.

Linking Question: How do I use technology to optimize an oil spill cleanup plan?

Elaborate—Simulate and Save

KEY IDEA: Simulations help us understand how technologies work without going into the field.

ACTIVITY: Students use a simulation to explain the way various oil spill technologies work.

Linking Question: How can explanations of one cleanup technology help explain other cleanup technologies?

expectations in the MS-ESS2 Earth's Systems and the MS-ESS3 Earth and Human Activity sections from the NGSS. There is a focus on the crosscutting concepts of patterns and cause and effect.

The Designing Environmental Solutions module helps students accomplish some of the standards in the MS-ESS3 Earth and Human Activity sections from the NGSS. There is a focus on the crosscutting concepts of patterns and systems and system models.

All three of the modules help students develop the practices of science and engineering as described in the Doing Technology section of this chapter.

In Technology in Practice, the process of "technology design" has the same meaning as "engineering design" in *A Framework for K–12 Science Education* (NRC, 2012) and the *Next Generation Science Standards* (NGSS Lead States, 2013). Through the lessons in the Doing Technology chapter, students acquire both the understanding of and the abilities to carry out engineering design. This helps students meet the new standards.

We recognize that the purpose of the NGSS is to provide a common set of learning expectations for curriculum, instruction, and assessment. The NGSS is based on *A Framework for K–12 Science Education: Practices, Crosscutting Concepts, and Core Ideas* (NRC, 2012), which projects a broad vision for the future of science education. In many cases, the Framework provides more expansive descriptions of what students are expected to know and be able to do than does the NGSS. That is the case with the practices of science and engineering, which weave throughout the new standards, and which all students are expected to master. The phases of the process of technology, as described in Technology in Practice, are very similar to the way that engineering design is described in the Framework (Table 7.1).

Table 7.1 Similarities Between "Technology Design" in Technology in Practice and Engineering Practices in the Framework

Technology in Practice	A Framework for K–12 Science Education
Identify the problem: "Scientists, engineers, and other people who do technology have a process they follow to solve problems. First, they have to identify the problem. People who do technology need a clear idea of what problem they want to solve." (Doing Technology, Technology in Practice)	*Asking questions and defining problems:* "Engineering begins with a problem, need, or desire that suggests an engineering problem that needs to be solved. Engineers ask questions to define the engineering problem, determine criteria for a successful solution, and identify constraints" (NRC, 2012, p. 50).
Come up with ideas to solve the problem: "People who do technology come up with ideas about how to solve the problem. It is important to come up with several possible ways to solve the problem. Engineers have to consider many factors. They have to think about cost, materials, time, space, and safety." (Doing Technology, Technology in Practice)	*Constructing explanations and designing solutions:* "Each proposed solution results from a process of balancing competing criteria of desired functions, technological feasibility, cost, safety, esthetics, and compliance with legal requirements. There is usually no single best solution but rather a range of solutions" (NRC, 2012, p. 52). *Developing and using models:* "Engineering makes use of models and simulations to analyze existing systems so as to see where flaws might occur or to test possible solutions to a new problem. Engineers also call on models of various sorts to test proposed systems and to recognize the strengths and limitations of their designs" (NRC, 2012, p. 50).
Design a solution: "Each idea [engineers] come up with must be carefully tested. Each plan is drawn or written down, which makes it easier to explain the ideas to others." (Doing Technology, Technology in Practice)	*Planning and carrying out investigations:* "Engineers use investigations both to gain data essential for specifying design criteria or parameters and to test their designs. Like scientists, engineers must identify relevant variables, decide how they will be measured, and collect data for analysis. Their investigations help them to identify how effective, efficient, and durable their designs may be under a range of conditions" (NRC, 2012, p. 50).

Technology in Practice	A Framework for K–12 Science Education
Carry out the solution: "Engineers and designers carry out each idea and see how well each one works." (Doing Technology, Technology in Practice)	*Analyzing and interpreting data:* "Engineers analyze data collected in the tests of their designs and investigations; this allows them to compare different solutions and determine how well each one meets specific design criteria—that is, which design best solves the problem within the given constraints" (NRC, 2012, p. 51). *Using mathematics and computational thinking:* "In engineering, mathematical and computational representations of established relationships and principles are an integral part of design" (NRC, 2012, p. 51).
Evaluate the solution: "They evaluate the pros and cons for each idea to see which one provides the best solution. To do this, engineers collect data, or evidence. They analyze the evidence and ask questions about how well each idea worked." (Doing Technology, Technology in Practice)	*Engaging in argument from evidence:* "In engineering, reasoning and argument are essential for finding the best possible solution to a problem. Engineers collaborate with their peers throughout the design process, with a critical stage being the selection of the most promising solution among a field of competing ideas. Engineers use systematic methods to compare alternatives, formulate evidence based on test data, make arguments from evidence to defend their conclusions, evaluate critically the ideas of others, and revise their designs in order to achieve the best solution to the problem at hand" (NRC, 2012, p. 52).
Share the results: "Sharing information is important in science and engineering. People who do technology write or tell about their own process. They communicate with words, pictures, and diagrams. They tell people about the problem and how they solved it. They also share how the solution works and whether they did anything to make it work better." (Doing Technology, Technology in Practice)	*Obtaining, evaluating, and communicating information:* "Engineers cannot produce new or improved technologies if the advantages of their designs are not communicated clearly and persuasively. Engineers need to be able to express their ideas, orally and in writing, with the use of tables, graphs, drawings, or models and by engaging in extended discussions with peers. Moreover, as with scientists, they need to be able to derive meaning from colleagues' texts, evaluate the information, and apply it usefully" (NRC, 2012, p. 53).

Key Features of the Program

Technology in Practice incorporates key features that align with the current research on STEM teaching and learning and that support the middle school philosophy (Armstrong, 2006; NRC, 2012). These key features include the following:

1. Use of the BSCS 5E Instructional Model

2. Meaningful collaborative learning strategies

3. Sense-making strategies to support understanding

4. Practical support for teachers

5. A broad role for assessment

1. Use of the BSCS 5E Instructional Model. We have developed and sequenced each chapter in each module using the research-based BSCS 5E Instructional Model (Bybee, 1997; Bybee & Landes, 1990) (see Figure 7.10). The 5E model is based on a constructivist philosophy of learning (Ausubel, Novak, & Hanesian, 1978; Vygotsky, 1962) and is supported by the findings from *How People Learn* (Bransford, Brown, & Cocking, 1999). One underlying tenet of this philosophy is that people build or construct their understanding across time beginning with previous experiences, and they use new experiences to deepen or revise that understanding.

In Technology in Practice, each chapter cycles through the 5Es as described below, and each activity exemplifies one of the Es, in sequence.

Engage: The students engage in an event or question related to the major concept of the chapter. This stage encourages students to begin thinking about what they already know and what they might learn.

Explore: The students participate in a common set of experiences on which they will draw as they begin to develop their understanding of the concept.

Explain: The students construct their explanation of the major idea they have been exploring through additional activities, discussions, and readings.

Elaborate: The students expand or deepen their understanding of the concept by applying it to new situations.

Evaluate: The students complete an activity that helps both the students and the teacher evaluate the students' understanding of the concept.

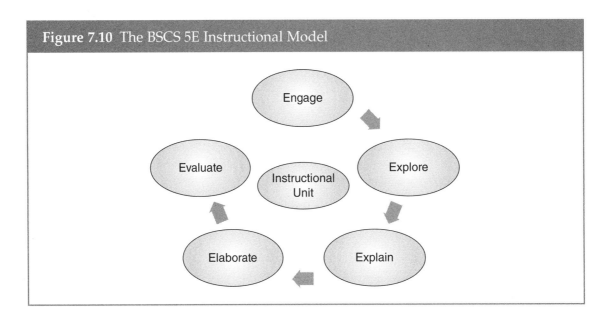

Figure 7.10 The BSCS 5E Instructional Model

2. Meaningful Collaborative Learning Strategies. Engineering, technology, and science are collaborative enterprises (see Figure 7.11). A single solution or design is often the result of many scientists, engineers, and technologists working together, communicating their results, sharing their ideas, and building on past ideas and successes. And certainly, today's workplaces require that employees work together with one another to accomplish tasks.

In the classroom, collaborative learning research indicates that collaboration among students increases the level of student success, especially for those populations that have traditionally been underserved by education. For those reasons, we have carefully incorporated meaningful collaborative learning strategies into the program. The model we use is based primarily on the work of Johnson and Johnson (1987), Adams and Hamm (1996), and Thousand, Villa, and Nevin (1994).

Working in teams also allows students to practice teamwork skills, which will become even more important when they enter the workforce in the next decade or so. At times, the student materials will highlight these teamwork skills and instruct students to reflect on their work as part of a team. Technology in Practice is composed of many hands-on and minds-on investigations that keep students working together and engaged in solving problems and creating solutions.

Figure 7.11 Engineering, technology, and science are collaborative enterprises

Copyright Ablestock.com.

3. Sense-Making Strategies to Support Understanding. In addition to collaborative learning strategies, Technology in Practice incorporates specific and targeted sense-making strategies that help students make sense of what they are learning and also help them organize information in ways that help them solve complex problems. To help students track their learning journey, the program encourages students to make extensive use of a technology notebook. Students use this notebook to capture their understanding as it deepens and to monitor their progress toward the learning goals. In particular, they use the notebook to record answers to questions throughout the program, capture their ideas and reflections, record data and draw illustrations, and complete the sense-making strategies embedded in the activities. Many of these sense-making strategies increase the participation and success of all students in the classroom. The specific sense-making strategies that we incorporated into this program include creating and using a personal glossary, data tables, analogy maps, and Venn diagrams, and using a strategy called Think, Share, Advise, Revise (TSAR).

The Personal Glossary supports students in developing their own definitions and descriptions of concepts and processes that are meaningful to them. They are encouraged to modify their entries as their understanding deepens. Learning how to set up a data table that aligns with the data they will collect and the problem they are working to solve provides students with the opportunity to develop a skill that will be useful in organizing data and solving problems throughout their lives. Analogy maps help students make sense of models they use in activities and relate those models to real-world phenomena. The Venn diagram is a useful way for students to illustrate their understanding about how certain concepts or processes may have things in common as well as aspects that distinguish them from one another. The TSAR strategy structures an interaction between students as they consider each other's ideas and offer advice for how to improve them. Together, this collection of sense-making strategies provides a small but powerful set of tools that aligns well with the types of activities in this program and supports students in their learning journey.

4. Practical Support for Teachers. Technology in Practice provides teachers with practical and thoughtful support and at the same time respects teachers' need to personalize and individualize materials occasionally. Our program provides teachers with the flexibility to do that.

For the program as a whole, we provide teachers with important background information about the philosophy of the program and its key features as well as an overview of the program. For each module, we provide targeted learning goals for students so teachers can see at a glance what concepts the student will explore and come to understand. For each chapter, we provide a chapter organizer that illustrates the flow of the activities and the key ideas. For each activity, each E, the support is more detailed. We provide an overview of the activity and a section called Before You Teach, which lists all the materials for the activity as well as any advance preparation that might be needed. We also include a very valuable section called As You Teach, which provides detailed outcomes and indicators of success so teachers can easily track how well the students are meeting the intended outcomes of a particular activity. We provide the teacher with strategies for getting started and support for each step of the process and procedure as needed. The program also includes suggested responses to questions that students have been asked to answer. All masters that students and teachers need are included in an easy-to-print format.

5. A Broad Role for Assessment. With respect to assessment, we know that American education is often driven by testing and grading, but tests and grades represent only one aspect of assessment. In this program, assessment has a broad role in supporting both the teacher and the student and includes an interactive and ongoing process between the teacher and the student. This process of embedded assessment allows the students and the teacher to have a more authentic measure of what the students know, value, and are able to do at different points throughout the program. The program includes questions and steps that can be used as formative assessments. The Evaluate activity of each chapter can serve as a summative assessment for the concepts learned in the chapter. For the teacher, the embedded assessments help inform their practice and determine the flow of the lessons. Broadening the role of assessment like this allows the teacher to identify the needs of students and modify lessons to meet those needs. Ongoing assessment also helps students monitor their own progress and identify areas where they need to deepen or refine their understanding. The collection of entries students make in their technology notebooks will become a portfolio that tracks their understanding.

Conclusion

Since the early 1990s, BSCS has incorporated engineering design and technology into curricular programs from kindergarten through high school. We applaud the inclusion of engineering design and practices in the *Framework for K–12 Science Education* and the Next Generation Science Standards. We hope that you see from the informative chapters in *The Go-To Guide for Engineering Curricula* that you do not have to create your own engineering curriculum to meet these standards. Technology in Practice can help you build engineering design into your curriculum seamlessly and with complete confidence that students will be motivated to learn. The modules use readily available materials and provide everything you need to take the plunge into technology design and engineering education.

References

Adams, D., & Hamm, M. (1996). *Cooperative learning: Critical thinking and collaboration across the curriculum.* Springfield, IL: Charles C Thomas.

Armstrong, T. (2006). *The best schools: How human development research should inform educational practice.* Washington, DC: Association for Supervisors and Curriculum Development.

Ausubel, D. P., Novak, J. D., & Hanesian, H. (1978). *Educational psychology: A cognitive view* (2nd ed.). New York: Holt, Rinehart and Winston.

Bransford, J. D., Brown, A. L., & Cocking, R. R. (Eds.). (1999). *How people learn: Brain, mind, experience, and school.* Washington, DC: National Academies Press.

Bybee, R. W. (1997). *Achieving scientific literacy: From purposes to practices.* Portsmouth, NH: Heinemann.

Bybee, R. W., & Landes, N. M. (1990). Science for life & living: An elementary school science program from Biological Sciences Curriculum Study. *American Biology Teacher, 52*(2), 92–98.

CAST. (2008). *Universal design for learning guidelines, version 1.0.* Wakefield, MA: Author.

Johnson, D. W., & Johnson, R. T. (1987). *Learning together and alone: Cooperative, competitive, and individualistic learning* (2nd ed.). Englewood Cliffs, NJ: Prentice Hall.

National Research Council (NRC). (2012). *A framework for K–12 science education: Practices, crosscutting concepts, and core ideas.* Committee on a Conceptual Framework for New K–12 Science Education Standards. Board on Science Education, Division of Behavioral and Social Sciences and Education, National Research Council (NRC). Washington, DC: National Academies Press.

NGSS Lead States. (2013). *Next generation science standards: For states, by states. Volume 1: The standards.* Washington, DC: National Academies Press.

Thousand, J. S., Villa, R. A., & Nevin, A. I. (Eds.). (1994). *Creativity and collaborative learning: A practical guide to empowering students and teachers.* Baltimore, MD: Paul H. Brookes.

Vygotsky, L. S. (1962). *Thought and language.* Cambridge: MIT Press.

8

Engineering in IQWST

David Fortus
Weizmann Institute of Science, Rehovot, Israel
Joseph Krajcik
Michigan State University, East Lansing, Michigan

IQWST: A Comprehensive and Coherent Middle School Science Curriculum

Investigating and Questioning our World through Science and Technology (IQWST) (Krajcik, Reiser, Sutherland, & Fortus, 2012) is an NSF-funded comprehensive and coherent sixth- through eighth-grade science curriculum that incorporates engineering activities. It was co-developed by a team consisting of science educators; scientists; an engineer; learning scientists; teacher educators; and specialists in technology and literacy, language, and culture. It is aligned with the Next Generation Science Standards (NGSS Lead States, 2013) and situates student learning in meaningful, extended investigations, in project-based science contexts (see Figure 8.1).

The IQWST materials support students in acquiring deep understandings of the big ideas and science and engineering practices as articulated in *A Framework for K–12 Science Education* (NRC, 2012). The curriculum is designed to support students as they use their knowledge and skills in scientific and engineering practices such as modeling, designing investigations and artifacts, constructing explanations, testing artifacts, analyzing data, and arguing.

The curriculum was developed using a learning-goals-driven design process, in which learning outcomes that drive the design of activities and assessments specified how students should be able to *use* the scientific ideas and practices outlined in the NGSS. The design principles that drove the development of the curriculum are based on research

Authors' Note: Many thanks go to Christine Gleason and Ann Novak for their support and feedback in enacting IQWST units and in helping prepare this chapter.

Figure 8.1 In the seventh-grade Energy unit, students develop a Rube Goldberg-like device that involves at least a number of pre-specified types of energy (design constraints) and as many different energy transformations as possible

Image courtesy of the Weizmann Institute of Science.

on teaching and learning, and specified the ways in which materials support teacher enactment and student learning. These principles included structuring units around explicit learning goals (articulated as learning outcomes); contextualizing inquiry in meaningful scientific and engineering problems; supporting the cognitive, social, and language challenges in science-based and engineering-based inquiry; anchoring all learning in experiences with phenomena; providing formative assessments of students' understanding; embedding rich literacy features; and supporting diverse learners.

The materials are organized around driving questions that motivate students to apply the science that they learn. The curriculum centers around experiencing phenomena, conducting investigations, using technology tools, and reading materials that extend students' first-hand experiences of phenomena and support science literacy. Teacher materials incorporate multiple educative features that support teacher learning of the science content and pedagogical approaches. Reviews by expert scientists and Project 2061 at AAAS provided formative feedback on scientific accuracy and instructional approaches.

The IQWST curriculum materials are published by Sangari Active Science. Detailed information on the curriculum is available at http://sangariglobaled.com/iqwst/.

Focus on Big Ideas

The IQWST units were explicitly designed to align with the national science standards, the *Benchmarks for Scientific Literacy* (AAAS, 1993, 2008) and the *National Science Education*

Standards (NRC, 1996). It was clear from the very start that the national science standards listed more topics at the middle school level than any student could be expected to learn in depth within the typical time allotted to science education during the three years of middle school. IQWST's goal was to help students learn what we considered the most important ideas; we called them big ideas. We therefore selected clusters of key middle school content standards that represented big ideas in science.

The process of selecting standards and clustering the units into big ideas uncovered and highlighted many of the connections between the various topics we had chosen as themes for the various units. For example, it became clear that when learning in earth science about the water cycle, it would be beneficial for the student to have already learned about light's ability to heat water in an earlier unit about light and its interaction with matter. Light as the source of energy that drives photosynthesis was also important to biology. Since energy is one of the crosscutting concepts identified by the Framework (NRC, 2012), almost all the units had a connection to energy transfer, transformation, and conservation. We decided how to sequence the various units mainly, but not only, by analyzing their interdependencies. For example, while all the developers would have preferred energy to be the focus of the first unit in the sequence, we knew from prior research that the concept of energy transformation would be extremely challenging to sixth-grade students, so we decided to delay the unit on energy until seventh grade. This mindful sequencing of the units, as well as the thoughtful sequencing of the various activities in each unit, are other examples of curricular coherence (Shwartz, Weizman, Fortus, Krajcik, & Reiser, 2008). The final sequence is shown in Table 8.1.

Table 8.1 Sequence of the IQWST Units

	First Unit	**Second Unit**	**Third Unit**	**Fourth Unit**
Sixth Grade	Light and Sight	Particle Nature of Matter	Eco-systems	Forces That Shape the Earth
Seventh Grade	Chemical Reactions	Energy	Cells and Organs	Weather and Climate
Eighth Grade	Plate Tectonics and Planetary Science	Genetics and Natural Selection	Photosynthesis and Respiration	Force and Motion

Seventh-Grade Energy Unit

Selection of big ideas. The seventh-grade Energy unit provides a good example of how the IQWST units were developed and structured. The first step in developing this unit was to select the most important big ideas. In doing so, we used the following criteria, which turned out to be very similar to criteria used to choose the core concepts for the *Framework*.

   a. Explanatory power within and across disciplines and/or scales: The key standards help one to understand a variety of different ideas within and/or between science disciplines.

b. Powerful way of thinking about the world: The key content standards provide insight into the development of the field, or have had key influence on the domain.

c. Accessible to learners through their cognitive abilities (age appropriateness) and experiences with phenomena and representations.

d. Building blocks for future learning: The key content standards are vital for future development for other concepts and help lay the foundation for continual learning.

e. Key content standards help the individual participate intellectually in making individual, social, political, and practical decisions regarding science, technology, and engineering.

Each cluster of key standards was broken down into small statements of concepts and principles, and each was then elaborated to define the limits of what we wanted to achieve in the unit. For example, some of the statements of the principles and concepts for the seventh-grade Energy unit are as follows:

- There are different types of energy.

  - Kinetic energy is associated with the speed of an object.
  - Thermal energy is associated with the temperature of an object.
  - Gravitational energy is associated with the elevation of an object.
  - Elastic energy is associated with the deformation of an object.
  - Chemical energy is associated with the chemical composition of a substance.
  - Light energy is associated with light waves.
  - Sound energy is associated with sound waves.
  - Electrical energy is associated with closed circuits with power sources.

- Energy can be transformed from one type to another.
- Atoms and molecules are perpetually in motion. Increased temperature means greater average kinetic energy due to increased random motion of atoms and molecules.
- Most energy transformations result in thermal energy being transferred out of or into the system in which the transformations took place.
- Most processes involve the transfer of energy from one system to another. Energy can be transferred in different ways.
- Energy cannot be created or destroyed. Whenever some energy seems to disappear from a place, some will be found to appear in another.
- Thinking about things as systems means looking for how every part relates to others. The energy output from one part of a system can become the input to other parts.
- Energy from the sun (and the wind and water energy derived from it) is available indefinitely. Because the flow of energy is weak and variable, very large collection systems are needed. Other sources either don't renew or renew only slowly.
- Different ways of obtaining, transforming, and distributing energy have different environmental consequences.

Anchoring activities. An anchoring activity provides the students with a common experience that can be returned to throughout the unit. It should be exciting and motivating, and it should provide students with opportunities to begin investigations. A good

Figure 8.2 The seventh-grade Energy unit is based on the driving question, "Why do some things stop and others keep going?"

Teacher's Edition

Physical Science

Why Do Some Things Stop While Others Keep Going?

Second Edition

Image courtesy of the Weizmann Institute of Science.

anchoring activity should be (a) aligned with the unit's driving question and learning goals; (b) feasible in a classroom; (c) intriguing; (d) ethical; and (e) complex enough to prevent students from understanding it fully without constructing new learning, but not too complex to make it inaccessible. A good anchoring activity often leads directly into the driving question of a unit and is often used to help students see meaning in the driving question.

The anchoring activity that is used for the seventh-grade unit on energy is as follows: Students watch a video of a complex machine (a Rube Goldberg machine). After discussing this video, students examine and "mess around" with a series of devices, some of which predictably stop working after a few seconds, and others that operate for an unexpectedly long time, perhaps not even stopping at all. Students pose questions that they would like to answer in order to understand how these devices work. These questions are recorded on a driving question board (Weizman, Shwartz, & Fortus, 2008). At the end of the lesson, students are introduced to the driving question—"Why do some things stop and others keep going?"—and asked to share what they already know about energy. This leads to the engineering task of trying to design something that will never stop (see Figure 8.2).

An engineering task drives the unit. After the anchoring activity, students then engage in a series of investigations that cycle back to the anchoring activity and the driving question. Each cycle helps them delve deeper into the science content to gain a deeper understanding of how energy is involved in everything in the world, how it can be transformed from one type to another, and how it can be transferred between systems.

After reading an essay on perpetual motion machines and discussing whether they think they could design such machines, the students then return to Rube Goldberg machines. Students are divided into engineering teams, and each team is given the responsibility for designing and building a small machine. These small machines are to be Rube Goldberg-like devices, such as a machine that allow the students to turn off an alarm clock while lying in bed. The goal of each engineering team is to develop a machine that involves at least a number of pre-specified types of energy (design constraints) and as many different energy transformations as possible. They are required to document the energy transformations and transfers that occur during the machine's operation.

This project's goal is to give students an opportunity to integrate and apply their knowledge of energy—its transfer, transformation, and conservation—by thinking about how machines use energy to accomplish a task. By doing so, they are given multiple opportunities to engage in various engineering practices, such as identifying and defining desired physical changes, generating alternative solutions, building prototypes and testing them, and evaluating different possible solutions.

At first, each group prepares a design plan, including diagrams, initial descriptions of their proposed machines, and a planned list of materials. The preparation of the design plan is scaffolded by an activity sheet.

After the design plans are approved and some building materials collected, the students develop a work plan (who does what) and start building their machines. Once again, their work is scaffolded by an activity sheet. For example, the activity sheet asks the students to make Energy Conversion Diagrams (ECDs) and Energy Transfer Diagrams (ETDs) for all the energy transformations and energy transfers that occur in their machines, and then asks if thermal energy is involved in any way in the machine's operation.

ECDs and ETDs are graphical representations of energy conversions and energy transfers in systems that were developed for IQWST. An example ECD is shown in Figure 8.3. Note two things: (a) An ECD implicitly assumes the existence of energy conservation since the total area of the wedges (the area of the circle) representing the different types of energy participating in the process is constant; and (b) the term *energy conversion* is used instead of *energy transformation* because the word *transfer* sounds to many students like an abbreviation of *transformation* and because the term *conversion* allows us to use currency conversion as an analogy of energy transformation (i.e., change from one form of energy to another).

Note that while thermal energy is not one of the pre-specified energy types that needs to be included in the design of every machine, students should know at this stage that thermal energy will be involved in every group's machines because every macroscopic, un-isolated system always transfers thermal energy to its surrounding (energy dissipation), even if it was not specifically included.

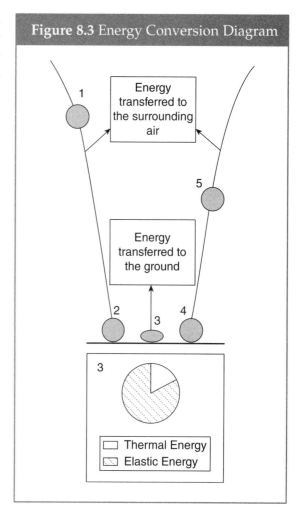

Figure 8.3 Energy Conversion Diagram

Image courtesy of the Weizmann Institute of Science.

Once the machines have been built, each machine is tested to be sure it works as planned. If not (which is almost always the case), modifications are made as needed. Often, the machines stop working before they were intended to, without completing the full chain of events as is typical of Rube Goldberg machines. This can be due to a mismatch between parts or a lack of sufficient energy to proceed. Having the students identify why their machines didn't work and what they need to do to fix them is often the most insightful part of the entire engineering project, with the students suddenly saying "Aha!" as they realize the importance of thinking of the relation of energy to their machine.

After the machines are built and tested, and their operation from an energy perspective described, all the machines are presented publicly. This can be done by each group of students presenting to the rest of the class, one class presenting to other classes, the students presenting to the parents in a science fair, and so on, as the teacher sees fit. An example poster presenting a machine is shown in Figure 8.4.

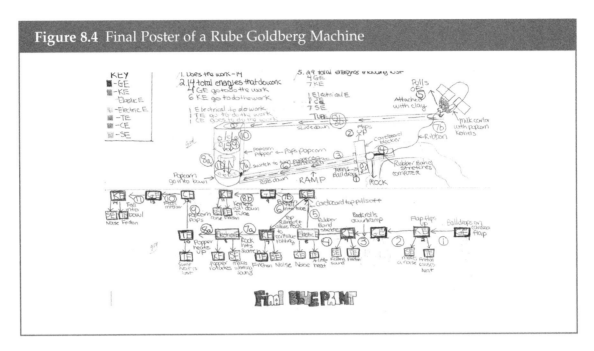

Figure 8.4 Final Poster of a Rube Goldberg Machine

Image courtesy of the Weizmann Institute of Science.

The Design Process in IQWST

Children tend to be natural designers. Have you ever seen some children trying to figure out how to pull a wagon behind a bicycle? When moving to a new house, have you ever tried to decide how to best organize the kitchen so that things you regularly use will be available easily but the kitchen won't be too cluttered? In both cases, the children and you were engaged in design. Design is essential to the engineering process.

Since we all use tools and materials purposefully in trying to adapt the environment to suit our needs, the capacity for design appears to be a fundamental human aptitude. However, we should distinguish between design as an everyday activity and Design (capital D), or engineering, as an activity in which professional designers/engineers engage. The distinction between the two lies in their differing degrees of formalization: Whereas everyday design is often spontaneous and intuitive, with the designer unaware that she is engaged in a problem-solving process that could perhaps be improved upon, Design or engineering is a formal process that may include many explicit stages and criteria for determining whether the outcomes of the design process are acceptable. Everyday designers often err in their decisions and considerations; formal engineering practices attempt to minimize the chances that engineers will do so as well.

In *A Framework for K–12 Science Education* (NRC, 2012), the National Research Council recognized engineering as a key component of science education. The Framework identified several key engineering practices and two core disciplinary ideas for engineering. The core engineering ideas include the following:

- Core Idea Engineering, Technology, and Science 1 (ETS1): Engineering Design

  o ETS1.A: Defining and Delimiting an Engineering Problem
  o ETS1.B: Developing Possible Solutions
  o ETS1.C: Optimizing the Design Solution

- Core Idea ETS2: Links Among Engineering, Technology, Science, and Society

  ○ ETS2.A: Interdependence of Science, Engineering, and Technology
  ○ ETS2.B: Influence of Engineering, Technology, and Science on Society and the Natural World

ETS1 signals design as a core disciplinary idea in engineering that all students need to understand and be able to use. As such, the Framework sees the design process as an engineer's basic approach to problem solving. Many of the practices involved in this process are identified in Figure 8.5 in the Design-Based Science (DBS) learning cycle. Central to these are identifying the problem, posing possible solutions, specifying constraints and limitations, describing design criteria, and constructing artifacts.

This focus in the Framework on Engineering as a core disciplinary idea affirms the value of teaching engineering ideas in K–12 science courses.

Whether design is done according to formal standards or not, it remains a form of ill-defined problem solving because there is no prescribed path leading from the requirement specifications to the final design product (see Figure 8.6). Often, there are no well-defined criteria of how to evaluate a design solution, so there is no clear definition of when an acceptable solution has been reached. Seldom can one determine if an engineering product is "correct" or "the only" or even "the best" response to the requirements. It must, however, be an acceptable answer to the requirements. Any engineering product is the result of a wide range of value judgments.

Simon (1999) felt that there was no fundamental difference between Design/engineering and many other real-world activities, which are by and large also ill-defined:

Design . . . is concerned with how things ought to be, with devising artifacts to attain goals. . . . Everyone designs who devises courses of action aimed at changing existing situations into preferred ones. The intellectual activity that produces

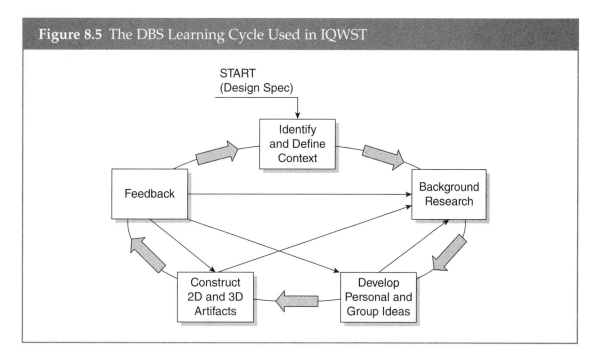

Figure 8.5 The DBS Learning Cycle Used in IQWST

Image courtesy of the Weizmann Institute of Science.

material artifacts is no different fundamentally from the one that prescribes remedies for a sick patient or the one that devises a new sales plan for a company or a social welfare policy for a state. (pp. 111–114)

Design/engineering is similar to science, which is also an ill-defined problem-solving activity:

There simply is no fixed set of steps that scientists always follow, no one path that leads them unerringly to scientific knowledge. . . . Some important themes pervade science, mathematics, and technology . . . they are ideas that transcend disciplinary boundaries and prove fruitful in explanation, in theory, in observation, and in design. (AAAS, 1990, p. 4)

There are actually more similarities than differences between scientific practices and engineering practices. Both are primarily means of supporting different forms of problem solving. In science, the problem is to develop a model or theory that supports the explanation and prediction of phenomena. In engineering, the problem is to design an artifact that meets predefined specifications. While both science and engineering do not follow linear processes, they can be shown to include the following steps, each of which may occur several times, in different order, and in conjunction with different steps. Table 8.2 compares the steps typically found in science and engineering problem solving (Fortus, Dershimer, Krajcik, Marx, & Mamlok-Naaman, 2004).

The similarities between engineering and science suggest that engineering could become a natural part of science classes, with students designing to apply science ideas and learning science to design solutions to engineering problems. Combining engineering and science has received much attention in the United Kingdom and in several other countries. In his description of the science and engineering practices in the *Framework for*

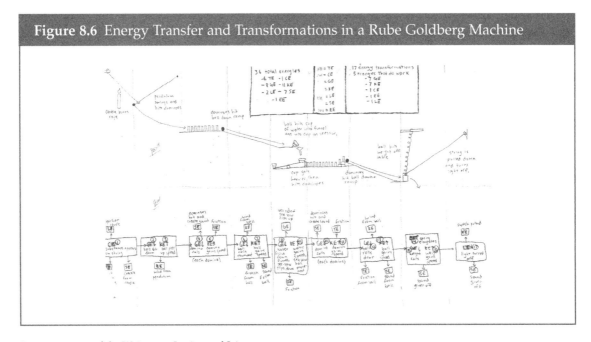

Figure 8.6 Energy Transfer and Transformations in a Rube Goldberg Machine

Image courtesy of the Weizmann Institute of Science.

Table 8.2 Steps in Scientific and Engineering Problem Solving

Scientific Problem Solving	Engineering Problem Solving
Pose questions.	Identify and define desired physical change and constraints.
Review existing knowledge base.	Gather and analyze existing technologies.
Develop theory and model.	Determine performance criteria.
Design investigations.	Generate alternative solutions and build prototypes.
Gather, analyze, and interpret data.	Test prototypes.
Consider alternative explanations.	Evaluate different solutions.
Communicate results in journals.	Apply for patent.

K–12 Science Education, Bybee (2011) compares them. For instance, regarding modeling, Bybee states that science involves the construction and use of models to explain natural phenomena, whereas engineering makes use of models to test and analyze an existing system under particular conditions or to test solutions to a problem.

Curriculum designers and teachers need to consider how to incorporate engineering practices into science curriculum materials. In general, there are two distinct ways to do so: Either the practices can be used at the end of a unit, where students apply the knowledge they have constructed during the unit to design an artifact, or a unit presents at its start a design goal that motivates student learning and that drives all learning activities (Fortus et al., 2004). Design-Based Science (DBS), used in the IQWST curriculum, is an exemplar of the second approach, structuring all learning activities around an instructional cycle based on the typical steps in most engineering problem-solving processes.

A Framework for K–12 Science Education stresses the use of models by engineers to test their design solutions; DBS refers to these models as student-generated artifacts. The artifacts in DBS are like the models stressed in the Framework. In both cases, learners or engineers build things that specify relationships among the parts of a system in order to test and revise their designs.

Scientific and Engineering Practices in IQWST

In addition to identifying the big ideas in science, we identified five central scientific and engineering practices: explanations/argumentation; modeling and design of artifacts; data gathering, organization, and analysis; investigation design and artifact testing; and literacy. Scientific and engineering practices (Fortus, Dershimer, Krajcik, Marx, & Mamlok-Naaman, 2005; Lehrer & Schauble, 2006) represent the disciplinary norms of scientists and engineers as they construct, test, communicate, and reason with scientific knowledge. As adapted to the classroom, scientific and engineering practices characterize how students use scientific understandings to make sense of, explain, and make material changes to the world. These practices also overlap with those from *A Framework for K–12 Science Education* (NRC, 2012) and the *Next Generation Science Standards* (NGSS Lead States, 2013).

Practices are important in IQWST for two complementary but distinct reasons. First, participating in scientific and engineering practices is a means to engage learners in developing and using conceptual understanding. Second, scientific and engineering practices define an important part of what it means to understand the disciplines of science and engineering themselves. Without engaging students in scientific and engineering practices while learning content, learners cannot develop an understanding of how to use the content; without embedding the scientific and engineering practices in meaningful content, learners cannot develop understanding of the practices. Understanding content depends on using the practices, and understanding the practices depends upon understanding their relation to content. When scientific and engineering practices and content are integrated together, learners develop integrated understanding (Fortus & Krajcik, 2012) in which ideas are connected to each other. The advantage to such understanding is that learners can now use their understanding to solve problems, explain phenomena, and learn more as they have a foundation on which to build and connect new ideas (Krajcik & Shin, 2013).

These five central practices are interwoven throughout the entire curriculum. Not all of the practices receive identical emphasis in different units. For example, the sixth-grade chemistry unit emphasizes modeling and data gathering, organization, and analysis. The seventh-grade physics unit emphasizes designing and testing material artifacts (engineering). Literacy is emphasized in every unit through the specifically crafted reading materials, worksheets, and homework. The integration of each practice in a given unit builds off the experience students have gained in engaging in this practice in earlier units. For example, the modeling practices integrated into the sixth-grade chemistry unit build off the modeling experiences that students will have had in the sixth-grade physics unit, which comes before it. Thus, the experience and proficiency at a scientific or engineering practice that can be expected of students at the end of the three-year sequence is much better than could have been obtained had each practice been learned in a collection of independent units, where each unit would have had to begin from scratch, assuming little to no prior middle school experience in any of the practices.

This careful and attentive sequencing of the various practices with the different units is another example of curricular coherence (Fortus & Krajcik, 2012). Studies have shown that by the end of middle school, if the recommended coherent sequence was followed, student have constructed a substantial understanding of the various practices, such as modeling and the ability to engage in modeling in a variety of situations (Schwarz et al., 2009).

Driving Questions

One of the key characteristics of project-based units is that they are built around a driving question. A good driving question should fulfill the following six criteria: (a) *Feasibility:* It must be feasible for students to design, perform investigations, and test artifacts to answer the question; (b) *Worth:* The driving question should deal with science and engineering content and practices that are aligned with the unit's learning goals; (c) *Contextualization:* The driving question should be anchored in the lives of learners; (d) *Interest:* The driving question should be interesting and exciting to learners; (e) *Ethics:* Investigating the driving question should not harm living organisms or the environment; and (f) *Sustainability:* The driving question should be able to sustain students' interest for a prolonged time.

We brainstormed a list of possible driving questions and evaluated each one using these six criteria. We then contacted scientists, science educators, teachers, and students; presented them with what we thought were the three best driving questions; and asked them to consider which driving question they thought would be best, without specifying any of the criteria listed above. In every case, all the reviewers rated the three possible driving questions in the same order as we had. For example, the driving question that was chosen for the sixth-grade physics unit on light was, "Can I believe my eyes?" The driving question that was chosen for the seventh-grade unit on energy was, "Why do some things stop and others keep going?"

Educative Features

Each lesson also includes many educative features (Davis & Krajcik, 2005). These usually come in the form of text boxes integrated into the flow of the lesson that provide the teacher with additional, just-in-time support. These boxes may suggest additional teaching strategies; suggest additional background content knowledge that is not meant to be shared with students, but rather to deepen a teacher's understanding of the science content or a specific activity; suggest common student conceptions that students might have about specific content or about inquiry processes; and be a check point to alert teachers to the concepts that students should understand by certain points in the lesson.

An example common student conception box is the following:

Common Student Conceptions

Students often forget that there is a lot of trial and error in engineering. It will be important for you to stress to your students in these design lessons that they should expect a lot of trial and error before getting things right.

An example teaching strategy box is the following:

Teaching Strategy

Students should know by now that thermal energy will be present in each group's machine simply because of energy dissipation. It might be a good idea to remind students about energy dissipation and thermal energy's properties so that they do not have to spend so much time worrying about how to incorporate this energy in their designs.

An example student checkpoint box is the following:

> ### Student Checkpoint
>
> While your students are working on revising their machines, you should make an effort to weave in various review points drawn from the entire unit. For example, remind students that thermal energy is present in the machines and that energy dissipation may be largely responsible for a lot of the revisions that need to be made. If students get stuck on how to solve a problem, help them think about it in terms of energy conversions and energy transfer.

An example background content knowledge box is the following:

> ### Teacher Background Knowledge
>
> Students might notice that the diameter of the spot on the wall gets bigger or smaller. This relationship between size of the spot and distance from the wall is because light actually travels outward from a source as a wave front. You can think of a wave front as the surface of a balloon. As you blow into the balloon its diameter expands, similar to the size of the circle of light on the wall. Light has the properties of both a wave and a particle. It is not important for sixth-grade students to explore the wave-particle dual properties of light. For the purpose of this unit, the path of light is treated as a straight line. This is called the ray model of light.

Engineering Task That Drives a Unit

The energy unit in IQWST is an example of an entire unit that is driven by a design problem. IQWST also engages students in design problems at the end of units to help solidify their understandings by having them apply the core science ideas that they have constructed. The seventh-grade chemistry unit is driven by the driving question, "How can I make new stuff from old stuff?" During this 8- to 10-week project-based science unit, students develop an understanding of the core disciplinary idea that in a chemical reaction, substances combine with each other and make new substances that have different properties from the original materials. Moreover, students learn a mechanism that can explain the various features of chemical reactions—the atoms in the starting materials combine in new ways to form new substances. The unit builds on core science ideas developed in the sixth grade, including the particle nature of matter and that different substances have different properties. The Stuff unit also engages students in a variety of scientific and engineering practices. Throughout the unit, students ask questions, develop and use models to explain phenomena, plan and carry out investigations, and analyze and interpret data to construct explanations and engage in argumentation from evidence. Students end the unit by engaging in a design problem where they need to redefine the problem ("How can I make new stuff from old stuff?"), specify criteria, and plan and carry out their solution.

To contextualize learning, students make soap from fat and sodium hydroxide. Students conduct an investigation in which they first make soap and then compare the properties of the materials they make with the starting materials and commercial soap. Students are then challenged at the end of the unit with the design challenge of improving their soap. To meet this challenge, students brainstorm criteria for determining what constitutes an improvement to their original product. They then need to specify criteria for testing their product. While the making and testing of soap engages students in blending core ideas of science with science practices, this last design challenge of improving the soap clearly engages learners in a chemical engineering problem that allows them to apply their understanding of both science and engineering while using engineering practices.

Figure 8.7 Troubleshooting a Rube Goldberg Machine

Image courtesy of the Weizmann Institute of Science.

These two illustrative examples, the seventh-grade energy example in which students design, build, and test a Rube Goldberg machine (see Figure 8.7), and the seventh-grade chemical reaction example in which students improve on a soap formula, show how the IQWST materials engage students in using the core disciplinary ideas of engineering and science blended with the use of science and engineering practices. We picked these two examples because they illustrate two ways in which engineering ideas and practices can be incorporated into curriculum material—either as the driver of a unit or at the end of a unit where students apply their understandings. In both conditions, however, it is the combination of blending core ideas in science and engineering with science and engineering practices that supports students in developing integrated understanding that will allow them to solve problems, explain phenomena, and learn more in their daily lives.

Conclusion

Engineering ideas and practices are new to science education in the United States. The recognition of core engineering ideas and practices in *A Framework for K–12 Science Education* and the inclusion of engineering standards in the Next Generation Science Standards stresses the importance of engineering in K–12 science education. The design process that is essential to professional engineers provides learners with a unique way of solving problems and testing potential solutions. Perhaps most essentially, engaging in engineering practices and the design process will help all learners understand that solving problems comes with constraints and limitations, and the importance of defining criteria.

Understanding constraints and limitations is critical to helping build a more sustainable global society. All problems have trade-offs, and humans all over the globe need to realize that making our world a sustainable place so that our children will also enjoy this planet only comes by making trade-offs. Although incorporating engineering practices into the science curriculum and implementing them in science classrooms will pose challenges for curriculum developers and teachers, engaging learners in engineering practices has many worthwhile benefits. In particular, these engineering ideas and practices will help learners become better problem solvers and learners who are aware that any situation has trade-offs and constraints. The IQWST curriculum, with its focus on engaging students in science and engineering core ideas and practices over the course of middle grades, has the potential to support students in developing these understandings and capabilities.

References

American Association for the Advancement of Science (AAAS). (1989). *Science for all Americans.* Project 2061, American Association for the Advancement of Science (AAAS). New York: Oxford University Press.

Bybee, R. (2011). Scientific and engineering practices in K–12 classrooms: Understanding a framework for K–12 science education. *Science and Children, 49*(4), 10–15.

Davis, E. A., & Krajcik, J. S. (2005). Designing educative curriculum materials to promote teacher learning. *Educational Researcher, 34*(3), 3–14.

Fortus, D., Dershimer, R. C., Krajcik, J. S., Marx, R. W., & Mamlok-Naaman, R. (2004). Design-Based Science (DBS) and student learning. *Journal of Research in Science Teaching, 41*(10), 1081–1110.

Fortus, D., Dershimer, R. C., Krajcik, J. S., Marx, R. W., & Mamlok-Naaman, R. (2005). Design-Based Science and real-world problem-solving. *International Journal of Science Education, 27*(7), 855–879.

Fortus, D., & Krajcik, J. S. (2012). Curriculum coherence and learning progressions. In B. J. Fraser, C. McRobbie, & K. G. Tobin (Eds.), *International handbook of science education* (2nd ed., pp. 783–798). Dordrecht, The Netherlands: Springer Verlag.

Krajcik, J. S., Reiser, B. J., Sutherland, L. M., & Fortus, D. (2012). *IQWST: Investigating and questioning our world through science and technology.* Greenwich, CT: Sangari Global Education/Active Science.

Krajcik, J. S., & Shin, N. (2013). Project-based learning. In R. K. Sawyer (Ed.), *The Cambridge handbook of the learning sciences* (2nd ed.). New York: Cambridge University Press.

Lehrer, R., & Schauble, L. (2006). Scientific thinking and science literacy: Supporting development in learning in contexts. In W. Damon, R. M. Lerner, K. A. Renninger, & I. E. Sigel (Eds.), *Handbook of child psychology* (6th ed., Vol. 4). Hoboken, NJ: Wiley.

National Research Council (NRC). (1996). *National science education standards.* National Committee on Science Education Standards and Assessment. Board on Science Education, Division of Behavioral and Social Sciences and Education, National Research Council (NRC). Washington, DC: National Academies Press.

National Research Council (NRC). (2012). *A framework for K–12 science education: Practices, crosscutting concepts, and core ideas.* Committee on a Conceptual Framework for New K–12 Science Education Standards. Board on Science Education, Division of Behavioral and Social Sciences and Education, National Research Council (NRC). Washington, DC: National Academies Press.

NGSS Lead States. (2013). *Next generation science standards: For states, by states. Volume 1: The standards.* Washington, DC: National Academies Press.

Schwarz, C. V., Reiser, B. J., Fortus, D., Davis, E. A., Kenyon, L., & Shwartz, Y. (2009). Developing a learning progression of scientific modeling: Making scientific modeling accessible and meaningful for learners. *Journal of Research in Science Teaching, 46*(6), 632–655.

Shwartz, Y., Weizman, A., Fortus, D., Krajcik, J. S., & Reiser, B. J. (2008). The IQWST experience: Using coherence as a design principle for a middle school science curriculum. *Elementary School Journal, 109*(2), 199–219.

Simon, H. A. (1999). *The sciences of the artificial* (3rd ed.). Cambridge: MIT Press.

Weizman, A., Shwartz, Y., & Fortus, D. (2008). The driving question board: A visual organizer in project-based learning. *Science Teacher, 75*(8), 33–37.

9

Project-Based Inquiry Science

Janet L. Kolodner
Georgia Institute of Technology
Barbara Zahm and Ruta Demery
It's About Time, Inc.

Figure 9.1 Students use a model to investigate topographic maps

Project-Based Inquiry Science (PBIS) is a research-informed, three-year, middle school science curriculum composed of 13 units. When used with fidelity, it provides opportunities for middle school students to apply big ideas in science, connect science to technology and engineering and the world around them, and become expert at many discipline-specific skills. PBIS can also help students appreciate the interconnectedness of the sciences and begin to develop the 21st-century skills that they will need to become productive members of the workforce and pursue higher education coursework. Like scientists and engineers, PBIS students work in collaborative groups to ask questions and define problems; and as they pursue answers and design solutions, they develop and use models, plan and conduct investigations, collect and analyze data, construct explanations, and discuss and present their findings.

Overview

How PBIS Builds STEM and 21st-Century Skills

In PBIS, students learn science content and science and engineering practices in the context of addressing engineering design and problem-solving challenges and answering big scientific questions. The 13 units can be mixed and matched in a variety of ways to cover three years of middle school science. Individual units have also been used successfully in after-school programs and summer camps.

Like real scientists who try to make sense of the natural world and real engineers who design devices and processes and solve problems, PBIS students work to understand situations and identify their criteria and constraints, refine problems they are asked to solve, ask questions and pursue answers, develop and use models, plan and conduct investigations, collect and analyze data, create explanations, and discuss and present their findings. In PBIS, learning these fundamental science and engineering practices is intricately merged with learning disciplinary core ideas and crosscutting concepts as outlined in *A Framework for K–12 Science Education* (NRC, 2012) and the subsequent *Next Generation Science Standards* (NGSS Lead States, 2013). While PBIS was developed before publication of the *Framework for K–12 Science Education* and NGSS, it was designed by some of the same researchers who influenced their development.

The individual curriculum units in PBIS present three types of projects: Some ask students to address an engineering design challenge, some ask them to solve an engineering problem, and some ask them to answer a driving science question. In engineering design units, students iteratively design, build, and test a device. In engineering problem-solving units, students are presented with a realistic community scenario and a problem they need to address. Driving-question units begin by presenting students with a complex science question with real-world implications. Students are then challenged to break down the question into smaller questions and develop answers to the questions they generate.

Three of the PBIS units are "Launcher Units." Launcher Units gradually introduce and develop science and engineering practices, as outlined in the *Framework for K–12 Science Education*, to provide a base upon which students can build mastery in these practices and use them efficiently and effectively during the rest of the school year. In each Launcher Unit, practices are introduced in the context of addressing a series of small engineering and science challenges.

The challenges that drive each unit, whether design, problem solving, or driving question, are carefully selected to lead students into investigation of specific disciplinary core ideas, use of appropriate engineering and science practices, and use of core 21st-century skills. To decide how to prioritize the use and learning of 21st-century skills within the context of STEM content and skills targeted for middle school, the developers of PBIS identified some of what citizens need to know and be able to do to engage productively in public discourse. For example, they considered what might be required for students to engage in public discourse on global climate change or public health, be able to choose government representatives or vote on referenda, know how to interact productively with a doctor to make medical decisions, understand ecological systems, or reason scientifically about causes and effects of human and technological activity.

In this chapter, we describe three of the 13 PBIS units. The intention is two-fold: to introduce several of the PBIS units and to help readers get a feel for what students experience as they are learning in the context of the PBIS approach. To learn more about Project-Based Inquiry Science, you can visit the "Welcome Page" of the PBIS CyberPD website (www.pbiscyberpd.org). In the Case Study video, you will be able to hear what teachers and administrators have to say about PBIS, and see how it is used in the classroom.

Vehicles in Motion (An Engineering Design Challenge Unit)

The Big Challenge in this unit is to design a vehicle and its propulsion system that can go straight, far, and fast, and carry a load. Students act like design engineers, and in the process, they learn about forces and motion.

Students begin this unit by identifying the criteria and constraints of the challenge. During a whole-class discussion, students offer ideas about how to address the challenge and some of what they know. To keep track of these ideas, and to monitor progress toward meeting the challenge, the class uses a Project Board with five columns, as shown in Figure 9.2. Students' ideas go in the "What do we think we know?" column of the Project Board; their questions go into the "What do we need to investigate?" column. (A similar Project Board is used in every PBIS unit.)

Each small group then receives a set of toy cars (each with different capabilities and propulsion mechanisms), a ramp, and different surfaces. They engage in an exploratory activity called "messing about." The goal of this small-group, guided-play activity is to lead students to become curious about why the cars behave differently and to uncover their prior knowledge as they try to explain those differences. Then they come together again as a whole class and discuss their experiences. The teacher facilitates the discussion, this time helping the class generate, for the Project Board, some well-formed questions about what makes things move, what allows them to keep moving, what slows them down, how different propulsion systems work, what a propulsion is, and so forth.

Many of the questions on the Project Board will be about making vehicles go straight, keeping them going, and measuring their speed, and it is this set of questions that is addressed in Learning Set 1. The students are given materials to build a coaster car and instructions for building a moderately performing one, and they iteratively work toward making it go straight, far, and fast. They design a procedure for measuring the speed of a vehicle, and iteratively move back and forth between their design goals and their need to learn new things. Then they return to the Project Board and record what they have learned, their evidence, their ideas about how to apply what they've learned to the Big Challenge, and additional questions they still need to answer for success.

Figure 9.2 Project Board for Vehicles in Motion

Design and build a vehicle that will go straight, far, and fast, and carry a load.				
What do we think we know?	**What do we need to investigate?**	**What are we learning?**	**What is our evidence?**	**What does it mean for the challenge or question?**

A question students may ask at this point is, "How do you get a car going?" Until now, they have been pushing their vehicles or letting them go on ramps. Learning Set 2 is devoted to propulsion and getting things going, and students are challenged in this learning set to optimize a propeller propulsion system. The question for the Learning Set is, "What factors affect the performance of a propeller-driven car?" This Learning Set is presented in additional detail to illustrate the fullness of students' experiences with PBIS and the way science and engineering practices, core ideas, and crosscutting concepts are integrated in the PBIS approach.

As at the beginning of the unit, students begin this Learning Set by "messing about." They are given propellers, and they explore in small groups to identify what might affect their car's behavior. As they become curious, they generate smaller questions that need to be answered: How does the number of blades on a propeller affect performance? The size of the blades? The number of times the rubber band is wound? After 20 minutes, they report to the class what they've experienced in their explorations and record their ideas and the questions they've generated in the first two columns of the Project Board. Then they work as a class to identify investigations they might do to learn more about those effects. Each group chooses (or is assigned) a question to answer.

At this point, the transition between engineering design and science investigation is completely natural and seamless. Working as scientific investigators, each group now designs and runs an experiment to answer their question and analyze their data (see Figure 9.3). When experimentation is complete, students prepare to present and share their results with the class. The whole class gets together again for these presentations. Because students need each other's investigative results to be successful propeller car designers, they listen intently and query each other about the gathering and interpretation of data (much as in a professional poster session). Sometimes, groups design their experiments badly, and no lessons can be drawn from them. Sometimes, groups design a nice experiment but run the procedures badly, and the data that are collected lack consistency. In either of these instances, students give each other advice about how to design or run the investigation better, and groups might repeat their investigations.

Figure 9.3 Students iteratively design and test their propeller-driven cars

Image courtesy of It's About Time.

For the purposes of this unit, it is important now for the class to reflect on and discuss what they are learning about propulsion and record what they have learned in the "What are we learning?" column, along with their evidence in the "What is our evidence?" column of the Project Board.

It is also important for students to consider why things happened as they did. Thus, the teacher asks students to explain their results. Students will provide pieces of explanations, but, in general, they realize that they do not yet know enough to provide complete explanations. This calls for a return to inquiry. This time, rather than running experiments, they read about the science that explains their cars' performance, getting together as a class again to discuss the science content they read and add these science foundations to the Project Board. The class discussion may be quite sophisticated; the teacher's job during that discussion is to help students articulate rigorous explanations tying the science they read to the phenomena they observed. The goal is for every student in the class to be able to attach a scientific explanation to the patterns observed in the experiments and recorded on the Project Board.

With investigation and explanation complete, activity returns to designing, and each group uses the results of the class's investigations to plan its propeller engine design. Each group prepares a chart that includes its design ideas and the science and experimental evidence that justifies each of those design choices. When the group is satisfied with its design, the students prepare a poster, this time presenting their design ideas along with the evidence that justifies each decision and their predictions about how their design will perform. The class discusses the ideas everyone has presented. Students return to their small groups, this time to refine their designs and then to build and test them.

In traditional classrooms, after solutions have been generated and discussed, the class moves on to its next topic or project. However, in Project-Based Inquiry Science, learners are given the opportunity to try again, often several times. The students discuss what they still need to learn and what on the Project Board might need to be refined. They might engage in some additional inquiry together to answer some remaining questions. Then small groups get back together and, using the advice of their peers, refine their propeller engines and again test their performance. This iterative refinement process continues, with refining and testing interspersed, as needed, with whole-class presentations and discussions until all groups have successfully built a working propeller engine. Through this set of processes, the class iterates toward better solutions and better science understanding.

At the end of the Learning Set, students once again return to the Project Board. In addition to recording what they have learned and their evidence, students record recommendations they have generated that address the Big Challenge. Students may also identify new questions they need to answer to fully address the challenge, and those go into the "What do we need to learn?" column.

The cycles continue in Learning Set 3 of Vehicles in Motion as students address the challenge of how a load will affect the performance of their car and investigate the relationship among force, mass, and acceleration. After Learning Set 3, they use everything they have learned (recorded on the Project Board) to refine their vehicles and their propulsion systems to meet the challenge.

The activities in this unit provide opportunities for not only learning about the disciplinary core ideas of motion and stability, but also learning science and engineering practices; 21st-century skills; and the crosscutting concepts of cause and effect, systems and system models, and stability and change. While mastery of these skills and knowledge cannot happen within the context of one unit, the same opportunities are afforded across all PBIS units. The movements from design and problem solving into inquiry and back are similar across PBIS units, as are the opportunities for sharing and reflecting as a class, so that the students can continually refine their understanding and capabilities.

Living Together (An Engineering Problem-Solving Unit)

In this unit, students are challenged to give advice to the council of a small town situated on a river as to whether or not they should permit a manufacturing company to locate in the town.

In addition to the challenge, at the beginning of the unit, students are introduced to a Big Question: How does water quality affect the ecology of a community? To help them clarify the question and begin to imagine what they need to learn to give advice to the town council, they look at five jars containing water samples and match them to photographs of different locations along a river. They consider what good water quality means.

Living Together brings a real-world problem into the classroom. "FabCo wants to move in. Sounds great! So, what's the problem?" This is an open-ended problem and affords a great deal of student creativity in finding a solution. As in all PBIS units, students begin their problem-solving cycle by gathering around the Project Board to record what they think they know and what they need to investigate. This activity helps them define and delimit the problem and start looking for alternative solutions.

Next, the students begin the first Learning Set, which focuses on "How do flowing water and land interact in a community?" To answer the question, students model a watershed and observe the effects of different types of land use—residential, commercial, and agricultural—on the river and its nearby land. They use the Rouge River in Michigan as a case study for how land use can affect a river. In the process, they learn about the effects of the river on land, land use on a river, and different sources of pollution. Each small group in the class is assigned a different land use in which to become "experts." Then, at the end of the Learning Set, each group makes recommendations about possible solutions to the problem. Groups listen to each other's recommendations, discuss how evidence and science knowledge support their claim, and help one another revise their claims and recommendations as needed. They return to the Project Board to record what they have learned and what else they need to investigate. They understand that they will need to consider trade-offs in negotiating a solution and that different people in the city may have different perspectives on what a good solution is.

In Learning Set 2, students focus on "How do you determine the quality of water in a community?" They investigate water-quality indicators—plant growth, pH, dissolved oxygen, temperature, turbidity, and fecal coliform bacteria. They learn about phosphates and nitrates, acids, bases, and the pH scale, and the range of pH that different organisms can tolerate. In Learning Set 3, students focus on "How do changes in water quality affect the living things in an ecosystem?" They design and conduct investigations on the effect of fertilizer on plant growth, measure the pH of different water samples, and design and run computer-generated population models of what happens when an ecosystem changes (see Figure 9.4). They learn about ecosystems, classifying organisms, photosynthesis and cellular respiration, and food chains and webs.

As in Vehicles in Motion, students move fluidly from a design and problem-solving activity into inquiry and back again, engaging in conducting investigations, providing possible solutions, and presenting and sharing their ideas. As appropriate, students update the Project Board during the course of each Learning Set, and then at the end of the Learning Set, students add to and refine their recommendations and identify what else they still need to learn to achieve the challenge.

At the end of the unit, students pull together what they have learned to make recommendations to the town council. As is true of most real-world problems, the many different perspectives from which to view the problem give rise to many different potential solutions. Because different people in the city find different trade-offs more palatable, the students end this unit with a city council meeting. They reorganize into new groups, each including an "expert" in one of the land uses and each group taking on the identity of one of the stakeholders—a fisher and organizer of the annual trout festival, an executive of the manufacturing company, a farmer, and an owner of a resort down the river from the town. Each group formulates a recommendation based on its stakeholder's point of view and presents it in a Solution Showcase. This completes the unit.

As in all PBIS units, science and engineering practices, disciplinary core ideas, and crosscutting concepts are interwoven throughout Living Together. For example, students discover the importance of energy and matter in a natural system as they track the transfer of energy as it flows through a food chain. The concept of stability and change is addressed when students observe how changes in one part of a system, the temperature

Figure 9.4 Students design and build a model to investigate the effect of land use on a river

Image courtesy of It's About Time.

and amount of dissolved oxygen in a river, can cause significant changes in another part, the population of trout.

Ever-Changing Earth (A Driving Science Question Unit)

In this unit, the context for inquiry is provided by a driving science question: "What processes within Earth cause geologic activity?" Students build their knowledge about Earth and the processes that shape it through modeling, data collection, analysis, and information sharing. The practices and concepts they learn are key to understanding and answering this Big Question.

Students work in pairs to familiarize themselves with a specific location and the Earth structures that represent the constructive forces of the different Earth processes in that location. They look at earthquake and volcano data in real time using the Internet and firsthand descriptions of the events. They observe and describe multiple years of data, and they use these data to explain the processes making the plates move and changing Earth's crust. They find patterns in the earthquake and volcano data and identify the plates and the ways they are moving. They think about how these movements lead to different kinds of changes to the crust, how earthquakes happen in different places, how volcanoes are shaped in different ways, and how the topography of the land is different. By connecting all of the information gathered through readings, investigations, and information sharing, students are able to ultimately create an explanation for the changes happening in the region of their Earth structures.

As they come to understand their assigned Earth structures and those in regions close to theirs, each pair contributes to a Big World Map that eventually includes an overlay outlining Earth's plates. Students create a file of work containing their prediction maps, along with each explanation they create throughout the process. The final product is a presentation of their explanation, which includes a display of all their maps, models, and other select works.

In this unit, students engage in many science practices. To answer the Big Question, students must locate the plate boundaries on Earth and identify the direction of their movement. Students examine earthquake data and use that to speculate about the location of the boundary in their region. Next, they look at the location and types of volcanoes. With each piece of additional information, students refine and present their ideas about where the boundaries are located. They piece their solution to the problem with the solutions of others to arrive at a complete solution. In doing so, they are engaging in a systematic process to iteratively refine a solution. Although this unit is developed within the context of a science question, the practices in which they engage as student scientists are very similar to those used by engineers.

The Ever-Changing Earth unit also helps students understand how technology, engineering, and science are connected. They use Earth-imaging programs to observe their region of study, they discover that GPS units can be used to measure the movement of seismic plates, and they read about how seismographs are used to measure the magnitude of an earthquake (see Figure 9.5).

This unit is replete with crosscutting concepts. Students use patterns to identify plate boundaries; investigate the cause and effect of plate movement; and appreciate the importance of scale, proportion, and quantity as they observe earthquakes and volcanoes over time and space. The concepts of stability and change are inherent in the plate movements, and Earth's interior provides an opportunity to investigate energy and matter.

Figure 9.5 Students use the technology of an Earth-imaging program to study geologic activity

Image courtesy of It's About Time.

Structure of PBIS Units

Every unit, whatever its Big Challenge or Question, has a similar engineering design structure and requires similar engineering, science, and 21st-century practices. Figure 9.6 provides a high-level overview of PBIS's structures. On the left is a design and problem-solving cycle, and on the right is an inquiry cycle. The cycles are joined by two sets of arrows, one showing that inquiry is carried out in the context of design or problem-solving needs, the other pointing out that what is learned through inquiry is then used in furthering a solution to the Big Challenge or answering the Big Question.

Notice that both are cycles: Addressing design challenges is iterative, and so is answering questions and inquiry. In each cycle are the steps one would normally expect. For example, in the science cycle, students clarify a question, make hypotheses, and develop and conduct an investigation. In the design cycle, students first need to understand the challenge, plan a design, then build and test the solution. Common to science and design are times for analyzing data and sharing findings.

Students work in small groups during the design, problem-solving, and inquiry steps and then come together as a class to make sense of their experiences, learn from each other, and plan next steps. The times for presentations and whole-class discussions are important for a variety of reasons. They come at times that are natural for reflection and when students need help from others. They give students a chance to ask questions and practice and debug argumentation, explanation, clear communication, questioning, and other important skills, and they give the teacher a chance for formative assessment. Throughout these activities, students are making sense of problems and persevering in solving them, reasoning abstractly and quantitatively, constructing viable arguments, and critiquing the reasoning of others.

With the exception of the shorter Launcher Units, each PBIS unit is 6 to 10 weeks long. Typically, students complete one launcher unit and three or four additional units during

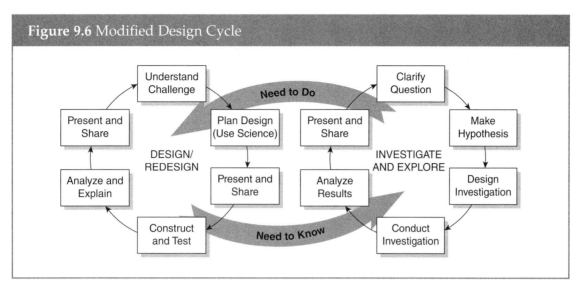

Figure 9.6 Modified Design Cycle

Adapted from Kolodner, Gray, and Fasse (2003).

a school year. The combination of units addresses the disciplinary core ideas for a single school year and guides students through the whole variety of science and engineering practices each year.

Each unit begins with an activity that helps students appreciate the importance of the challenge or question, gets them excited about it, and makes them curious. This is followed by an activity that elicits what students think they know about the challenge and the smaller questions they have to answer for success. Units are made up of Learning Sets that include activities and readings to answer questions students have generated. In each Learning Set, students focus on understanding the subchallenge or subproblem or the smaller question and then moving iteratively through the cycles. At the end of each Learning Set, students reflect on what they have learned, how they might apply what they've learned to addressing the Big Challenge or answering the Big Question, which questions they've answered, which they still need to answer, and what additional questions they have. Then they begin a new Learning Set.

Addressing the Three Dimensions of the NGSS

After completing the PBIS units, students should be able to meet almost all of the Performance Expectations outlined in the Next Generation Science Standards (NGSS). A performance expectation is a sentence that combines three dimensions: science and engineering practices, core disciplinary ideas, and crosscutting concepts.

Science and Engineering Practices. The NGSS identify eight practices that describe the skills that students are expected to develop as they engage in science and engineering activities. In PBIS, these practices are not just found in isolated inquiry activities, but permeate the entire PBIS curriculum. Table 9.1 shows examples of how students are engaged in science and engineering practices in PBIS.

Core Disciplinary Ideas. Each of the PBIS units also addresses specific core disciplinary ideas in the NGSS. For example, in Learning Set 3 of Vehicles in Motion, the students are presented with the engineering challenge of designing a propeller car that will carry a load. To meet this challenge, students plan, design, and conduct an experiment to answer the question, "What effect does adding mass to your propeller car have on its acceleration?" This activity helps students meet a performance expectation in physical science and in engineering design:

MS–PS2–2. Plan an investigation to provide evidence that the change in an object's motion depends on the sum of the forces on the object and the mass of the object.

MS–ETS1–4. Develop a model to generate data for iterative testing and modification of a proposed object, tool, or process such that an optimal design can be achieved.

Table 9.1 Science and Engineering Practices in Project-Based Inquiry Science

Scientific and Engineering Practices	Examples From Project-Based Inquiry Science
Asking questions and defining problems	PBIS is built on the principle that students need to identify and ask their own questions and define problems. This is seen throughout PBIS. For example, activities at the beginning of each PBIS unit help students delimit the problems they are expected to solve. Students identify the criteria and constraints of the challenge they are given and review and revise the criteria and constraints as they progress through the unit. Students also generate their own specific questions that they will investigate to complete the unit's project, record these questions, reflect on them, and continue to build on these questions throughout each unit.
Developing and using models	Modeling is an integral part of PBIS. For example, in Living Together, students model a watershed to discover how water can affect land and how land use can affect water quality. In Digging In, students model erosion control around a basketball court. They iteratively return to their models to make additional adjustments throughout the unit. Students are always reminded to be cognizant of the strengths and drawbacks of the models.
Planning and carrying out investigations	Students plan and carry out investigations throughout all the PBIS units. For example, in Good Friends and Germs, students plan an investigation to discover where in their classroom they can find germs.
Analyzing and interpreting data	After students complete an investigation, the text prompts the students to analyze their data, look for patterns, and draw inferences. These Analyze Your Data features are found in all PBIS units. Students also analyze data from tests to determine similarities and differences among several design solutions to identify the best characteristics of each that can be combined into a new solution to better meet the criteria for success.

Scientific and Engineering Practices	Examples From Project-Based Inquiry Science
Using mathematics and computational thinking	Mathematical and computational thinking is used whenever quantitative data are generated. For example, in Genetics, students take a sampling of rice and calculate and graph the ratio of length to width. Later in the unit, they calculate the frequency of traits in a model of a sample population. In Vehicles in Motion, students take measurements to calculate the speed of their cars and then graph their results.
Constructing explanations and designing solutions	Creating explanations is at the heart of PBIS and takes place frequently in all units. The Create an Explanation feature reminds students when an explanation is required. Students are provided with a Create Your Explanation page that helps them organize their thinking as they make a claim, provide evidence from their observations, and review science knowledge as they craft their explanation. In many units, students also iteratively design and build models or solutions. They evaluate their models and solutions to determine how well they meet the criteria and constraints of the problem.
Engaging in argument from evidence	In PBIS, students are given many opportunities to engage in scientific argumentation. They discuss the results of their investigations, their interpretations of their results, their explanations, as well as their solutions to the unit projects during the prescribed social practices that are a part of the PBIS classroom culture. In PBIS, students are always expected to cite evidence when they are presenting their arguments.
Obtaining, evaluating, and communicating information	Communication is another hallmark of the PBIS classroom. There are numerous social practices in which the students engage during a PBIS unit. For example, students participate in Conferences (small-group discussions); Communicates (large-group discussions); Share Your Data, Share Your Explanation, and Investigation Expos (presentations of the results of an investigation); and Solution Showcases (presentations of projects).

Crosscutting Concepts. This challenge in Vehicles in Motion also addresses several crosscutting concepts. These include cause and effect, stability and change, as well as form and function. Students are also introduced to the concept of systems and subsystem models when they build and consider the function of the wheel and axle subsystem and the propeller-driven propulsion subsystem. The function of the coaster and propeller car also deals with the concept of conservation of energy. Figure 9.7 illustrates how the three dimensions are merged in the NGSS and in PBIS.

Instructional Materials

The curriculum consists of 13 units (see Figure 9.8). For each unit, there is a four-color, hardcover student edition. The student edition includes all the activities and readings that are required to address the unit's Big Challenge and/or answer the Big Question. For

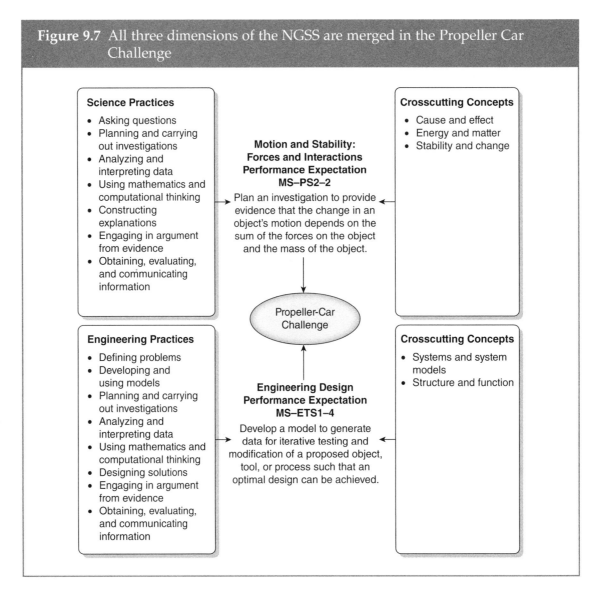

Figure 9.7 All three dimensions of the NGSS are merged in the Propeller Car Challenge

Image courtesy of It's About Time.

each unit, there is also a Teacher's Planning Guide. This guide provides comprehensive "educative resources" that support teachers in implementing the curriculum with fidelity. It includes classroom management suggestions and content background support. The guide also provides guidance for differentiated instruction for struggling learners, advanced learners, and English-language learners. Both student editions and teacher's planning guides are available electronically online.

Also available are an EXAMVIEW® test generator for all 13 units, content videos, NetLogo® software, IAT Technology Lab Extensions that provide detailed equipment (data logger and probeware) setup as well as step-by-step procedural instructions for 20 activities, and tested and convenient material kits for use with each PBIS unit.

There is "24/7" teacher video support that includes introductory and other pedagogical videos, equipment setup videos, and unit walkthrough videos. In-person professional development workshops are also available, as well as an online Getting

Started course that prepares teachers to begin implementing the program. Following is a list of all 13 units.

Launcher Units

Digging in—Within the context of Earth science, students solve design challenges and learn fundamental principles about matter, atoms, molecules, volume, density, erosion and deposition, volcanoes, and rocks and minerals.

Diving Into Science—Within a physical-science context, students meet design challenges and explore concepts of mass, surface area, air resistance, and forces.

Animals in Action—Within a life-science context, students study the practices of biologists and learn such fundamental science ideas as adaptations and interdependence of living things, and the crosscutting concept of biological structure and function.

Engineering Design Units

Vehicles in Motion—Students explore principles of motion and force, including relative motion, velocity, acceleration, Newton's laws, friction, gravity, balanced and unbalanced forces, and net force. They use these principles to improve their design of cars.

Moving Big Things—Students explore what makes things move and define balanced and unbalanced forces. Through investigations and analysis of simple machines, students qualitatively define mechanical advantage and learn about Newton's laws of motion and energy transformations.

Energy—Students explore the following types of energy: kinetic, elastic potential, gravitational potential, thermal, chemical, light, sound, and electrical. They learn that energy has the ability to do work or cause a change. And they investigate conservation of energy and read about renewable and nonrenewable energy sources.

Figure 9.8 Thirteen Hardbound PBIS Units

Image courtesy of It's About Time.

Engineering Problem-Solving Units

Weather Watch—Students learn how weather is measured, the difference between weather and climate, and the factors that affect the weather and climate. They discover that latitude, the tilt of Earth's axis, and the proximity to large bodies of water affect surface temperatures. They investigate the causes of precipitation, including transfer of thermal energy, the water cycle, and the effect of winds and ocean currents on weather and climate.

Living Together—Using some of the practices and skills employed by ecologists, students learn about food chains and webs, ecosystems, biomes, photosynthesis and cell respiration, classification of living things, water quality and its effect on living organisms, and the effects of human activity on ecosystems.

Genetics—Students investigate the processes of sexual and asexual reproduction, Mendelian inheritance, Punnett squares, meiosis and mitosis, chromosomes and DNA, how traits and the environment interact, evolution and natural selection, variation, natural and artificial selection, and the promises and potential threats of genetic engineering.

Air Quality—Through numerous investigations and case studies, students learn about the nature and composition of air and other matter, states of matter, atomic theory, bonding, the periodic table of the elements, and many other fundamental chemistry topics, as well as sources and effects of pollution. Students apply their knowledge by investigating air quality in their own community and examining the sources, effects, and potential solutions to pollution problems.

Good Friends and Germs—Using the practices of epidemiologists, students investigate communicable diseases and their effects on people. Students explore bacteria and viruses that cause disease, cell structure and theory, levels of organization of living organisms, structure and function, interdependence of human body systems, and how to track a disease. Students use this information to develop a set of recommendations for staying healthy.

Driving Question Units

Ever-Changing Earth—Students use a variety of methods, including software, the Internet, and two-dimensional maps to observe differences in topography, and earthquake and volcano patterns. In the process, they learn about the structure of Earth, the theory of plate tectonics, interactions of Earth systems, and the history of Earth.

Astronomy—As part of exploring the potential for the impact of objects in space, students learn about evidence of collisions in the solar system; the components of the solar system (including the sun, Earth, Earth's moon, other planets and their satellites, comets, and asteroids); the motion of those components; and the existence of other galaxies. Based on this understanding, students determine whether a fictional asteroid will hit Earth.

Foundations of PBIS: What Scientists Know About Learning

PBIS has its roots in two educational approaches: Project-Based Science and Learning by Design™. Project-Based Science suggests that students should learn science through engaging in the same kinds of inquiry practices scientists and engineers use, in the context of scientific problems relevant to their lives, using tools authentic to science (Krajcik, Blumenfeld, Marx, Bass, & Fredricks, 1998). Learning by Design™ engages students in design practices, including the use of iteration and deliberate reflection (Kolodner, Camp et al., 2003, Kolodner, Gray, & Fasse, 2003).

These two educational approaches were merged with support from the NSF to become a coherent, three-year middle school science curriculum (Kolodner et al., 2008). They were well suited to be united since they were both well grounded in two fundamental strands of modern research on how people learn: the research literature on mental processes (cognition) involved in learning and the research literature on engagement.

Research on mental processes led to five principles that drove the development of PBIS.

1. Learning is a process of iteratively constructing, revising, and connecting together mental models—models of what we know.

2. Becoming fluid at reasoning skills is an iterative process of composing and debugging sequences of "how-to's"—mental logic for carrying out reasoning.

3. The above implies that we can only learn on the edges of what we already know.

4. Learners know they need to learn something when they can't do something they want to do or something turns out differently than they expected, or something happens that they can't explain.

5. A great deal of reflection and interpretation, and therefore time, is needed to recognize the need to learn and to troubleshoot and revise one's mental models.

These principles suggest that to promote learning, activities should be sequenced so that learners have a chance to repeatedly practice using knowledge and skills they are learning in a variety of contexts and to iteratively and incrementally construct understanding. Learners need to periodically reflect on their reasoning so that they become aware of the ways in which their understanding and capabilities need to be deepened or corrected. These principles also suggest that the more learning activities are aligned to learners' goals, the more attention learners will put into building accurate, complete, and connected mental models. The principles further tell us that the better aligned learning activities are with contexts in which mental models and skills will be used, the more accurate, complete, and connected will be the mental models and skills learners are developing.

Research on engagement sheds light on helping learners become and remain engaged. This second research strand suggests that units need to be long enough for learners to apply and debug the mental models and cognitive skills they are constructing. This, in turn, requires that learners remain engaged with learning activities for sustained periods of time. Some of the principles that arose from this literature are similar to suggestions that arise from the literature on mental processes involved in learning, and some are new:

1. Since we want learners to learn scientific reasoning, we should have learners engage in scientific reasoning as scientists would (disciplinary authenticity) using the tools scientists would use and having access to the same kinds of resources (real-world authenticity).

2. Learners should be doing scientific reasoning in contexts that interest them and make sure to help them connect those contexts to what they already know (personal authenticity).

3. Scaffolding in units should help learners gauge what they know and what they are still unsure of (assessment authenticity).

4. When learners have opportunities to make choices about how to participate, they engage more readily.

5. Help learners and teachers form classroom communities, starting at the beginning of the year, that are sustained through repeated engagement in the classroom activities.

6. Give learners opportunities to help each other understand and learn by working in small groups, whole-class discussions, and by making presentations.

7. Provide scaffolding through hints and prompts that will help them be successful at working together and at helping each other learn.

8. Have learners identify what might come next before telling them what to do. This can be accomplished by use of a Project Board to keep track of questions students have raised and what they are learning.

Evidence of Effectiveness

PBIS is based on a significant body of educational research.[1] Furthermore, there is compelling evidence showing that PBIS meets the goals that were set by the developers. Evaluation evidence shows that these materials engage students well and are manageable by teachers, and that students learn both content and how to engage in engineering and science practices. In every summative evaluation, student performance on posttests improved significantly from pretest performance (Blumenfeld, Fishman, Krajcik, Marx, & Soloway, 2000; Kolodner, Camp et al., 2003; Kolodner, Gray, & Fasse, 2003). In one set of results, performance by a project-based class in Atlanta doubled on the content test while the matched comparison class (with an excellent teacher) experienced only a 20% gain. Most exciting about the Atlanta results is that performance assessments show that PBIS students score higher on all categories of problem solving and analysis and are more sophisticated at engineering and science practice and managing a collaborative scientific investigation.

A Chicago group has also documented significant change in process skills in project-based classrooms. Students become more effective in constructing and critiquing scientific arguments (Sandoval & Reiser, 1997) and in constructing scientific explanations using discipline-specific knowledge (Smith & Reiser, 1998).

Researchers at Northwestern and Georgia Tech have also investigated the change in classroom practices that are elicited by PBIS-type units. Analyses of students' artifacts indicate that students are engaging in ambitious learning practices, requiring weighing and synthesizing many results from complex analyses of data, and constructing scientific arguments (Edelson, Gordin, & Pea, 1999; Kolodner, Camp et al., 2003; Kolodner, Gray, & Fasse, 2003; Reiser et al., 2001; Ryan & Kolodner, 2004).

Other findings show that PBIS students are engaged in planning, performing, monitoring, and revising their investigations, and reporting on their investigation processes as well as their results (Loh et al., 1998; Kolodner, Camp et al., 2003; Ryan & Kolodner, 2004). In general, the classrooms engaging in project-based activities reveal substantial moves toward a scientific discourse community in which students focus on arguing from evidence, critiquing ideas, and conjecturing, rather than simply reporting on what they have read or been told (Kolodner & Gray, 2002; Tabak & Reiser, 1997).

Future Modifications

Project-Based Inquiry Science aligns extremely well with almost all the Performance Expectations of the Next Generation Science Standards. You can view the correlation of PBIS to NGSS by visiting the It's About Time website, www.iat.com. Additional digital resources, including e-books, simulations, and videos, are in development.

Conclusion

Project-Based Inquiry Science integrates engineering and technology seamlessly into science instruction. A major emphasis in technology education is learning the practices of designers, which include making informed decisions, prioritizing and trading off criteria against each other, working in a team, communicating ideas and results, and so on. This emphasis is evident in PBIS, because although the disciplinary core science ideas are all incorporated into the units, the curriculum is aimed toward developing scientific literacy by also focusing on the practices of scientists and engineers. This is one of the curriculum's greatest strengths and an important reason why it is so well suited to supporting the Next Generation Science Standards.

Note

1. Bransford, Brown, and Cocking (1999); Anderson (1982); Schank and Abelson (1977); Laird, Newell, and Rosenbloom (1987); Schank (1999); and Vygotsky (1978). Researchers on engagement included Papert (1993); Resnick, Bruckman, and Martin (1996); Holland, Lachicotte, Skinner, and Cain (1998); Shaffer and Resnick (1999); Lave and Wenger (1991); and Wenger (1998).

References

Anderson, J. R. (1982). Acquisition of cognitive skill. *Psychological Review, 89*(4), 369–406.

Blumenfeld, P., Fishman, B., Krajcik, J., Marx, R.W., & Soloway, E. (2000). Creating useable innovations in systemic reform: Scaling-up technology-embedded project-based science in urban schools. *Educational Psychologist, 35*(3), 149–164.

Bransford, J. D., Brown, A. L., & Cocking, R. R. (Eds.). (1999). *How people learn: Brain, mind, experience, and school*. Washington, DC: National Academies Press.

Edelson, D. C., Gordin, D. N., & Pea, R. D. (1999). Addressing the challenges of inquiry-based learning through technology and curriculum design. *Journal of the Learning Sciences, 8*(3-4), 391–450.

Holland, D., Lachicotte, W., Jr., Skinner, D., & Cain, C. (1998). *Identity and agency in cultural worlds*. Cambridge, MA: Harvard University Press.

Kolodner, J. L., Camp, P. J., Crismond, D., Fasse, B. B., Gray, J., Holbrook, J., Puntambekar, S., & Ryan, M. (2003). Problem-based learning meets case-based reasoning in the middle school science classroom: Putting learning by design into practice. *Journal of the Learning Sciences, 12*(4), 495–547.

Kolodner, J. L., & Gray, J. (2002). Understanding the affordances of ritualized activity structures for project-based classrooms. In *Proceedings of the International Conference of the Learning Sciences* (pp. 221–228). Mahwah, NJ: Lawrence Erlbaum.

Kolodner, J. L., Gray, J., & Fasse, B. B. (2003). Promoting transfer through case-based reasoning: Rituals and practices in Learning by Design™ classrooms. *Cognitive Science Quarterly, 3*, 119–170.

Kolodner, J. L., Starr, M. L., & 12 additional authors. (2008, July). Implementing what we know about learning in a middle school science curriculum for widespread dissemination: The Project-Based Inquiry Science (PBIS) story. Panel summary in Proceedings of the International Conference of the Learning Sciences, Utrecht.

Krajcik, J., Blumenfeld, P., Marx, R., Bass, K., & Fredricks, J. (1998). Inquiry in project-based science classrooms: Initial attempts by middle school students. *Journal of the Learning Sciences, 7,* 313–350.

Laird, J. E., Newell, A., & Rosenbloom, P. S. (1987). Soar: An architecture for general intelligence. *Artificial Intelligence, 33*(1), 1–64.

Lave, J., & Wenger, E. (1991). *Situated learning: Legitimate peripheral participation.* New York: Cambridge University Press.

Loh, B., Radinsky, J., Russell, E., Gomez, L. M., Reiser, B. J., & Edelson, D. C. (1998, January). The progress portfolio: Designing reflective tools for a classroom context. In *Proceedings of the SIGCHI Conference on Human Factors in Computing Systems* (pp. 627–634). ACM Press/Addison-Wesley.

National Research Council (NRC). (2012). *A framework for K–12 science education: Practices, crosscutting concepts, and core ideas.* Committee on a Conceptual Framework for New K–12 Science Education Standards. Board on Science Education, Division of Behavioral and Social Sciences and Education, National Research Council (NRC). Washington, DC: National Academies Press.

NGSS Lead States. (2013). *Next generation science standards: For states, by states. Volume 1: The standards.* Washington, DC: National Academies Press.

Papert, S. (1993). *The children's machine.* New York: Basic Books.

Reiser, B. J., Tabak, I., Sandoval, W. A., Smith, B. K., Steinmuller, F., & Leone, A. J. (2001). BGuILE: Strategic and conceptual scaffolds for scientific inquiry in biology classrooms. In S. M. Carver & D. Klahr (Eds.), *Cognition and instruction: Twenty-five years of progress* (pp. 263–305). Mahwah, NJ: Lawrence Erlbaum.

Resnick, M., Bruckman, A., & Martin, F. (1996). Pianos not stereos: Creating computational construction kits. *Interactions, 3*(6), 40–50.

Ryan, M. T., & Kolodner, J. L. (2004, June). Using "rules of thumb" practices to enhance conceptual understanding and scientific reasoning in project-based inquiry classrooms. In *Proceedings of the 6th International Conference on Learning Sciences* (pp. 449–456). International Society of the Learning Sciences.

Sandoval, W. A., & Reiser, B. J. (1997). Evolving explanations in high school biology. Presented at the annual meeting of the American Educational Research Association, Chicago. Available at http://www.letus.org/bguile/Papers/Bguile_papers.html.

Schank, R. C. (1999). *Dynamic memory revisited.* New York: Cambridge University Press.

Schank, R. C., & Abelson, R. (1977). *Scripts, plans, goals, and understanding.* Mahwah, NJ: Lawrence Erlbaum.

Shaffer, D. W., & Resnick, M. (1999). "Thick" authenticity: New media and authentic learning. *Journal of Interactive Learning Research, 10*(2), 195–215.

Smith, B. K., & Reiser, B. J. (1998). National Geographic unplugged: Classroom-centered design of interactive nature films. In *Proceedings of CHI '98* (pp. 424–431). New York: ACM Press. Available at http://www.media.mit.edu/explain/papers/CHI98_Landlord.PDF.

Tabak, I., & Reiser, B. J. (1997). Complementary roles of software-based scaffolding and teacher-student interactions in inquiry learning. In *Proceedings of the 2nd International Conference on Computer Support for Collaborative Learning* (pp. 292–301). International Society of the Learning Sciences.

Vygotsky, L. S. (1978). *Mind in society: The development of higher psychological processes.* Cambridge, MA: Harvard University Press.

Wenger, E. (1998). *Communities of practice: Learning, meaning, and identity,* Cambridge, UK: Cambridge University Press.

10

Engineering Design in SEPUP's Middle School Issue-Oriented Science Program

Barbara Nagle
The Lawrence Hall of Science
University of California, Berkeley

Figure 10.1 In the Issues and Earth Science course, students design, build, test, and redesign a wind vane

The Science Education for Public Understanding Program (SEPUP) develops issue-oriented science instructional materials for middle and high school classrooms. SEPUP is a program of the Center for Curriculum Development and Implementation at the University of California, Berkeley's Lawrence Hall of Science. SEPUP courses are developed with the input of scientists and tested by classroom teachers, who teach the curricula in their classrooms and provide feedback for revision of the materials.

SEPUP's middle school program is a three-year comprehensive science sequence comprised of Issues and Earth Science (IAES), Issues and Life Science (IALS), and Issues and Physical Science (IAPS). These courses were developed with funding from the National Science Foundation and were prepared through an iterative cycle of development, classroom testing, and revision in national field test sites. The courses are intended to prepare all students to learn and apply science to their own lives and to their local communities.

The complete sequence or portions of the sequence have been adopted in a number of states and school districts. Some districts use the SEPUP materials to implement one or more complete courses, while others use individual units from the courses to develop customized and coordinated sequences that align with their middle school standards. The shared pedagogy of the three courses and the SEPUP assessment system with holistic rubrics used across the sequence facilitate customization while helping to maintain coherence across the units.

SEPUP instructional materials include comprehensive courses, individual units from these courses, supplemental modules, and single-concept kits. In this chapter, we focus on SEPUP's three comprehensive middle school science courses. Detailed information about SEPUP and a link to the publisher, Lab-Aids, Inc. of Ronkonkoma, New York, is available at http://sepuplhs.org/.

SEPUP Goals and Instructional Model

SEPUP's instructional materials are based on SEPUP's philosophy that *all* students deserve an opportunity to learn science and understand how it relates to their present and future lives. SEPUP has developed an instructional model that we call issue-oriented science. The goals for SEPUP's issue-oriented science materials are to

- engage students in the process of learning science;
- encourage students to use scientific evidence to make decisions; and
- help educate tomorrow's citizens about the application of science to everyday life.

At the middle school level, these issues range from personal decisions, such as whether to take a medicine that has certain side effects, to community problems, such as how to treat toxic waste or where to site a nuclear waste facility.

The SEPUP instructional model is shown in Figure 10.2. To **motivate** students, a personal or societal issue provides a theme for each SEPUP unit, and students' questions are addressed in the subsequent series of activities. Each activity begins with a **challenge**, a specific question or goal. To tackle the challenge, students **collect evidence** in guided or open-ended investigations. They run experiments, collect data, work with models, and work on projects. Reading activities provide background information, extend investigations, and help students build their conceptual knowledge and make connections between concepts and their everyday lives. Throughout the instructional activities, students **analyze evidence**, from their own investigations and from secondary sources. These activities help them **build scientific knowledge** and make connections to help them address the central issue. At the end of a unit, students **use their evidence** and new knowledge in a culminating activity or activities that require them to reach a decision or to solve the original problem. Through these activities, they learn how science affects people's lives.

SEPUP instructional materials do not advocate a particular position on issues, but encourage students to support their views with relevant evidence. SEPUP selects issues that

- require an understanding of important scientific concepts and processes;
- require an application of evidence;
- are interesting and accessible to diverse groups of students; and
- are open-ended and complex enough to foster discussion and debate.

The SEPUP Middle School Courses

Issues and Earth Science (IAES)

In each of the middle school courses, the first unit introduces students to some of the practices of science important to the course. The introductory unit in Issues and Earth Science is Studying Soil Scientifically. The unit focuses on observation and measurement (gathering qualitative and quantitative data) as students investigate soil composition and

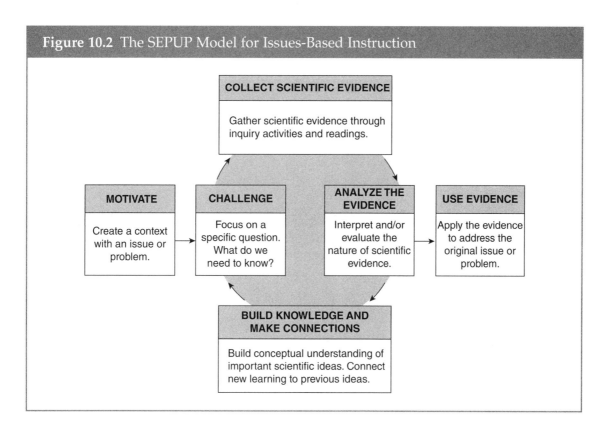

Figure 10.2 The SEPUP Model for Issues-Based Instruction

COLLECT SCIENTIFIC EVIDENCE

Gather scientific evidence through inquiry activities and readings.

MOTIVATE

Create a context with an issue or problem.

CHALLENGE

Focus on a specific question. What do we need to know?

ANALYZE THE EVIDENCE

Interpret and/or evaluate the nature of scientific evidence.

USE EVIDENCE

Apply the evidence to address the original issue or problem.

BUILD KNOWLEDGE AND MAKE CONNECTIONS

Build conceptual understanding of important scientific ideas. Connect new learning to previous ideas.

fertility. These processes relate to the scientific and engineering practice of analyzing and interpreting data to determine similarities and differences in findings. As the course proceeds, additional scientific and engineering practices are introduced.

IAES includes two activities that engage students in the complete engineering design process—designing, testing, and redesigning a solution to a problem—as well as several activities that include evaluation of selected components of a solution. The first design activity is part of a unit on Erosion and Deposition. The issue-oriented challenge at the heart of this unit is to use an understanding of erosion and deposition to recommend where a fictional community should build new homes—on a hill, on a seaside cliff, or in a marshy area near a river. Students prepare a topographical map of a physical landform and then use what they have learned to analyze historical topographical maps to determine what changes have taken place in the fictional community's proposed building sites. In order to prepare for the design activity, they use stream tables to investigate erosion and deposition in rivers, and learn more about these processes at varying time scales through a reading and by engaging in a role-play on the effects of Hurricane Katrina on the Mississippi River Delta.

With that background and purpose in mind, the students are ready for their first major design activity. In Activity 32, "Modeling Erosion," the students use sand and water in a plastic tub to model the erosion of a cliff and a beach, as shown in Figure 10.3. They then design, build, test, and redesign a structure to reduce erosion of the model beach. The questions that follow the activity ask students to apply what they have learned to the fictional scenario and to compare and evaluate their design solutions.

In the second engineering design activity of this course, Activity 67, "Measuring Wind Speed and Direction," students design and build a wind vane or anemometer. The wind vane is shown in Figure 10.1. Figure 10.4 shows a student testing his anemometer.

This activity also emphasizes the complete engineering design cycle. Students work in pairs to develop and draw plans for their design, exchange with another pair to review

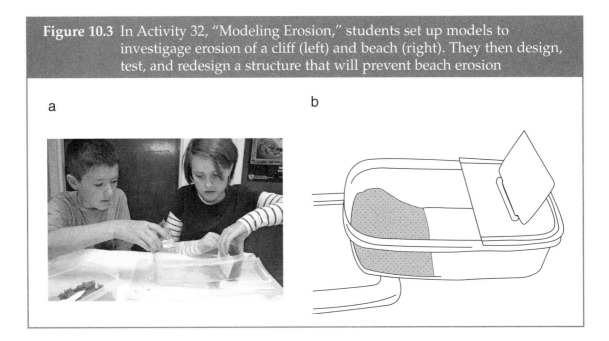

Figure 10.3 In Activity 32, "Modeling Erosion," students set up models to investigage erosion of a cliff (left) and beach (right). They then design, test, and redesign a structure that will prevent beach erosion

and improve their plans, build their instruments, test them and evaluate their performance, and redesign and retest one or more times.

As the unit nears its end, students use the information they have gathered from hands-on activities and other sources to prepare a Geologist's Report for building sites under consideration by the community. In the final activity, "Building in Boomtown," students use what they have learned about erosion; deposition; weathering; the topography of the sites; and brief reports from a geologist, engineer, and ecologist on the characteristics of each site. Each group prepares and presents a plan for building on one of the sites. Then each student makes his or her own recommendation of a building site. The presentations are assessed for students' abilities to weigh evidence and trade-offs in their selection of a site, and to communicate their ideas. This assessment engages students in authentic activities in which they apply concepts about erosion and deposition and the practices of science and engineering to suggest a solution to a problem. This unit demonstrates how an issue can be used to integrate science and engineering.

Figure 10.4 A student tests his anemometer

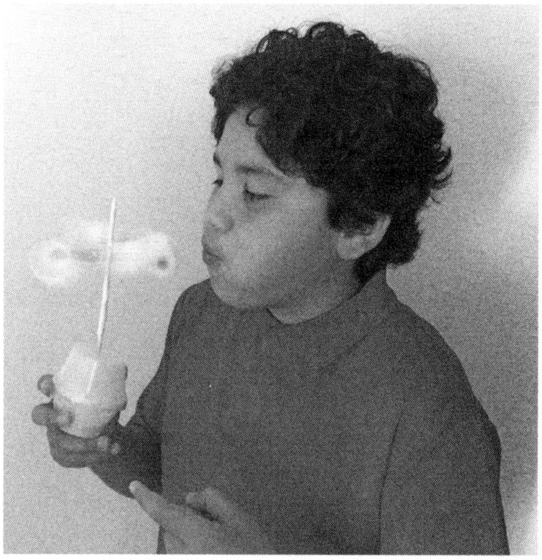

Through the design activities in IAES, students begin to develop an understanding of the design process that is also used in IALS and IAPS. Both activities include elements that build toward Engineering Design performance expectations. For example, analysis questions at the end of each activity ask students to identify common features of successful designs.

The units in Issues and Earth Science are summarized below:

A. Studying Soil Scientifically—Students study different types of soils in the context of designing a school garden. Science content includes observation, measurement, soil composition, and soil fertility.

B. Rocks and Minerals—Students investigate properties of rocks and minerals and consider the relative value of mined versus manufactured diamonds. Science content includes the rock cycle, formation of rocks and minerals, observation, and data collection.

C. Erosion and Deposition—Students study the destructive forces of wind, waves, and water on landforms as they decide on the safest location for new homes in a coastal community. Science content includes topography, erosion, deposition, and landforms.

D. Plate Tectonics—Students study the structure of the Earth in preparation to identify potential sites for the safe storage of radioactive waste. Science content includes Earth's history, earthquakes, volcanoes, plate tectonics, and Earth's structure.

E. Weather and Atmosphere—Students investigate the root cause of local and extreme weather conditions. Science content includes weather, climate, atmosphere, oceans, clouds, the water cycle, and the sun as a source of energy.

F. The Earth in Space—Students reflect on Earth's rotation and revolution and how these affect what they observe in the sky, then apply this knowledge to considering the advantages and disadvantages of alternative calendars. Science content includes Earth, moon, day and year, seasons, tides, and the tilt of Earth's axis.

G. Exploring the Solar System—Students study the solar system as they weigh the hazards and benefits of space exploration. Science content includes space exploration, telescopes, space objects, the sun, the solar system, gravity, planetary motion, and remote sensing.

Issues and Life Science (IALS)

IALS (SEPUP, 2012b) begins with a unit titled *Studying People Scientifically*. This unit introduces scientific practices and the relationships between science and health and medical issues. It focuses specifically on how scientific evidence and trade-offs are involved in decisions about developing safe and effective medications as students examine data from simulated clinical trials. Students engage in the practices of science and engineering, including analyzing and interpreting data to determine similarities and differences in findings, and engaging in argument from evidence.

In IALS, the engineering design activities are clustered in a culminating unit on Bioengineering. Students apply scientific concepts they learned earlier about the human body and cell biology to their design projects. The unit was intentionally designed to engage students in the complementary nature of scientific ideas and the development of technology and meet the National Science Education Standards (NSES) for Science and Technology in the context of the life sciences. For this reason, the unit is an excellent match to the science and engineering practices in the NGSS.

The Bioengineering unit begins with an activity titled "You, An Inventor?" Students invent solutions for performing daily activities with a broken and immobilized arm and for solving another problem of their own choosing. In the second activity, "Bioengineering Case Studies," they read four case studies. Two of these case studies involve artificial limbs specialized for running or rock climbing, and prepare students for four activities that include the complete design, test, and redesign cycle. They work in groups of four students to design artificial heart valves, artificial bones, an energy bar, and (after dissecting a chicken wing) a robotic arm.

Each design activity provides students with design criteria and a procedure for testing the design. Each activity includes a planning and design phase, construction of a prototype, evaluation and comparison of the prototypes, at least one cycle of redesign and testing, and a presentation of the final design to the class. The artificial bone activity, part of which is shown in Figure 10.5, stresses the relationship between scientific investigations and the engineering design process, in which engineers sometimes set up controlled tests of individual variables as they move toward an optimal design.

An activity on "Technology and the Life Sciences" helps students deepen their understanding of the relationship between science and engineering. They read short passages about the work of 16 individuals who have made key contributions to science and technology. As they discuss each person's work, they decide whether they would characterize their work as science, bioengineering, inventing, or some combination. They end the activity discussing the complementary relationship between science and technology and thinking about how understanding science and technology might be useful in careers that interest them.

Figure 10.5 Illustration From the Text for How to Test the Strength of an Artificial Bone (Left) and a Student Conducting a Variation of the Activity (Right)

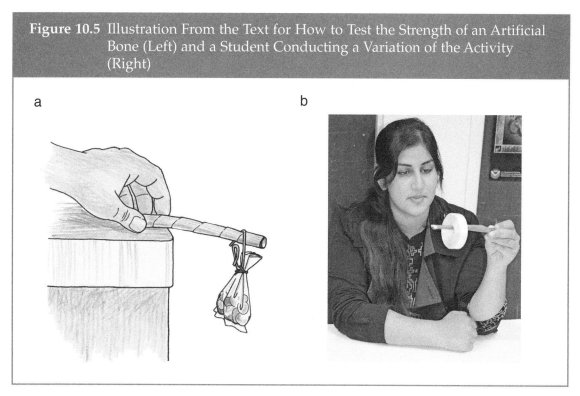

The units in Issues and Life Science are summarized below:

A. Experimental Design: Studying People Scientifically—Students analyze data from simulated clinical trials. Science content includes observations and data collection, formulation of hypotheses, experimental design, placebos, and the nervous system.

B. Body Works—Students explore the role of organ systems and chemical processes within the body as they learn about heart disease, nutrition, and exercise. Science content includes human body systems, structure and function modeling, and cardiovascular disease.

C. Cell Biology and Disease—Students study microbiology, cell structure and function, and causes of disease. Science content includes microscopy, cell structure and function, microbes, disease, antibiotic resistance, and emerging diseases.

D. Genetics—Students study fundamental concepts of genetics as they learn about genetic testing and the use of DNA for identification. Science content includes asexual and sexual reproduction, nature and nurture, and DNA fingerprinting.

E. Ecology—Students consider what happens when a new species is introduced into an ecosystem. Science content includes how species are introduced, biological classification, energy flows in food webs, habitats, producers and consumers, and the carrying capacity of populations.

F. Evolution—Students consider the basic lines of evidence for evolution as they determine whether an extinct species should be brought back to life. Science content includes adaptation, endangered species, extinction, geological time, the law of superposition, natural selection, and the fossil record.

G. Bioengineering—Students design tools and products as they learn how biotechnology can improve people's lives. Science content includes design parameters, bioengineering, prototypes, science and technology, and invention.

Issues and Physical Science (IAPS)

IAPS (SEPUP, 2012c) begins with a unit titled Studying Materials Scientifically. This unit introduces scientific practices, classroom safety when working with chemicals, and the use of chemicals to produce useful products. It focuses specifically on evidence and trade-offs related to the use of hazardous chemicals.

Figure 10.6 Student Working With a Solar Energy Collector

IAPS includes five activities in which students suggest or evaluate solutions to problems, and five activities that engage them in some or all of the three engineering phases—design, test, and redesign. Four of the engineering design activities are in the Energy unit of the course. This unit integrates activities on types of energy and energy transfer with issues related to energy efficiency and household energy use.

The first design activity, an ice-preserving contest, involves student teams in designing, testing, presenting their designs and getting feedback from another team, and redesigning a container to prevent the transfer of energy. In the second design activity, students are given a simple setup to measure the calories stored in a snack food, test the apparatus, and then suggest improvements to the apparatus.

In the third activity, shown in Figure 10.6, students test, redesign, and retest a solar heating apparatus. After collecting data with this solar collector, students suggest improvements to the collector's design. In the fourth design activity, they use model homes to test designs for keeping the homes warm or cool.

The final engineering design activity in IAPS is in the unit on Force and Motion. Students design crash test dummies and redesign them based on feedback from other students. The units in Issues and Physical Science are summarized below:

A. Studying Materials Scientifically—Students investigate the properties of different materials, then apply their knowledge to evaluate the safe handling and storage of cleaning products. Science content includes laboratory safety, handling of hazardous materials, density, identifying unknown substances, and the properties of substances.

B. The Chemistry of Materials—Students study the environmental impact associated with making and disposing of computer circuit boards. Science content includes physical and chemical properties of materials, elements and compounds, chemical reactions, the chemistry of materials, conservation of mass, and the Periodic Table.

C. Water—Students investigate biological and chemical contamination of water sources and apply what they learned to decide on a process for treating industrial wastewater. Science content includes water quality elements and compounds, atoms and molecules, solubility, acids and bases, mixtures and solutions, and the particle theory of matter.

D. Energy—Students explore a range of energy generation and use issues and apply their knowledge to designing an energy-efficient home. Science content includes types of energy, energy transfer and transformations, electrical energy, measuring energy, energy efficiency, magnetic fields, and motors and generators.

E. Force and Motion—Students develop understanding of force and motion in the context of automobile safety and apply their understanding to the investigation and prevention of vehicle collisions. Science content includes Newton's laws, inertia, force, friction, experimental design, and automobile safety.

F. Waves—Students investigate the transmission of various kinds of waves and apply their knowledge to reducing the dangers of excessively loud sounds and ultraviolet light. Science content includes wave properties, types of waves, sound, light, and the electromagnetic spectrum.

SEPUP and the Next Generation Science Standards

At the time the courses were first developed, content was guided by the National Science Education Standards, referred to as the NSES (NRC, 1996). In addition to the core science standards in Life, Physical, and Earth and Space Sciences, the SEPUP courses include strong correlations to the standards on Inquiry, Science and Technology, Science in Personal and Social Perspectives, and History and Nature of Science. The Next Generation Science Standards, or NGSS (NGSS Lead States, 2013), build on the previous work done in developing the NSES, but go further in integrating scientific and engineering practices and crosscutting ideas with core conceptual understanding. The NGSS are based on *A Framework for K–12 Science Education: Practices, Crosscutting Concepts, and Core Ideas*—referred to in this chapter as the NRC Framework (NRC, 2012).

Connections to Core Ideas. SEPUP's issue-oriented instructional model aligns well with the NGSS, which integrate core ideas with crosscutting concepts and scientific and engineering practices, and with the NRC Framework, which emphasizes the role of design in solving human problems, and of designers in developing criteria, evaluating solutions, and determining the trade-offs involved in a design or solution. The NRC Framework identifies four criteria for core ideas and indicates that any core idea should meet two or more of these criteria. These criteria, listed below, have always been important in SEPUP's curriculum design. Note that Criterion 3 refers specifically to relevance and to personal or societal concerns.

1. Have broad importance across multiple sciences or engineering disciplines or be a key organizing principle of a single discipline.

2. Provide a key tool for understanding or investigating more complex ideas and solving problems.

3. Relate to the interests and life experiences of students or be connected to societal or personal concerns that require scientific or technological knowledge.

4. Be teachable and learnable over multiple grades at increasing levels of depth and sophistication. That is, the idea can be made accessible to younger students but is broad enough to sustain continued investigation over years. (NRC, 2012, p. 31)

Connections to Engineering Design. The NRC Framework was released before the most recent revision of the SEPUP middle school program, and the engineering design activities were revised for the 2012 editions to more fully develop engineering practices, including an emphasis on the three major phases of the engineering design process described in the NRC Framework:

- DESIGN: Creates design, prototype, or plan, noting constraints of proposed use
- TEST: Tests design, prototype, or plan, collecting qualitative or quantitative data
- REDESIGN: Evaluates prototype, design, or plan, suggests further changes as needed

Connections between activities in the three SEPUP middle school courses and the engineering design process are shown in Table 10.1.

Connections to Performance Expectations. The phases of the engineering design process are reflected in various NGSS performance expectations that integrate core ideas with science and engineering practices. The NGSS document stresses that instruction

Table 10.1 Connections Between SEPUP's Middle School Courses and Engineering Design

IAES Unit, Activity Title and Description	Suggest or Evaluate a Solution	Engage in the Design Process		
		Design	Test	Redesign
SEPUP Issues and Earth Science Course				
A. Studying Soils Scientifically, Activity 11: Garden Action—Recommend a soil improvement plan	✓			
C. Erosion and Deposition, Activity 32: Modeling Erosion—Design a coastal breakwater		✓	✓	✓
C. Erosion and Deposition, Activity 35: Building in Boomtown—Recommend a site plan for housing development		✓		
D. Plate Tectonics, Activity 49: Comparing Site Risk—Evaluate sites for nuclear waste disposal	✓			
E. Weather and Atmosphere, Activity 67: Measuring Wind Speed and Direction—Design and build a wind vane and anemometer		✓	✓	✓
G. Exploring Space, Activity 98: Choosing a Mission—Recommend a space mission	✓			

SEPUP Issues and Life Science Course				
C. Cell Biology and Disease, Activity 48: Wash Your Hands, Please!—Design an improved hand-washing procedure		✓	✓	
E. Ecology, Activity 88: Presenting the Facts—Suggest a plan for preventing zebra mussel spread	✓			
G. Bioengineering, Activity 104: Designing Artificial Heart Valves—Design, produce, and test artificial heart valves that meet set criteria		✓	✓	✓
G. Bioengineering, Activity 105: Designing Artificial Bones—Design, produce, and test an artificial bone		✓	✓	✓
G. Bioengineering, Activity 107: Designing an Energy Bar—Design, make, and evaluate energy bars		✓	✓	✓
G. Bioengineering, Activity 108: Getting a Hold on Design—Design a prosthetic limb		✓	✓	✓
SEPUP Issues and Physical Science Course				
B. The Chemistry of Materials, Activity 12: Evaluating Materials—Recommend a material for a drink container	✓			
B. The Chemistry of Materials, Activity 13: Product Life Cycle—Construct a product life cycle for a drink container	✓			
B. The Chemistry of Materials, Activity 29: The Green Computer Decision—Evaluate options to recommend a "green" computer	✓			
C. Energy, Activity 60: Ice-Preserving Contest—Design an ice preservation chamber		✓	✓	✓
C. Energy, Activity 63: Measuring Calorie—Improve a calorimeter			✓	✓
C. Energy, Activity 69: Solar Heating—Design a better solar collector		✓	✓	✓
C. Energy, Activity 70: Collecting Solar Energy—Design a home to stay warm in the winter and cool in the summer		✓	✓	
C. Energy, Activity 72: Improving Energy Efficiency—Recommend an energy improvement plan for a home	✓			
D. Force and Motion, Activity 73: Choosing a Safe Vehicle—Evaluate vehicle safety features	✓			
D. Force and Motion, Activity 85: Crash Testing—Design a crash test dummy		✓	✓	✓

should incorporate frequent use of the scientific and engineering practices in other contexts than the specific pairings in the performance expectations for life, physical, and earth and space sciences. For example, the introduction to the earth and space sciences performance standards states,

> These performance expectations blend the core ideas with scientific and engineering practices and crosscutting concepts to support students in developing useable knowledge to explain ideas across the science disciplines. While the performance expectations shown in middle school earth and space science couple particular practices with specific disciplinary core ideas, instructional decisions should include use of many practices that lead to the performance expectations. (NGSS Lead States, 2013, p. 51)

As shown in Table 10.2, many SEPUP middle school activities directly support students in achieving these performance expectations.

Table 10.2 Connections Between SEPUP's Middle School Courses and Performance Expectations

NGSS Performance Expectation	SEPUP
MS-ETS1–1. Define the criteria and constraints of a design problem with sufficient precision to ensure a successful solution, taking into account relevant scientific principles and potential impacts on people and the natural environment that may limit possible solutions.	Can be incorporated into existing design activities in all courses.
MS-ETS1–2. Evaluate competing design solutions using a systematic process to determine how well they meet the criteria and constraints of the problem.	Included in the three middle school courses.
MS-ETS1–3. Analyze data from tests to determine similarities and differences among several design solutions to identify the best characteristics of each that can be combined into a new solution to better meet the criteria for success.	Included in the three middle school courses.
MS-ETS1–4. Develop a model to generate data for iterative testing and modification of a proposed object, tool, or process such that an optimal design can be achieved.	Included in the three middle school courses.
MS-ESS3–3. Apply scientific principles to design a method for monitoring and minimizing a human impact on the environment.	Can be included as a component of students' proposed plans for IAES Activity 35, Building in Boomtown, with minor modifications.
MS-LS2–5. Evaluate competing design solutions for maintaining biodiversity and ecosystem services.	A new activity for the Ecology unit of IALS will enhance the issue of invasive species and address this performance expectation.

NGSS Performance Expectation	SEPUP
MS-PS1–6. Undertake a design project to construct, test, and modify a device that either releases or absorbs thermal energy by chemical processes.	A new activity will build on concepts and practices students learn in the Materials and Energy units of IAPS to enhance the correlation to this performance expectation.
MS-PS2–1. Apply Newton's Third Law to design a solution to a problem involving the motion of two colliding objects.	A new activity for the Force and Motion unit will integrate the issue of automobile collisions.
MS-PS3–3. Apply scientific principles to design, construct, and test a device that either minimizes or maximizes thermal energy transfer.	Activities in IAPS address this standard.

The SEPUP Assessment System and the NGSS

The SEPUP Assessment System provides teachers with tools for formative and summative assessment of student learning. This research-based system was developed in collaboration with the Berkeley Evaluation and Assessment Research (BEAR) group in the UC Berkeley Graduate School of Education (Wilson & Sloane, 2000), and has been cited in nationally known publications such as *Knowing What Students Know* (NRC, 2001b) and *Classroom Assessment and the National Science Education Standards* (NRC, 2001a). The assessment tasks are embedded in the program activities, and many engage students in authentic tasks of scientists and engineers, thereby naturally integrating the practices of science and engineering (Dimension 1) with crosscutting concepts (Dimension 2) and core ideas (Dimension 3). Each unit includes a culminating assessment that engages students in applying concepts and practices to a personal or social issue or problem, and many units engage students in the engineering design process. The assessment system provides powerful formative feedback that helps teachers monitor what students have achieved at the end of each unit. The components of the assessment system are shown in Figure 10.7.

Table 10.3 shows how each of the eight SEPUP assessment targets, or student progress variables, relates to the Practices of Science and Engineering (Dimension 1: Practices), Crosscutting Concepts (Dimension 2), and Core Ideas (Dimension 3) of the Framework.

Conclusion

As shown above, the SEPUP middle school sequence currently addresses many of the core ideas and performance expectations in the Next Generation Science Standards, as well as the major phases of the engineering design process. With some modification, the program will address several more of the performance expectations, and activities to directly address the remaining performance standards will integrate well into the existing content and issues of the units.

Figure 10.7 Components of the SEPUP Assessment System

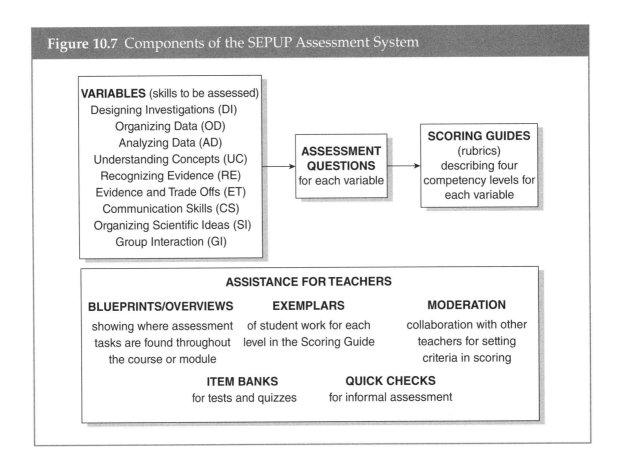

VARIABLES (skills to be assessed)
Designing Investigations (DI)
Organizing Data (OD)
Analyzing Data (AD)
Understanding Concepts (UC)
Recognizing Evidence (RE)
Evidence and Trade Offs (ET)
Communication Skills (CS)
Organizing Scientific Ideas (SI)
Group Interaction (GI)

ASSESSMENT QUESTIONS
for each variable

SCORING GUIDES
(rubrics)
describing four competency levels for each variable

ASSISTANCE FOR TEACHERS

BLUEPRINTS/OVERVIEWS
showing where assessment tasks are found throughout the course or module

EXEMPLARS
of student work for each level in the Scoring Guide

MODERATION
collaboration with other teachers for setting criteria in scoring

ITEM BANKS
for tests and quizzes

QUICK CHECKS
for informal assessment

The most important connection, however, is with the overall goal of the Next Generation Science Standards, which is for students to see the importance of science and engineering in relation to the critical issues that they see in the world today, and that they will be called upon to confront in the future. This goal is described in the introduction to the NGSS as follows:

> Many recent calls for improvements in K–12 science education have focused on the need for science and engineering professionals to keep the United States competitive in the international arena. Although there is little doubt that this need is genuine, a compelling case can also be made that understanding science and engineering, now more than ever, is essential for every American citizen. Science, engineering, and the technologies they influence permeate every aspect of modern life. Indeed, some knowledge of science and engineering is required to engage with the major public policy issues of today as well as to make informed everyday decisions, such as selecting among alternative medical treatments or determining how to invest public funds for water supply options. In addition, understanding science and the extraordinary insights it has produced can be meaningful and relevant on a personal level, opening new worlds to explore and offering lifelong opportunities for enriching people's lives. In these contexts, learning science is important for everyone, even those who eventually choose careers in fields other than science or engineering. (NRC, 2012, p. 7)

Table 10.3 Relationship Between SEPUP Assessment Variables and the Framework

SEPUP Assessment Variable	Relationship to the Framework
Understanding Concepts	**Practice 2:** Ability to make, use, and evaluate models **Practice 6:** Constructing explanations and designing solutions **Dimension 2:** Ability to connect ideas through crosscutting concepts **Dimension 3:** Core ideas
Designing Investigations (includes Designing Procedures)	**Practice 1:** Asking questions (in science) and defining problems (in engineering) **Practice 3:** Planning investigations **Practice 6:** Constructing explanations and designing solutions
Organizing Data	**Practice 3:** Planning investigations **Practice 8:** Communicating information
Analyzing Data	**Practice 4:** Analyzing data **Practice 5:** Using mathematics, information and computer technology, and computational thinking **Practice 7:** Engaging in argument from evidence
Organizing Scientific Ideas	**Practice 8:** Communicating information
Communication Skills	**Practice 8:** Communicating information
Recognizing Evidence	**Practice 4:** Analyzing data **Practice 6:** Constructing explanations and designing solutions **Practice 7:** Engaging in argument from evidence
Evidence and Trade-offs	**Practice 4:** Analyzing data **Practice 7:** Engaging in argument from evidence

References

National Research Council (NRC). (1996). *National science education standards.* National Committee on Science Education Standards and Assessment, Board on Science Education, Division of Behavioral and Social Sciences and Education, National Research Council (NRC). Washington, DC: National Academies Press.

National Research Council (NRC). (2001a). *Classroom assessment and the national science education standards.* Committee on Classroom Assessment and the National Science Education Standards, Center for Education, Division of Behavioral and Social Sciences and Education, National Research Council (NRC). Washington, DC: National Academies Press.

National Research Council (NRC). (2001b). *Knowing what students know: The science and design of educational assessment.* Committee on the Foundations of Assessment (J. Pelligrino, N. Chudowski, & R. Glaser, Eds.), Board on Testing and Assessment, Division of Behavioral and Social Sciences and Education, National Research Council (NRC). Washington, DC: National Academies Press.

National Research Council (NRC). (2012). *A framework for K–12 science education: Practices, crosscutting concepts, and core ideas.* Committee on a Conceptual Framework for New K–12 Science Education Standards. Board on Science Education, Division of Behavioral and Social Sciences and Education, National Research Council (NRC). Washington, DC: The National Academies Press.

NGSS Lead States. (2013). *Next generation science standards: For states, by states. Volume 1: The standards.* Washington, DC: National Academies Press.

SEPUP. (2012a). *Issues and earth science.* Lawrence Hall of Science, University of California at Berkeley. Ronkonkoma, NY: Lab-Aids®, Inc.

SEPUP. (2012b). *Issues and life science.* Lawrence Hall of Science, University of California at Berkeley. Ronkonkoma, NY: Lab-Aids®, Inc.

SEPUP. (2012c). *Issues and physical science.* Lawrence Hall of Science, University of California at Berkeley. Ronkonkoma, NY: Lab-Aids®, Inc.

Wilson, M., & Sloane, K. (2000). From principles to practice: An embedded assessment system. *Applied Measurement in Education, 13*(2), 181–208.

11

Techbridge

Engaging Girls in STEM in Out-of-School Time

Emily McLeod and Linda Kekelis

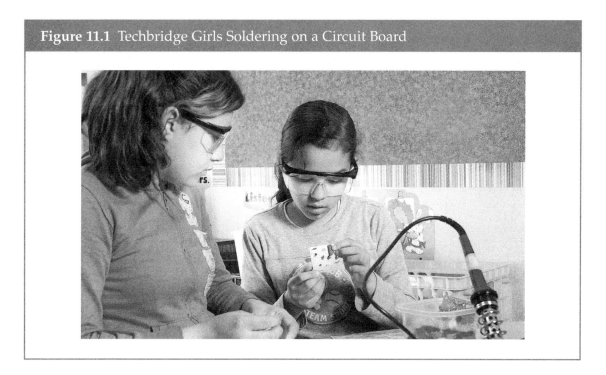

Figure 11.1 Techbridge Girls Soldering on a Circuit Board

Image courtesy of Techbridge.

W hat if a new way to harness wind energy was in the mind of a middle school girl in Oakland? If the breakthrough for treating cystic fibrosis was waiting to be developed by a girl in your community, would it happen? If we put more resources into inspiring girls in science, technology, engineering, and mathematics (STEM), many more of today's engineers in the United States might be female (U.S. Department of Commerce, 2011).

Techbridge is an Oakland-based nonprofit organization that seeks to expand the representation of women and underrepresented minorities in STEM. Through innovative programming, Techbridge inspires girls to pursue academic and career paths in STEM that will better prepare them for 21st-century jobs. The Techbridge curriculum has been developed for after-school and summer programs for girls in Grades 5–12. To date, Techbridge has served more than 5,000 girls, primarily targeting students from communities in need, and reached another 15,000 girls through a partnership with Girl Scout councils nationwide. Techbridge also works with families, role models, teachers, and partners to provide girls with guidance and support on their paths to academic and professional fulfillment.

From its start, Techbridge has engaged girls as co-creators of the curriculum, sparking their interest in engineering, promoting inquiry, and incorporating real-world applications so girls can see how STEM careers make the world a better place. And a difference can often be seen in the lives of the girls themselves. For example, at the beginning of her time in a Techbridge program, Estephania was a shy ninth grader. She was curious about how things work and was intrigued by Techbridge's challenging curriculum. Raised in a family where no one had graduated from high school, Estephania started to think about how studying science could lead to a fulfilling technical career, and was encouraged by role models.

She participated in Techbridge for four years and became the first in her family to graduate from high school. Now she is on the pre-med track at UC Berkeley and remains involved with Techbridge as an alumna. Estephania recently told us,

> Before I joined Techbridge, I was somewhat interested in science but didn't have the drive that Techbridge gave me to pursue a career in science. In Techbridge, I went on field trips that enabled me to picture myself in the shoes of engineers and scientists. I wanted to be like the Techbridge role models that I met. If I wasn't involved in Techbridge, I'm positive that I wouldn't be so passionate about science, or have been so determined to be the first-generation high school graduate in my family.

The curriculum currently consists of 13 units (with more under development). It can be used with both girls and boys and is suitable for use in a variety of out-of-school time settings, including after-school programs, summer programs, and Girl Scout councils. All units are appropriate for middle school students; the curriculum is highly adaptable, and many activities can be simplified for use with younger grades, while others can be made more in-depth and complex for high school students. The units can be led by after-school line staff, teachers of all backgrounds, Girl Scout troop leaders, or others.

Further information about Techbridge is available at www.techbridgegirls.org, and videos can be found at www.youtube.com/user/Techbridge.

Sample Unit: Electrical Engineering

What It Looks Like

In a classroom, pairs of girls work intently together on a project at tables and on the floor. The room buzzes with focused conversation and excitement. Girls visit stations around the room to choose from a variety of supplies: recycled materials such as scrap wood, plastic bottles, and old CDs; motors, battery holders, and other electronic equipment; even the "fur" and stuffing from motorized stuffed animals they dissected earlier.

Take a closer look, and you can see that the girls are building electronic toys, working from original designs that they sketched themselves as part of the engineering design process. One pair is building a motorized watercraft with two propellers. They turn on a switch to test it, and the propellers whirr, but there's a problem: "Hey, they are spinning in different directions!" exclaims one of the girls. The other says, "Maybe we got the positive and negative wires mixed up when we connected one of the propellers to the motor?" They discuss their ideas for fixing the circuit with a facilitator, go back to work, and a few minutes later, the propellers are both spinning correctly. Later, the girls take their toy to a nearby fountain to test it, make observations, and take notes for a redesign.

About the unit. The above is a scene from a group completing "Electronic Toy Design," one of the activities in the Techbridge Electrical Engineering unit. Electrical engineering can be a challenging and satisfying career, and the first step on the path toward this career is developing an understanding of electricity and circuits. The unit demystifies these topics for kids and gives them a chance to develop confidence as they begin by building simple circuits, and then take on more complex projects that require them to work independently and create their own circuit designs.

Concepts covered in the unit include electron flow, polarity, and series and parallel circuits, as well as the engineering design process. Kids also learn how various electrical components work and become familiar with the terminology used to describe them, and about what electrical engineers do. Skills developed through the unit include circuit building and design, drawing of circuit diagrams, and soldering. Projects kids can create include a light-up LED butterfly, a color-changing lantern, an electronic buzzer game board, and electronic toy prototypes.

A sample path through the unit. Techbridge curriculum units are divided into a series of discrete activities of varying length and complexity. Many activities are stand-alone and can be completed by participants with little or no prior experience with the subject. However, after-school programs that meet on a regular basis or summer programs can use a series of activities from the same unit, creating an experience that gives participants the chance to deepen and build on their knowledge from one activity to the next. Here is one series of activities from the electrical engineering unit:

> The program begins with "Create a Circuit," an introductory activity. Pairs of girls are given a variety of basic components, such as batteries, motors, LEDs, and resistors, one by one, and are challenged to use the components to create working circuits (see Figure 11.1). As they experiment, girls develop questions about what they observe and work to answer those questions together. The activity introduces circuits in a fun, exploratory way and gives girls a chance to

Figure 11.2 Girls Working on a Snap Circuits Challenge

Image courtesy of Techbridge.

practice their questioning skills. At the end of the activity, girls watch a video of an electrical engineer and talk about the kinds of work done by electrical engineers.

Next, girls work on "Snap Circuits Challenges" (see Figure 11.2). Pairs are given a variety of challenges to complete using Snap Circuits, or kits containing electronic components that snap together. For example, a pair of girls is challenged to create a circuit containing a switch-activated alarm. The class periodically breaks to talk about what the girls have built and to discuss concepts such as polarity and series and parallel circuits. Girls also learn and practice how to draw circuit diagrams.

Once girls are familiar with circuitry basics, they are ready to learn how to solder. Soldering is an empowering skill for girls to learn, and it connects them to practices used by electrical engineers. During "Soldering a Simple Circuit," an introductory activity, they solder together LEDs, switches, and batteries to make a circuit that can be placed in a stuffed animal or card (see Figure 11.3).

Girls next work on the "LED Butterfly," investigating and building a butterfly decoration that uses a battery and LEDs. The activity reinforces what girls have learned about polarity and strengthens their soldering and circuit-building skills.

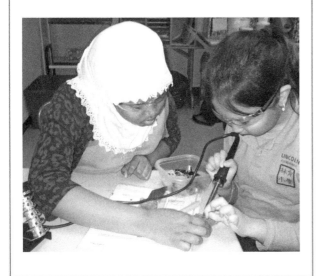

Figure 11.3 Girls Working on a Soldering Project Together

Image courtesy of Techbridge.

At the beginning of the following session, girls compete in teams to answer questions about circuits during a game of "Circuitry Jeopardy," one of the unit's icebreakers. Techbridge units include fun, short icebreakers that help girls get to know and get comfortable with one another.

Now that girls are comfortable soldering circuits, they move on to the "Tilt Lantern" activity. Teams learn about a new component, the tilt switch, by investigating and observing a small lantern that turns on when held upright and shuts off when turned upside down. They develop hypotheses about how the lantern works and open it up to determine whether they were correct, and then they build their own tilt lanterns. Because this group is experienced and comfortable with circuits, the facilitator has them sketch out the circuit and build it using their sketches as a guide. The activity helps girls develop skills in investigation, observation, and the development of hypotheses, and also gives them a chance to work more with parallel circuits.

As the capstone project for the unit, girls complete the "Electronic Toy Design" activity. Before beginning the design process, girls reverse-engineer electronic toys, developing a hypothesis about how they work and dissecting the toys to determine if their hypothesis was correct. They meet a role model who describes her work as an electrical engineer. The role model visits the program a couple more times to support girls as they work on their toys. Girls learn about the engineering design process and use all of the steps in the process as they design, build, test, and redesign their toys (see Figure 11.4). This project gives girls the opportunity to apply many of the concepts they've learned over the course of the unit. It also allows them to work creatively and independently as they take responsibility for investigating, designing, and troubleshooting their projects.

Figure 11.4   Girls test out prototypes of water toys

Image courtesy of Techbridge.

Goals

The Techbridge curriculum is designed to meet the following goals:

- **Increase the number of girls and underrepresented minorities pursuing STEM careers.** Currently, women earn less than 30% of college degrees granted in engineering and computer science. Just 28% of those working in science and engineering careers are women, and only 10% working in the field are minority women (National Science Foundation, 2013). It's crucial to find ways to increase the number of women and minorities pursuing STEM careers: This untapped talent pool can increase innovation and discovery, the STEM career pathway can be higher paying, and there are often more job opportunities available. The Techbridge curriculum gives girls the opportunity to see that careers in STEM can be exciting and have a real impact on the world. Role models help them imagine how they can get there.
- **Engage girls in the practices of science and engineering.** The curriculum introduces girls to a variety of engineering and technology fields, with a focus on disciplines where women are underrepresented. Projects promote inquiry; girls are encouraged to investigate questions and discover how things work. They also learn how to develop experimental methods to carry out their investigations, and to participate in the engineering design process by brainstorming, designing, building, and redesigning. Throughout the curriculum, girls engage in these practices that mirror those used by scientists and engineers—practices highlighted as crucial in

A Framework for K–12 Science Education (NRC, 2012) and *Next Generation Science Standards* (NGSS Lead States, 2013).

- **Spark interest in science and engineering topics through a focus on real-world topics.** In elementary school, both girls and boys have similar levels of interest in science, but by the end of the middle school years, boys are about twice as interested in pursuing STEM careers (NSF, 2007). Many of Techbridge's projects are design-based and focus on topics relevant to the girls, exposing girls to engineering in daily life and building early interest in STEM.

- **Inspire and motivate program participants through career exploration and role models and field trips.** STEM activities, no matter how engaging and self-directed, may not lead to career interests. Girls want to make the world a better place, and by seeing how science and technology provide the tools for innovation and real problem solving, they can develop an interest in STEM professions. Our dynamic programming offers girls career exploration through role models, field trips to technology companies, and interactive activities that invite girls to imagine their future in engineering. From designing a career card to interviewing a role model, career activities invite girls to make connections between hands-on activities and STEM careers.

Connection to Next Generation Science Standards

One of the primary goals of the Techbridge curriculum is to engage girls in the practices of scientists and engineers as a way to excite them about STEM careers and help them to see the real-world impact such careers can have.

> The actual doing of science or engineering can . . . pique students' curiosity, capture their interest, and motivate their continued study; the insights thus gained help them recognize that the work of scientists and engineers is a creative endeavor—one that has deeply affected the world they live in. (NRC, 2012, p. 42)

To this end, the engineering design process is a crucial component of many activities across the curriculum. As girls use the engineering design process, they engage in a number of the science and engineering practices identified in the Framework and the NGSS: defining problems, designing solutions, planning and carrying out investigations, analyzing data, and communicating information (see Figure 11.5).

For example, during an activity in the "Girls Go Global" unit, pairs design and build a water carrier for a hypothetical user (a girl in a developing nation) with specific needs. As part of the testing process, they develop a survey to gather feedback about whether the carrier meets the design constraints they identified, and have another pair test the carrier and complete the survey. Pairs redesign and retest their carriers. This process helps girls to meet NGSS performance expectation MS-ETS1–2: *Evaluate competing design solutions using a systematic process to determine how well they meet the criteria and constraints of the problem.*

During another activity from the same unit, girls build and test biomass-burning stoves, taking the temperature of the water before and after their fuel burns (see Figure 11.6), and redesigning and retesting stoves to determine whether the redesign is more efficient (gets

Figure 11.5 The Techbridge Engineering Design Process

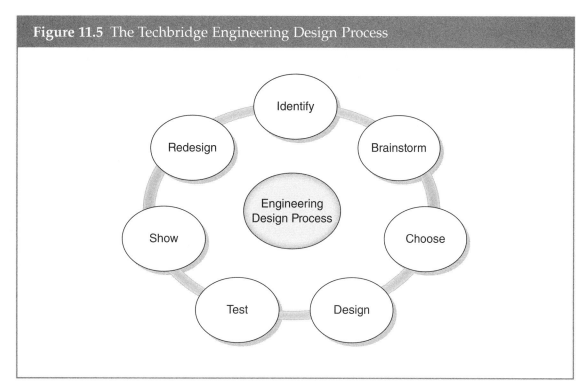

Image courtesy of Techbridge.

the water hotter while using the same amount of fuel). The activity helps girls meet NGSS performance expectation MS-ETS1–3: *Analyze data from tests to determine similarities and differences among several design solutions to identify the best characteristics of each that can be combined into a new solution to better meet the criteria for success.*

Activities in the units may also connect to the NGSS performance expectations related to science concepts; for example, the stove activity also connects to MS-PS3–3: *Apply scientific principles to design, construct, and test a device that either minimizes or maximizes thermal energy transfer.*

Curriculum Materials

The Techbridge curriculum consists of 13 units, with additional units being added on a regular basis. Each unit covers a different engineering, science, or technology topic, such as Mechanical Engineering, Chemical Engineering, or Design Challenges. Each unit contains the following components:

Icebreakers. These are short, fun activities designed to promote interactions across different groups that help them practice teamwork and learn new STEM skills. Techbridge evaluations have shown that these activities are important in helping create a safe, inviting space where girls feel comfortable working with others. We have found that "when teachers and students worked together to bridge the differences [among groups of students]—the Techbridge experience reduced stereotypes and divisions between different groups of students" (Kekelis, Ancheta, Heber, & Countryman, 2005, p. 243).

Figure 11.6 Testing the Temperature of Water Heated by a Biomass-Burning Stove

Image courtesy of Techbridge.

There are icebreakers within each of the units, and also an Icebreaker unit that includes more than 50 icebreakers. For example, in "Common Bonds," the activity begins with one girl standing at the front of the room and naming three things about herself. Another girl who shares one of those three things in common then comes to the front of the classroom and links arms with her, states three things about herself, and so on. By the end of the activity, the group of girls has formed a linked chain, and they have all learned something about the others in the group.

Activities. Activities range in length from short, introductory activities that take 15 minutes to more complex projects that stretch over several hours. Each activity includes step-by-step instructions for facilitators, information about the STEM content behind the activity, and tips from Techbridge staff about how to facilitate the activity and how to troubleshoot issues that may arise. Activities include handouts for participants and a list of discussion questions that can be used to encourage them to think more deeply about the work.

Materials and equipment. Techbridge activities are designed to be completed in after-school spaces or classrooms, so no specialized lab equipment is required. Some activities use basic tools such as digital scales and thermometers, while others use computers, soldering irons, or hot glue guns. Materials vary depending on the topic covered—some activities use electronic components such as LEDs and switches, while others use common household items such as straws, paper clips, and rubber bands.

Each activity includes a detailed materials list, along with suggestions for where to purchase less common items. The materials cost varies. Some activities can be completed at little or no cost, while other projects (such as those in which participants create an object to take home) may cost a few dollars or more per child.

Who Can Lead These Activities and What Support Will They Need?

Teachers. Teachers, particularly science or engineering teachers, have content knowledge and experience that will allow them to use the activities with relative ease.

After-school line staff. Activity guides are written to support line staff with limited STEM background, but with a desire to learn and introduce youth to science and engineering. As needed, line staff can learn about content for the activities they are delivering. However, depending on their experience level, they may need guidance on leading an organized lesson with specific learning objectives.

Girl Scout troop leaders and partners. Girls Go Techbridge programs-in-a-box are designed to be led by staff and volunteers with limited STEM experience. Each program contains supports including information about the science and engineering behind the activities, connections to the engineering design process, reflection questions and possible answers, and ties to career skills featured in the activities.

Program Models

After-school programming. The units can be used in after-school programs that meet weekly or at other intervals. The activities can be the main focus of the program, or used as part of a menu of options that encompasses other subject areas. The length of activities varies; depending on the length of the program, multiple activities may be completed in a session, or one activity may stretch over several sessions. Most of the Techbridge units are designed around a theme, and ideally, several activities from the same unit will be completed so participants can deepen and build on their knowledge of the subject. However, many activities can also be completed as stand-alone activities. A combination of short-term and long-term projects seems to best maintain the interest of kids.

Summer programming and weekend workshops. The curriculum can also be used as part of more immersive experiences in the summer or on weekends. In this context, all or many of the activities from a unit can be taught in a relatively short time frame, giving participants the chance to dive deeply into a subject and build on what they are learning from activity to activity.

Girl Scout councils. Techbridge has taken its curriculum and created programs-in-a-box to teach middle school girls science and engineering skills. The program, Girls Go Techbridge, approaches innovation through design challenges that introduce the engineering design process and foster creativity and critical thinking. A key success is the flexibility of the program, which can be implemented in a variety of settings; serve many types of girls; and be led by staff, role models, and volunteers with limited STEM experience. To support leaders without STEM backgrounds, Leaders' Guides include information about the science and engineering behind the activities and questions to prompt reflection. Family resources, available in Spanish and Chinese, offer ideas for engaging girls in science and engineering along with projects to try at home and information about careers.

There are five programs-in-a-box, each of which offers 9–12 hours of programming:

- **Power It Up** introduces electronics and circuitry, soldering, and energy usage.
- **Make It Green** introduces green design and shows how engineers help make the world a better place.
- **Design Time** presents the engineering design process and provides the opportunity to brainstorm and build prototypes.
- **ThrillBuilders** introduces simple machines and concepts like force and gears, and highlights careers in mechanical engineering.
- **Engineers to the Rescue** exposes girls to sustainable forms of energy along with engineering specialties.

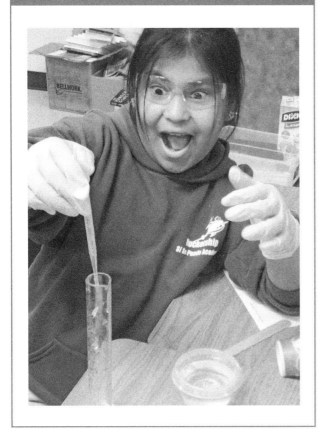

Figure 11.7 A girl works on the "Make a Superball" activity from the Chemical Engineering unit

Image courtesy of Techbridge.

Techbridge also offers professional development through the Girls Go Techbridge train-the-trainer model, which familiarizes trainees not only with the hands-on design challenges, but also with practicing inquiry, skill-specific feedback, and connecting activities to specific careers in engineering (via role-play) and real-world applications. While this project was developed for Girl Scout councils, other groups can use the program boxes to support STEM.

Brief Unit Descriptions

The following are descriptions of the other Techbridge units currently available for purchase.

Career Exploration. How does sunblock work? Who designed the iPod? How do bridges stay up during earthquakes? In this unit, kids learn about the people who know the answers to these questions: chemical engineers, computer scientists, civil engineers, and many others in the field of science and technology. From working on goal-setting icebreakers, to creating advertisements for college majors, to designing board games about their roads to careers, kids explore a future in science and technology in ways that fuel their inspiration and excitement.

Chemical Engineering. The activities in this unit introduce kids to chemical manipulation and chemical processes, letting them use their knowledge of chemistry and problem solving to explore the world of chemical engineering. Basic principles, like the importance of following instructions in a lab, are made fun for kids as they create peanut brittle. Other challenges include discovering the chemical formula for the bounciest ball (see Figure 11.7) and creating a chemical combination to launch a rocket into the sky.

Computer Science. In this unit, kids learn how computers are a crucial part of our daily lives, and how software engineers write the code that makes them work. They develop basic programming skills by using tools such as Scratch and have the opportunity to build a simple webpage using HTML. During the unit, kids learn essential programming concepts such as algorithms, loops, and conditional statements. For more advanced groups, there are activities incorporating wearable electronics and Arduinos.

Design Challenges. Quick—what can you make with a skewer, a paper clip, a Dixie cup, and push pins? In this unit, kids are challenged to design and construct structures and products with limited materials and time constraints. They learn about mechanical energy and chemical reactions as they make self-propelled cargo boats and bungee jumps for eggs (see Figure 11.8). The Design Challenges unit encourages kids to think creatively, and it is full of activities that emphasize the importance of teamwork.

Digital Media. Lights, camera, animate! The activities in Digital Media invite kids to explore the many features of a digital camera and discover what they can do with images. They'll also experience firsthand the fun and creativity involved in creating animations as they make their very own claymation film. They'll be involved in every step of the process, including writing the story, drawing storyboards, modeling using clay figures, directing the action, and using stop-motion animation software.

Environmental Engineering. In this unit, kids learn about the many aspects of environmental engineering. From designing a solar-powered car to figuring out how to build a filter to clean dirty water, kids engage in a variety of hands-on activities that help them see how engineers make the world a better, greener place. Kids participate in activities that reveal human impact on the environment and the current strategies people implement to reduce this impact.

Figure 11.8 Testing During the "Egg Bungee Jump" Activity From the Design Challenges Unit

Image courtesy of Techbridge.

Girls Go Global. In this unit, kids take on the role of engineers working on pressing problems around the world. They learn about the challenges that people in developing nations may face meeting daily needs related to water, food, energy, and sanitation, and learn about solutions being created by engineers and designers across the globe. Throughout the unit, kids design, build, and test their own solutions, such as biomass-burning stoves, water carriers, and LED lights.

Green Design. The Green Design project provides an opportunity to introduce green building practices and engages kids in activities that emphasize energy conservation and material reuse. Each kid constructs a scale model of one room of a house that incorporates green construction practices and materials. As kids work through the activities within the unit, they learn about ways to help make the world a better place through the use of science and engineering.

Mechanical Engineering. From playground equipment to cars, mechanical engineers help make all the stuff around us work. This unit introduces kids to the basics of mechanical engineering through activities based on simple machines. Kids design their own cars, and power them through a variety of energy sources. They also explore the four-stroke engine and review basic care and maintenance of the family car.

Product Design. How does a product go from being an idea to on the store shelf? In this unit, kids explore the world of product design by taking on several roles within the design process. They analyze existing designs by taking apart hair dryers and other household appliances, and research, design, and prototype their own toy inventions. Throughout the activities, kids get hands-on experience with the engineering design process and gain an appreciation for being creative within a structured format.

Structural Engineering. Towers out of spaghetti. Bridges out of straws. Domes out of gumdrops. Building structures from everyday materials brings to life the field of structural engineering. Just like the professionals, kids plan for safety, performance, and cost of materials. They also test important parameters of each structure, such as how fast a marble can roll through a foam roller coaster and how long their structure stands through an earthquake.

Career Exploration: Role Models and Field Trips

A hallmark of Techbridge is its integration of career exploration, including field trips to STEM companies, role model visits, and interactive activities that invite girls to imagine their future in STEM. It takes the right combination of career guidance and personal connection to create successful experiences for youth and role models. Techbridge offers training and support to role models and partners to ensure these outreach activities are effective. Techbridge also offers the online Role Models Matter Toolkit, which includes downloadable resources, at http://techbridgegirls.org/rolemodelsmatter/.

Professional Development

Techbridge also helps build the capacity of other organizations to support STEM programming in out-of-school time for girls and boys through professional development. By advancing effective practices and collaborating with partners, Techbridge has helped introduce design-based activities that make engineering, technology, and science accessible and engaging for youth, and emphasizes career exploration through role models and career activities.

The organization hosts a summer institute that introduces participants to the curriculum and shares strategies for recruiting and engaging girls, incorporating role models, and supporting family outreach. Participants have used the curriculum for in-school and after-school programs as well as programs at museums and youth-serving organizations.

Future Developments

The Techbridge curriculum development process is an iterative one, and units are revised on an ongoing basis. Currently, units are being updated to strengthen connections to science content; encourage open-ended, girl-driven projects; and incorporate more opportunities for NGSS-connected practices such as data collection and investigation design.

Conclusion

The Techbridge curriculum and program can have a powerful impact on kids' enthusiasm for and engagement with STEM. Techbridge conducts surveys with girls in our after-school programs, and the results show that high-quality science and engineering programming can make a real difference, not just around STEM engagement, but also around problem solving, teamwork, and persistence. By implementing engineering curricula such as those from Techbridge or other providers in this book, you can inspire the youth in your own community to get excited about STEM—and maybe even pursue degrees and careers in the field. For more information, please send questions to info@ techbridgegirls.org.

References

Kekelis, L., Ancheta, R. W., Heber, E., & Countryman, J. (2005). Bridging differences: How social relationships and racial diversity matter in a girls' technology program. *Journal of Women and Minorities in Science and Engineering, 11*(3).

National Research Council (NRC). (2012). *A framework for K–12 science education: Practices, crosscutting concepts, and core ideas.* Committee on a Conceptual Framework for New K–12 Science Education Standards. Board on Science Education, Division of Behavioral and Social Sciences and Education, National Research Council (NRC). Washington, DC: National Academies Press.

National Science Foundation (NSF). (2007). Press release 07–108: Back to school: Five myths about girls and science. Retrieved July 30, 2013, from www.nsf.gov/news/news_summ.jsp?cntn_id=109939.

National Science Foundation, National Center for Science and Engineering Statistics. (2013). *Women, minorities, and persons with disabilities in science and engineering: 2013* (Special Report NSF 13–304). Available at http://www.nsf.gov/statistics/wmpd/.

NGSS Lead States. (2013). *Next generation science standards: For states, by states. Volume 1: The standards.* Washington, DC: National Academies Press.

U.S. Department of Commerce, Economics and Statistics Administration. (2011). *Women in STEM: A gender gap to innovation* (ESA Issue Brief #04–11). Retrieved June 2, 2014, from http://esa.doc.gov/sites/default/files/reports/documents/womeninstemagaptoinnovation8311.pdf.

12

WaterBotics®

Underwater Robots Built With LEGO® Materials

Jason Sayres, Mercedes McKay, and Arthur Camins
Center for Innovation in Engineering and Science Education (CIESE)
Stevens Institute of Technology
Hoboken, New Jersey

Figure 12.1 WaterBot® Picking up a Wiffle Ball

Image by Mark Dye, courtesy of Stevens Institute of Technology.

Authors' Note: This material is based upon work supported by the National Science Foundation under Grant Numbers 0624709 and 0929674. Any opinions, findings, and conclusions or recommendations expressed in this material are those of the authors and do not necessarily reflect the views of the National Science Foundation.

Underwater robotics is a timely, relevant, and exciting field that incorporates a very broad spectrum of engineering, science, and information technology disciplines. Recent news stories have highlighted numerous innovative applications of underwater robotics: assisting in the search for the downed Malaysian jet in 2014, responding to underwater disasters such as the 2010 Gulf oil spill, exploring the wreckage of the Titanic, and even swimming with and studying sharks out in the wild. Underwater robots have also aided in the rescue of swimmers drowning in rough waters and the recovery of other robots trapped while exploring places too dangerous for humans to enter. These examples demonstrate how science and engineering solve real human problems, and the contexts they provide can be used to increase student engagement. The design and construction of underwater robots is thus ideal for student projects since the work is readily connected to real-world applications, the content is highly interdisciplinary, and the underwater environment presents unique challenges not found in terrestrial robotics programs. Educators around the country are now using underwater robotics as the basis for rich and rewarding STEM projects.

WaterBotics® is a 20- to 26-hour underwater robotics program in which students design, construct, and program an underwater, remotely operated vehicle (ROV) using LEGO® materials and the LEGO® MINDSTORMS® robotics platform. Students apply a variety of science, engineering, and technology concepts as they design, build, and test their robots in a child's swimming pool. Their experiences are connected to real-life contexts and potential career paths.

The WaterBotics® curriculum was developed by the Center for Innovation in Engineering and Science Education (CIESE) at Stevens Institute of Technology in Hoboken, New Jersey, through two successive National Science Foundation grants. It has already impacted thousands of middle and high school students nationwide, more than 50% of whom are girls.

Information on WaterBotics® may be found on the project's website at http://waterbotics.org/.

How Does a WaterBotics® ROV Work?

In WaterBotics®, the robots built by students are called ROVs because they are not autonomous. Students remotely control the robots they build with custom controllers that they also build and program with the help of the LEGO® MINDSTORMS® system. This technology is based on a programmable microcontroller, called the NXT, along with a variety of sensors that plug into it. These sensors measure events like button presses, rotations, light intensity, or distance, and a program running on the NXT receives the resulting data and uses them to make decisions and perform actions, such as spinning a motor or making a sound (see Figure 12.1).

Students use the NXT and sensors to create a device that is similar to a video game controller, shown in Figure 12.2. They then program the robot to move based on how the sensors are manipulated. For example, pushing a particular button may make the robot turn left, whereas pushing another button may make it turn right. Alternatively, they could design their controllers to include a steering wheel to handle left and right movement, and the buttons would be used to make the robot dive and resurface. Design and redesign choices are all up to the students!

But how then does the NXT communicate with the robot in the water? Although there are several ways of accomplishing this, WaterBotics® employs a control scheme that takes advantage of the well-designed infrared (IR) technology used within the LEGO® Power Functions line of products. An illustration of the setup is shown in Figure 12.3.

Image by Mark Dye, courtesy of Stevens Institute of Technology.

Figure 12.2 The NXT Programmable Microcontroller

First, an IR transmitter is attached to the NXT. Its job is to send commands for the robot's movement. Next, a watertight case is configured to hold an IR receiver and a power supply, and the robot's motors are connected to the case using cables.

When the receiver gets a command from the transmitter, it directs power to one or more motors. As these motors rotate, they spin propellers, which then push water and, in turn, cause the robot to move.

The instructor prepares all of the IR receiver cases ahead of time. Students focus their attention on designing and building the robot, attaching it to the IR receiver case, and making and programming their controller.

Missions and the Iterative Design Process

Building a fully functional underwater ROV is a complex undertaking, even when using the exceptionally user-friendly materials of the LEGO® platform. Therefore, to help ensure success, especially for students with little to no experience, the curriculum splits up the overall design challenge into a series of four missions.

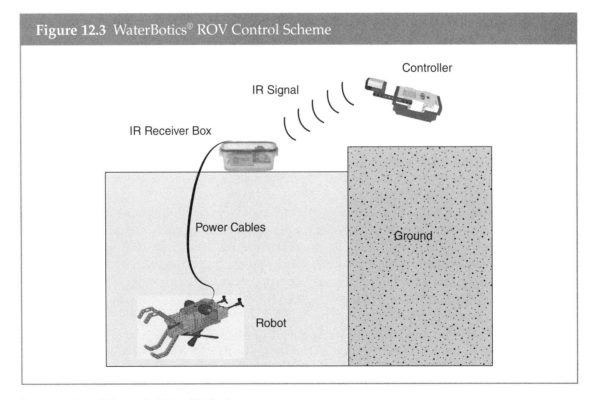

Figure 12.3 WaterBotics® ROV Control Scheme

Image courtesy of Stevens Institute of Technology.

Each mission tasks students with the creation of a robot that possesses a specific subset of the capabilities of the final ROV. These "bite-sized" design challenges are much less intimidating and are arranged to build on one another so that they progressively increase in complexity and eventually lead to a robot with complete functionality. This allows students to build on previous work and to ease into an accomplishment that might have otherwise seemed beyond their reach. They also gain an understanding of systems and subsystems, which are critical components of engineering design.

Another benefit of this mission structure is that it models and engages students in a tried-and-true method used in real-life engineering—the iterative design process. Students design, test, and redesign. They build and test subsystems on the way to a final complex challenge. As they engage in iterative design, they are taught about its role in the creation of technology and products. By understanding how the process is applied to this particular project, students will hopefully be able to apply it to future projects and thus gain confidence in taking on even tougher design challenges.

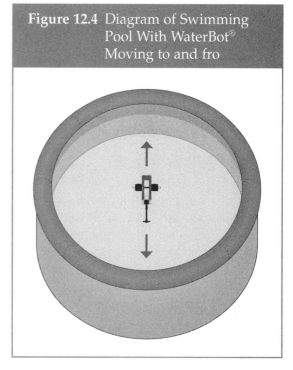

Figure 12.4 Diagram of Swimming Pool With WaterBot® Moving to and fro

Image courtesy of Stevens Institute of Technology.

To provide relevance and increase engagement, each mission is modeled after a real-life application of underwater robots. In addition, specific engineering careers are described in each mission so that students can visualize where their newfound interest in science and engineering might lead!

Mission 1: Rescue!

The first mission presents a seemingly simple challenge—build a robot that will float on the surface of the water and be able to move forward and backward in order to rescue a distressed swimmer, as illustrated in Figure 12.4. Yet there is more involved in accomplishing this task than is immediately apparent to students. Fortunately, the underlying complexities—creating a stable structure, ensuring flotation, generating propulsion, building a controller, programming it, and understanding how the IR communication works—are revealed incrementally, allowing students to deal with each aspect in turn without feeling overwhelmed.

The Initial Build. At the start of the mission, the class is divided into teams of three to five students. Each team is given an IR receiver case, a motor, one or more propellers, and a generous supply of LEGO® pieces. Their first task is to simply build a basic structure for their robot with four design features: the motor, at least one propeller, the ability to connect and disconnect easily from the IR receiver case, and the sturdiness to remain intact in the water.

To test for durability, students are directed to drop each robot from a height of 6 inches onto a solid surface. If a single piece pops off, students must redesign the structure to be reinforced, usually with beams and pins rather than bricks.

Once all robots have passed the drop test, they are connected to their IR receiver cases and placed in the water. Students note how well they float and whether they are lopsided.

If so, they can use pieces of pool noodle foam as floats and large washers as weights to properly balance their robot.

Visual Programming. With the robots floating serenely in the water, the students grow eager to get them moving. Thus, the next phase begins—learning about the NXT and using it to power the motors.

Fortunately, sample programs are included on the NXT in order to demonstrate the capabilities of the various sensors. Students are guided through the operation of the programs to learn about the most important sensors and to get an idea of how they interact with the NXT.

At this point, students are ready to learn about programming. The NXT can be programmed using a variety of languages, such as C, Java, or Labview. However, the default programming interface is a custom, icon-based graphical environment called NXT-G. While this is a notable departure from text-based languages, it still manages to cover many of the same concepts, such as branching and loops. In fact, writing a program in NXT-G is surprisingly similar to constructing a flow control diagram. A sample program is shown in Figure 12.5.

Two programming lessons are presented, which give students just enough information to be able to complete the first mission. They learn how to get the NXT to read the sensors, make decisions, and send commands to the motors through the IR transmitter. Optional step-by-step screencasts for each lesson are provided on the WaterBotics® website so that instructors can show them to their students rather than lecture. Alternatively, if enough computers are available, students may use them directly to learn at their own pace.

Putting It All Together. Once the preparatory lessons are completed, the students are ready to get all of the various parts working together and enable their robot to swim for the first time (see Figure 12.6). It is up to them to construct a controller, program it, get it

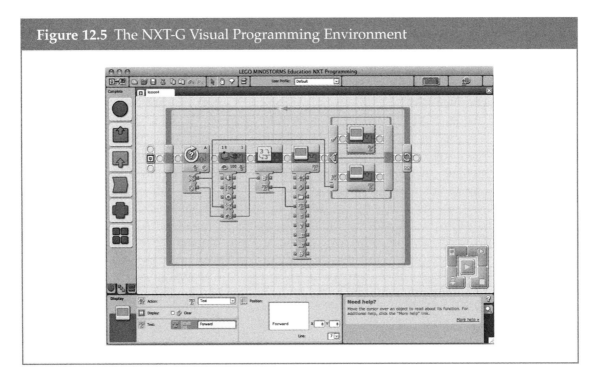

Figure 12.5 The NXT-G Visual Programming Environment

Image courtesy of Stevens Institute of Technology.

Figure 12.6 Creating a WaterBot® From Kit Materials

Image by Mark Dye, courtesy of Stevens Institute of Technology.

to communicate with their robot, and begin to direct the robot back and forth across the water. As needed, the instructor moves around the room to assist teams.

With their robots able to move satisfactorily, the students then work toward the basic objective of the mission. To simulate a drowning swimmer, each team is given a ping-pong ball that will be placed in the water. They are challenged to design a platform or holding bin on their robot to hold the "swimmer." Once ready, the robot will start from the end of the pool opposite the ping-pong ball and move forward toward it. When it gets close, a student can place the ball on the holding area of the robot, simulating the swimmer grabbing on. Finally, the robot is directed back to the start.

Students feel a sense of accomplishment as their robot performs its first successful rescue. However, since the motors don't spin quickly by default, most of the robots are initially quite slow. Students are challenged to make improvements. A "just-in-time" lesson introduces how gears can be used to change the rotation speed of the propellers and thus the speed of their robots. This lesson can take one of several forms: a mini-lab, a video, an illustrated handout, or even an enjoyable class activity in which the students act as the gears themselves.

Redesign, Achievements, and Culmination. After learning about gears, students are motivated to make the robots faster! This improvement aligns with the real-world context of the mission, since a faster robot would likely have a better chance of rescuing a drowning person. However, students typically have their own improvements in mind as well. They may want their robot to be able to rescue more than one person at a time or to be able to hold significantly more weight.

To give students flexibility in their robot designs and optimizations, they are presented with the idea of **achievements**. These are specific goals for their robots to accomplish within the context of the mission. For example, one achievement is to rescue a person within 20 seconds; another is to rescue five or more people in one trip. Each mission has seven or eight achievements for which students may strive, but only one must be accomplished for the mission to be considered a success.

With an understanding of the variety of modifications they can make, students are given ample unstructured time to go through numerous design-test-redesign cycles until their robots gain the characteristics they desire and complete the achievements they find relevant. The mission culminates in a friendly showcase in which students demonstrate their robots, describe their design goals, list the achievements they successfully completed, identify areas for improvement, and receive supportive feedback and encouragement from their peers.

Now that students have successfully designed a basic swimming robot, it's time to turn up the level of difficulty.

Mission 2: Clean Up!

The design challenge introduced in the second mission is for teams to take their current robots and—with the help of an additional motor and one or more extra propellers—modify them to enable two-dimensional movement (see Figure 12.7). The mission goal is to create a robot that can clean up floating pollution. Exactly how they accomplish this is up to them. The key idea is that there are multiple solutions to problems. The only requirement is that each robot must gather the pollutants, simulated by ping-pong balls, from the water's surface and return to its starting location.

ROV Rotation and a Formal Brainstorming Process. While there are numerous ways to get a robot to turn or move sideways, students often don't know where to begin. To help them get started, they are guided through a hands-on activity in which they physically model one of the most common techniques used to create ROV rotation. In this activity, pairs of students act as propellers on a robot. Each student is only allowed to move forward or backward, thus simulating each propeller's thrust capabilities. Students experiment with and observe the effect of different combinations of "thrust" on the "robot." This helps give students a gut-level instinct for how such a propeller system works and stimulates ideas for other approaches.

Before the students start to work on modifying their robots' propulsion systems, they are introduced to a more formal brainstorming process that encourages creativity and minimizes premature criticism. This technique is similar to one that has been used by professional design firms. It helps participants come up with ideas that they may not have previously considered, occasionally resulting in highly innovative designs that actually work.

At the end of the brainstorming session, each team will pick the solution they consider the best and begin to modify their robot to create the next prototype (see Figure 12.8). Once again, students conduct repeated drop tests and make modifications until their robot holds together. Then, after some testing for flotation and balance in the water, they are ready to work on a new version of their controller and program.

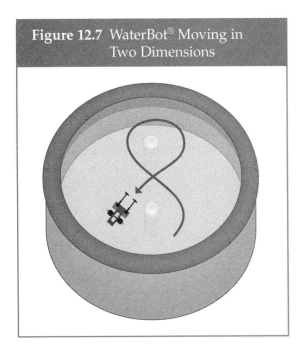

Figure 12.7 WaterBot® Moving in Two Dimensions

Image courtesy of Stevens Institute of Technology.

Figure 12.8 Students working on a more complex propulsion system for their WaterBot®

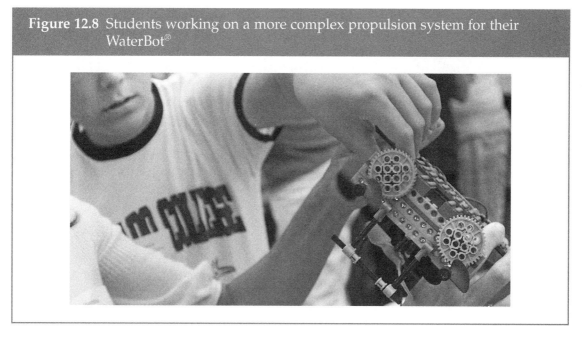

Image by Mark Dye, courtesy of Stevens Institute of Technology.

A New Programming Concept and a Tighter Design Cycle

Now students engage in another just-in-time programming lesson on the use of nested switch structures—similar to nested if/then statements in conventional languages—which will allow them to handle multiple sensors more efficiently. As with the previous programming lessons, there are multiple alternatives that the instructor may use—printed lessons, screencast walkthroughs, or self-paced study—to help students become comfortable with the new material.

After the lesson, teams work on their controller and program, and finally get the robot to make some initial runs through the challenge. They are then allowed some extra time for redesign, further testing, and final optimizations as they work toward completing one or more of the mission achievements.

Students tend to move rapidly through this mission, since they have become much more comfortable with how the subsystem components interact. They enjoy applying their newly acquired knowledge and skills. In short, this is the mission where they begin to "get it," and the enthusiasm is palpable. As their robots gain much more functionality, the students begin to see where the project is heading. By the end of this mission, they are eager to progress to the next stage.

This is fortunate, because the next mission is perhaps the most challenging one!

Mission 3: Mine Sweep!

After having successfully designed and built robots that move freely on the surface of the water, it's obvious to students that the next step is to give their robots the capability of diving under the water and exploring the depths. To this end, each team is given an additional

Figure 12.9 The rules become more complex as the WaterBot® dives under water

Image courtesy of Stevens Institute of Technology.

motor and a large propeller, and the official task is to enable their robot to go under the water and move around in a fully controllable manner (see Figure 12.9). The goal of this mission is to create a robot that can detonate or disable underwater mines, which are simulated by plastic cups resting on the bottom of the pool.

Buoyancy and Stability. Successfully completing this mission is actually more difficult than it sounds, because once fully submerged, the robots act in an almost completely unpredictable manner unless properly configured. Without understanding the science behind this behavior, this new outcome tends to be frustrating and demotivating to students. Therefore, before they begin to work on their robots, they are taken through a series of demonstrations and hands-on investigations to help them understand the critical concepts of buoyancy and stability.

Using a container of water, a few LEGO® pieces, some pool noodle foam chunks, and a few pennies, students build a small structure and practice achieving neutral buoyancy. When successful, their structure should hover in place when submerged, neither sinking to the bottom nor floating to the surface.

Students also practice achieving stability. Using the same small structure, they are now challenged to configure it so that when submerged, it is not only neutrally buoyant, but stable as well. This means the top of the structure should remain at the top, and upon being turned upside down, it should right itself.

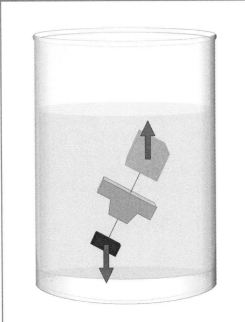
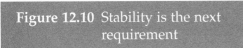

Figure 12.10 Stability is the next requirement

Image courtesy of Stevens Institute of Technology.

After the demonstrations and student investigation, the instructor may additionally choose to show some videos on these topics, distribute lesson handouts, or even run a buoyancy simulation. All of these extra features are available on the project website.

With a basic understanding of buoyancy and stability, teams are now given time to brainstorm ideas for getting their robot to move in three dimensions. Once again, they will use the more formalized brainstorming technique introduced in the previous mission.

Finally, it's time to build the prototype. The class is given a bit more time for this stage than in the other two missions, due to the difficulty of getting the buoyancy and stability right. While they're working, the instructor goes from team to team, helping those in need and testing each of the robots for good, strong stability.

Final Programming Lesson and Application of Concepts

Next, it's time for the final programming lesson. The topic is on "wires" as a means to pass data around in the graphical programming environment. Similar to how function parameters are used in text-based programming languages, the advantage of using wires is that they allow for more refined use of sensor data. For example, a typical application is to allow a rotation sensor to directly control a motor, such that the more the sensor is turned, the faster the motor spins. This can enable robots to have variable turning rates or fine-tuned vertical movement.

After the lesson, the students are given a generous amount of time to make adjustments to their controllers and programs, get their robots moving, redesign as needed, and try to complete one or more achievements (see Figure 12.11).

At this point, students have integrated the important science, engineering, and programming concepts into impressive ROVs that are capable of moving in three dimensions. All that's left to do is to give the robots the ability to manipulate the world around them.

Mission 4: Collect!

In this last mission, the students complete the final stage in the development of their ROVs. Their goal is to create a robot that can transport underwater samples to a collection bin. When finished, the robots are able to dive to the bottom of the pool, pick up one or more wiffle balls resting on the bottom of the pool, lift them up, carry them to an underwater bin, and drop them in (see Figure 12.12).

No More Instruction—Only Innovation. Students have gained knowledge, experience, and confidence, so they are now ready to work with greater independence. Therefore, rather than engage in guided learning activities, once the mission goals are explained to the students, they conduct one last brainstorming session to come up with their own ideas for a grabber or manipulator.

Next, they are given unstructured time to work on their robots, controllers, and programs as they try to complete one or more mission achievements. Most teams simply modify their existing robots, but a few decide to scrap everything and go back to the drawing board.

During this final mission, if they have not already done so, teams typically split to divide the labor—one subgroup to work on the robot and the other on the controller. This has the added benefit that students tend to instinctively choose to work on the aspects of the ROV that align with their own interests and talents, increasing their personal investment and motivation.

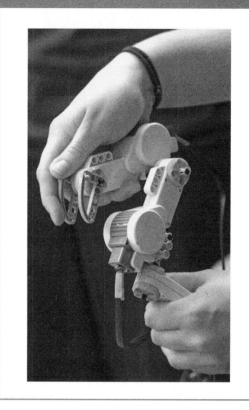

Figure 12.11 Students redesign their controller

Image by Mark Dye, courtesy of Stevens Institute of Technology.

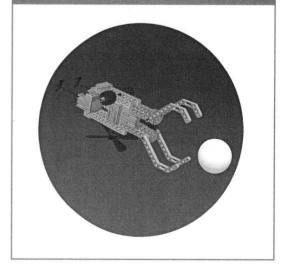

Figure 12.12 Retrieving an Object Underwater

Since this is the final chance for the students to show off their work (see Figure 12.13), instructors are encouraged to invite parents and family to attend the mission wrap-up, since their presence and encouragement can significantly add to the sense of pride students get from the project. And of course, their family members are invariably delighted and impressed to see what they have accomplished. It's a great high note to end on.

Connections to the Next Generation Science Standards

Although the WaterBotics® curriculum was developed before the Next Generation Science Standards (NGSS Lead States, 2013) were drafted, its focus on the engineering design process and iterative development aligns strongly with the emphasis on engineering called for in the NGSS. Additionally, since several fundamental physical science concepts are integral to WaterBotics® and are explicitly addressed within the curriculum, there are natural connections to the corresponding standards in the NGSS. Table 12.1 lists the engineering and physical science standards that are addressed by WaterBotics® and the connections to project activities and practices.

Connections to NGSS Engineering Design Core Ideas

WaterBotics® aligns well with the performance expectations in the NGSS, but it connects even more explicitly to the Engineering Design Disciplinary Core Ideas that

Figure 12.13 Carrying Out the Final Mission

Image courtesy of Stevens Institute of Technology.

Table 12.1 WaterBotics® Connections to NGSS: MS.Engineering Design

NGSS Standard	WaterBotics® Connections
MS-ETS1–1. Define the criteria and constraints of a design problem with sufficient precision to ensure a successful solution, taking into account relevant scientific principles and potential impacts on people and the natural environment that may limit possible solutions.	Each of the missions presents a design problem with clear constraints, such as the number of motors allowed, whether the robots must remain on the surface of the water, and the actual tasks that must be accomplished. Key science principles that are essential for each robot's success are either taught explicitly, demonstrated, or experimented with in the context of a separate hands-on activity.
MS-ETS1–2. Evaluate competing design solutions using a systematic process to determine how well they meet the criteria and constraints of the problem.	Students are encouraged to observe the robots from other groups and compare them to the functionality of their robots. At the end of each mission, students are encouraged to discuss the strengths and weaknesses of their designs as well as comment on those of other groups. Typical metrics for comparison are speed, maneuverability, and innovation.
MS-ETS1–3. Analyze data from tests to determine similarities and differences among several design solutions to identify the best characteristics of each that can be combined into a new solution to better meet the criteria for success.	The most significant piece of data in each mission is the time it takes for a robot to complete the mission's main challenge. When a robot is first able to complete the challenge, it is timed, and this value serves as a baseline. After each modification to the robot, it is then timed again to determine whether the redesign was effective. Other data used in the evaluation of design changes are less formal but just as important, such as the perceived maneuverability of the robot, the ease of use of the controller, and the consistency of the robot's performance.
MS-ETS1–4. Develop a model to generate data for iterative testing and modification of a proposed object, tool, or process such that an optimal design can be achieved.	The core design materials are LEGO® pieces, which allow students to build functional prototypes that can be used immediately for testing and modified directly. This allows for a tight design-test-redesign cycle, and typically results in rapid improvement of a robot's design and functionality. At the end of the project, the final LEGO® robot may in turn serve as the model for a more advanced underwater robot made of more durable materials and used in a real-world environment, such as a full-sized swimming pool or lake.
MS-PS2–1. Apply Newton's Third Law to design a solution to a problem involving the motion of two colliding objects.	Newton's Third Law is explicitly discussed in connection with how the flow of the water caused by the propellers causes propulsion and makes the robot move in the opposite direction.

(Continued)

Table 12.1 (Continued)	
NGSS Standard	**WaterBotics® Connections**
	Also explored is how the robot's motion is impeded when the flow of water is backward, causing it to collide with the robot. Various graphic illustrations and video demonstrations are used to reinforce this concept and help students plan solutions to address the problem.
MS-PS2–2. Plan an investigation to provide evidence that the change in an object's motion depends on the sum of the forces on the object and the mass of the object.	While this is not formally addressed in the WaterBotics® curriculum, students are exposed to this concept in practice since they observe that more massive robots tend to move more slowly. This becomes especially apparent in the later missions, as the robots grow in size and mass. The effect of the sum of forces on an object is observed when the flow of water from the propellers hits the back of the robot, reducing its motion. And once two propellers are used to move the robot in two dimensions, students observe how the combination of forces affects a robot's movement and rotation.

inform those standards. As a reminder, there are three middle school Disciplinary Core Ideas:

- ETS1.A: Defining and Delimiting Engineering Problems
- ETS1.B: Developing Possible Solutions
- ETS1.C: Optimizing the Design Solution

This is exactly the process that is followed in each of the four missions. Therefore, in participating in a WaterBotics® project, students are not only introduced to these ideas, they are taken fully through their implementation a total of four times. As a result of this experience, it is very likely that students will not only understand the engineering design process, but also internalize it as a successful approach to creating innovative technology.

Additional Physical Science Connections Outside of NGSS

In addition to the physical science connections to the NGSS, WaterBotics® covers several other important concepts:

- Gears and Gear Ratios
- Buoyant Force Versus Gravity
- Positive, Negative, and Neutral Buoyancy
- Stability Under the Water
- Center of Mass, Torque, and Rotational Motion

Although these concepts are not explicitly addressed in the NGSS, they may help to determine which types of classes WaterBotics® might fit into as a project-based enhancement activity or the target audience to which it would appeal if implemented during a summer camp. For example, it could help to enhance a classroom segment on the mechanics of water, or it could serve as an outreach activity for an organization that is concerned with marine science promotion, such as an aquarium or science museum.

Educator Supports and Recommended Background Knowledge

While WaterBotics® provides a rich and compelling experience for students, due to its numerous moving parts and multidisciplinary concepts it can be a complex project to set up and implement. For that reason, the curriculum includes a comprehensive and diverse collection of support materials in a variety of formats.

One of the first chapters in the WaterBotics® curriculum is dedicated to high-level planning, including timing and scheduling requirements, equipment needs, location and workspace arrangement, and appropriate staffing levels and training. This information can also help educators decide when to run a project and which environments would be most effective.

The following chapter deals entirely with equipment and technology setup and installation. Using clear explanations and an abundance of photos and graphic illustrations, instructors are shown how to assemble and test the IR receiver cases, set up the underwater environment, and install all the required software.

The next several chapters cover the project missions. Within each mission chapter, detailed activity/lesson plans are provided. These plans list time estimates for preparation and implementation, equipment needs, setup instructions, and a step-by-step activity walkthrough. Heavily illustrated student handouts accompany the science and programming lessons so that students may either follow along or learn on their own, depending on instructor preference.

The final two chapters contain all of the student handouts as well as extra content for instructors, such as optional lessons, inventorying advice, and troubleshooting tips.

In addition to the curriculum, the WaterBotics® website contains numerous support materials:

- Screencasts that walk through the programming lessons can be used in conjunction with the lessons themselves or as a replacement.
- Videos demonstrating the central physical science concepts can be used by instructors to aid them in creating their own live demonstrations, or they may simply be shown to students directly.
- Sample programs are provided for the missions so that if students get stuck and the instructor is unable to help them progress, they can look over an appropriate sample program to get ideas for potential solutions, or they can even use the program as the basis for a new attempt.
- An interactive buoyancy simulation can be used to explore how the buoyant force and gravity combine to produce positive, neutral, or negative buoyancy.
- Optional online surveys, logs, and assessments that were used for the purposes of the most recent research grant are available for instructors to use with their students.

All of the above resources can be managed via a simple course management system that allows educators to set up classes, add students, assign surveys and evaluations, upload images, and enable resources for students to access at the appropriate time.

Although WaterBotics® contains a significant amount of instructor and student support materials, it is recommended that instructors have some minimal experience with robotics, engineering, programming, or the physical science concepts involved in the project. While educators without this background have successfully implemented the program, the learning curve is reduced significantly as the experience level of the educator rises.

Formal Versus Informal Learning Environments

WaterBotics® was originally designed to be implemented in formal classroom environments, such as regular in-school, science or technology graded courses. However, as the curriculum evolved, adjustments were made and material added so that it could also be used within informal, extracurricular settings, such as summer camps or after-school programs. Each of these educational environments presents different opportunities and challenges, and it is worth taking a moment to consider how WaterBotics® best fits into each.

Formal Implementation. WaterBotics® has four goals when used as a component of formal courses. First, we strive to promote engagement through compelling, hands-on learning activities. Second, we want learning that is memorable, simultaneously deepening students' understanding of core science and engineering ideas and practices. Third, we hope to spark interest in science and engineering careers. Fourth, we want to bolster students' self-confidence in science and engineering, especially among those who come from backgrounds traditionally underrepresented in those disciplines.

Since these are ambitious but achievable goals, it is important to consider the challenges and limitations inherent in an in-school environment up front.

Probably the most significant factor to consider is the ability to set up a pool either within the classroom or somewhere nearby. The pool setup that is recommended for most implementations is a 6.5-foot diameter kiddie pool tucked into a slightly larger kiddie pool and filled with about 150 gallons of water. The second pool is there to catch minor spills and to act as a safeguard in case the inner pool develops a leak (see Figure 12.14). This setup has proven to be very effective at preventing water from going where it shouldn't.

But even with these safeguards, some schools will simply not allow a pool in a classroom, especially one with computers or other sensitive equipment. Therefore, other alternatives are presented in the curriculum, such as using small water-filled bins to do low-level testing, or setting up a pool in another area of the school that can accommodate it.

Another issue to consider is the amount of time required for implementation. As stated earlier, a full run of WaterBotics® takes about 20–26 hours. For those with limited instructional time, one solution is to cut out one or more missions. Although this will reduce the effectiveness of the project, it may be better to have a partial implementation rather than none at all.

However, implementation in a formal environment offers significant opportunities and advantages.

When the WaterBotics® is integrated into a core, required course, students with little to no previous experience or interest in robotics or engineering—who might pass up voluntary programs—gain valuable knowledge, skills, and self-confidence. The natural connections to science and engineering and the opportunities to build on them help answer the perennial student question, "Why do I need to learn this?" Additionally, students from all represented demographic groups in the school participate—not just those from a self-selected group.

Running WaterBotics® in an elective course also has some advantages. The self-selection process can help to ensure high initial enthusiasm, greater investment in optimization, and a more sophisticated level of achievement—albeit for the volunteer participants. Elective courses also frequently permit greater flexibility, permitting the instructor to utilize the full range of potential extension activities within the curriculum.

Informal Implementation. In an informal environment, such as a summer camp or after-school project, the primary goal of WaterBotics® is usually to generate enthusiasm and self-confidence, and to instill an interest in robotics, engineering, and/or science. While there may be a desire to have students learn specific concepts, there are usually no high-pressure measurements taken, such as grades or evaluations.

As with formal environments, the pool setup can be a challenge. However, since educators in informal settings often have more control over or selection of their environment, the pool is usually less of an issue, and more often than not the recommended pool setup described earlier can be used. Some locations will have restrictions, though, so this needs to be considered.

Figure 12.14 Students test their design in a small pool within a larger pool

Image by Mark Dye, courtesy of Stevens Institute of Technology.

Another advantage of informal projects is that there are typically fewer time constraints, which allows for the curriculum to be fully implemented. This is especially true for a week-long summer camp, in which daily sessions of five to six hours each easily provides enough time for the students to complete all four missions.

Informal programs, especially camps, can be tailored to attract participants from specific demographics. For example, it is common to have camps exclusively for girls or ones that provide scholarships for students from low-income families. By tailoring the audience and picking an appropriate theme, it is possible to attract youth who may be typically hard to reach for a robotics program.

A final consideration for informal projects, especially those that run for long hours, is that WaterBotics® —and really, any complex project—can prove to be overwhelming and intense. To address this concern, the curriculum contains advice on when to use breaks, and it provides examples of team-building or other social activities that are designed to allow students to release some pressure and get to know one another better.

Future Improvements

WaterBotics® is a research-based and well-tested curriculum. It has been used extensively with middle and high school students nationwide, both in formal classroom environments and in informal education settings. In response to growing interest by educators of elementary students, Stevens is currently developing a "lite" version of WaterBotics® that may be used with younger-aged students or, alternatively, with older students in situations where time is more limited. The lite version will keep much of the engineering and science content but remove some of the programming components.

A new website component—the WaterBotics® Virtual Event Showcase (WAVES)—was pilot-tested during the 2013–2014 school year. This application allows participants to upload videos of their robots to YouTube, TeacherTube, or Facebook, and then link the videos within the WaterBotics® website so they may be viewed by students from other project locations. Each video has simple encouragement badges that can be awarded—such as "Like," "Creative," or "Funny"— to provide positive feedback, recognition, and motivation. The videos are searchable by region, keyword, or badges to encourage both teachers and students to explore.

Ultimately, WAVES will result in a compelling collection of videos that demonstrate the range of innovation that is possible in a WaterBotics® project.

Conclusion

WaterBotics® is a unique curriculum developed by the Center for Innovation in Engineering in Science Education at Stevens Institute of Technology that provides students with an exciting exploration of the content-rich field of underwater robotics. Through two National Science Foundation grants, it has been shown to significantly increase students' interest and engagement in STEM learning and careers.

The core strengths of WaterBotics® are its strong focus on the engineering design process; the tight integration of science, engineering, and technology concepts; the fundamental appeal and approachability of LEGO® materials, and the utilization of a unique and fascinating environment. Although it was developed before the release of the NGSS, it has several strong alignments, especially with the engineering standards. Educators looking to put together a serious but fun project that addresses important parts of these new standards would be well-served by WaterBotics®.

References

NGSS Lead States. (2013). *Next generation science standards: For states, by states. Volume 1: The standards.* Washington, DC: National Academies Press.

13

Engineering Now

Peter Y. Wong, PhD
National Center for Technological Literacy
Museum of Science, Boston, Massachusetts

Figure 13.1 Student Balances Frame on Blimp

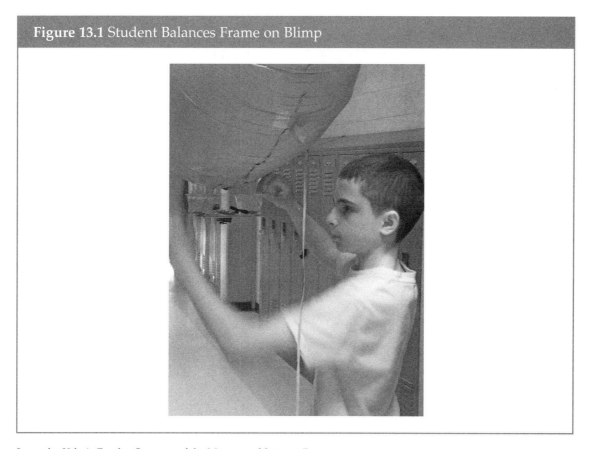

Image by Valerie Franks. Courtesy of the Museum of Science, Boston.

Engineering Now is a series of supplemental engineering units that can be used throughout Grades 6–8 by science and technology teachers. Each unit has a technology theme, kicks off with a WGBH *Design Squad* video, has hands-on and team-based activities (see Figure 13.1), and wraps up with career connections and a *LabTV* video. Students share their design solutions in the classroom, with museum staff, and on the web. Engineering Now is currently published by the Museum of Science, Boston.

Goals

Engineering Now is a new standards-based, classroom-tested curriculum. The main goal for the curriculum is to address the NGSS in the middle school classroom (Grades 6 to 8) while supporting Common Core State Standards in Mathematics and English Language Arts (NGA and CCSSO, 2010). Other important features of the curriculum include flexible integration into a broad range of middle school curricula, accessible professional development for teachers, and engaging design challenges for students.

Engineering Now consists of 10 units. Each unit has a design challenge related to modern technologies and industries and kicks off with a WGBH *Design Squad* video. A unit consists of eight lessons and spans approximately two weeks for classes with 50-minute periods. Teacher guides include reproducible pages for students, videos for classroom use, a physical kit with materials for hands-on activities, and ancillary materials to support customization.

Students work in teams and go through the engineering design process to solve a technical problem. The design solutions are creative and unique but also must meet quantitative criteria and constraints. Students are engaged with the video, hands-on materials, readings, and classroom discussions; document their work using sketches; and connect their design choices to research findings.

Teachers guide the students through their challenge and help them reflect on relevant science and engineering content and practices. Teachers are supported with background science and engineering material, teacher clipboard sheets with answers to questions that students are likely to bring up, and digital ancillary materials. At the end of the unit, the teachers point out potential careers in STEM related to the design challenge.

The first four units that will be released are related to familiar topics in the middle grades: Construction, Manufacturing, Transportation, and Bioengineering. The second set consists of Aerospace, Energy, Biomechanics, and Agricultural Engineering. Finally, Communication and Environmental Engineering will be rolled out.

Instructional Materials

Each unit consists of a teacher guide with black-line reproducible pages for students and teacher and a kit with physical resources for the design challenges. Each unit has eight lessons:

Lesson 1: Explore the Design Challenge

Lesson 2: Research One Science and/or Engineering Topic

Lesson 3: Research Another Science and/or Engineering Topic

Lesson 4: Brainstorm and Select Design

Lesson 5: Build and Test a Prototype

Lesson 6: Communicate and Critique

Lesson 7: Redesign and Test Solution

Lesson 8: Career Connections and Assessment

Teacher Pages: Each lesson features a summary, a vocabulary list, preparation tips, background information, and procedural information. Additional background information and sample questions with answers are provided in convenient, one-page Teacher Clipboard pages.

Student Activity Sheets: Following the teacher pages, you'll find the student activity sheets. They help facilitate collaboration within a team of students. Consider having teams create their own team names and use folders to hold their student activity sheets.

Optional Student Activity Sheets: Optional student activity sheets are included in some lessons to help extend or further explore the content. Further Investigation sheets help inform students' designs (and are found in Lessons 1–4). Making Connections sheets broaden students' understanding of topics covered (and are typically Lessons 5–8).

Cable Cars: Physical Science Meets Transportation Engineering

Students watch the *Design Squad* episode "Winner Takes All," which features two teams competing to create a new sled for a commercial retailer.

Lesson 1: Explore the Design Challenge. Students learn about the engineering design process by watching a *Design Squad* episode and completing student activity sheets. They define the problem explored in the unit: designing a cable car and cable car transportation system for the town of Piedmont.

Lesson 2: Research Vehicle Subsystems. Teams explore the subsystems in vehicles and modify a basic cable car design with various materials. They evaluate the changes in average speed and capacity.

Lesson 3: Research Cable Car System Design. Teams explore plans for a cable car transportation system using a mathematical model. They learn that the cable car design impacts their system route.

Lesson 4: Brainstorm and Select Design. Teams consider the criteria and constraints for designing a cable car and its system route. They brainstorm and share ideas for a cable car, and each team selects and sketches one cable car design. Students then complete a formative assessment.

Lesson 5: Build and Test a Cable Car System. Teams complete their designs and test their cable cars (see Figure 13.2). They then use their data to design a system route. Teams document their design solutions to prepare for their presentations.

Lesson 6: Communicate and Critique. Each team presents its cable car transportation system in a design review. Students evaluate each other's designs and look for ideas that might inform their own team's redesign.

Lesson 7: Redesign and Test Your Cable Car System. Teams make changes to their cable cars and/or system routes and test them to see if there are any improvements. Teams create a project summary report, which includes the process, their experiences, and final results.

Lesson 8: Career Connections and Assessment. Students watch a brief video about real-life engineers and discuss the problems they solve using transportation technologies. Students then complete a summative assessment.

Resilient Shelters: Earth Science Meets Construction Engineering

Students watch the *Design Squad* episode "DS Unplugged," which features two teams competing to make bridges without power tools.

Lesson 1: Explore the Design Challenge. Students learn about the engineering design process by watching a *Design Squad* episode and completing student activity sheets. They define the problem explored in the unit: designing a food shelter for a remote community to withstand a flood and protect the food supply.

Lesson 2: Research Materials for Building. Teams investigate how to build a food shelter using a paper template. They evaluate the resiliency of building materials based on wet and dry strength tests.

Lesson 3: Research Methods of Joining. Teams read about different designs for foundations. They compare and contrast different methods of joining materials.

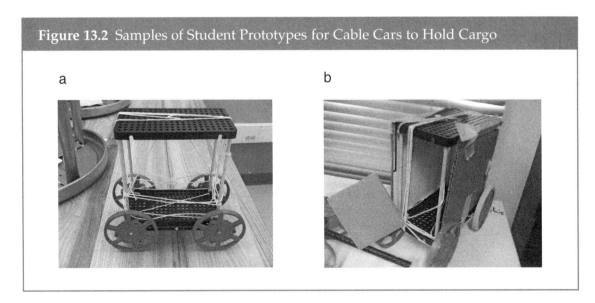

Figure 13.2 Samples of Student Prototypes for Cable Cars to Hold Cargo

a   b

Images by Jacob Milliron. Courtesy of the Museum of Science, Boston.

Lesson 4: Brainstorm and Select Design. Teams consider the criteria and constraints for designing a resilient food shelter. They brainstorm and share ideas for a shelter, and each team selects and sketches one design. Students complete a formative assessment.

Lesson 5: Build and Test Food Shelter. Teams complete their designs and test their food shelters in flooding conditions (see Figure 13.3). They document their design solution and prepare for a presentation.

Lesson 6: Communicate and Critique. Teams have a design review in which each team presents its food shelter. Students evaluate each design and look for ideas that might inform redesign.

Lesson 7: Redesign and Test Food Shelter. Teams make changes to their food shelter and test it to see if there are any improvements. Each team creates a summary report of its project including the process, the experience, and final results.

Lesson 8: Career Connections and Assessment. Students watch a brief video about real-life engineers and discuss the problems they solve using construction technologies. Students complete a summative assessment.

Pump Production: Physical Science Meets Manufacturing Engineering

Students watch the *Design Squad* episode "Pumped," which features two teams competing to make a pump for a water slide.

Lesson 1: Explore the Design Challenge. Students learn about the engineering design process by watching a *Design Squad* episode and completing student activity sheets. They

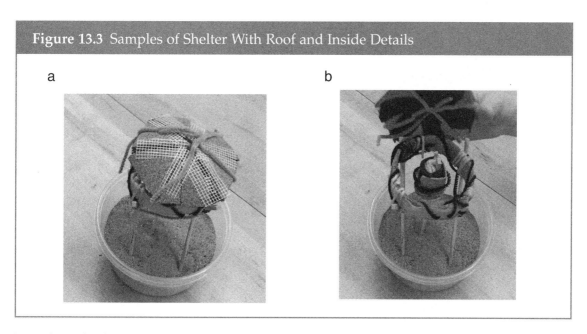

Figure 13.3 Samples of Shelter With Roof and Inside Details

a

b

Images by Jacob Milliron. Courtesy of the Museum of Science, Boston.

define the problem explored in the unit: designing a manufacturing process for pumps to be used in remote communities.

Lesson 2: Research Quality Control. Teams explore different methods for cutting standard-size gaskets for their piston pump designs. They calculate their method's productivity and efficiency.

Lesson 3: Research Materials and Joining. Teams construct different pistons using different materials and joining methods. They evaluate the materials' physical properties and give the pistons a "green score."

Lesson 4: Brainstorm and Select Design. Teams consider the criteria and constraints for designing a pump manufacturing process. They brainstorm and share ideas, and each team selects and sketches one design plan. Students complete a formative assessment.

Lesson 5: Build and Test a Pump Manufacturing Process. Teams complete their designs and test their pump manufacturing process according to their detailed sketches. Teams begin to create a presentation for communicating their designs.

Lesson 6: Communicate and Critique. Each team presents its process for manufacturing pumps. Students evaluate each team's design and look for ideas that might inform redesign.

Lesson 7: Redesign and Test the Pump Manufacturing Process. Team members work together to operate their piston pumps to produce a continuous flow. Teams make improvements and test their redesigns as needed. Teams create a summary report of their project including the process, their experience, and final results.

Lesson 8: Career Connections and Assessment. Students watch a brief video about real-life engineers and discuss the problems they solve using manufacturing technologies. Students complete a summative assessment.

Active Ingredient: Life Science Meets Bioengineering

Students watch the *Design Squad* profile "Dr. Howard Pryor and the Artificial Liver," which features a researcher who is a medical doctor and bioengineer.

Lesson 1: Explore the Design Challenge. Students are introduced to the field of bioengineering by watching a video and completing student activity sheets. They solve a mystery about why people attending a conference became ill by identifying evidence that supports a diagnosis. Students define the problem explored in the unit: designing a medicinal formulation to treat lactose intolerance.

Lesson 2: Research Digestion of Medicines. Teams investigate the pH of fluids that model digestive system conditions.

Lesson 3: Research Active and Other Ingredients. Teams investigate the components of a formulation. They compare the properties of two different active pharmaceutical ingredients (APIs), as well as the properties of various binders and disintegrants.

Lesson 4: Brainstorm and Select Design. Teams consider the specific criteria and constraints that must be met by their formulation designs. They brainstorm and share ideas for formulations based on their research, and each team selects two formulations to prototype. Each student completes a formative assessment.

Lesson 5: Build and Test Formulation. Teams prepare formulations to test (see Figure 13.4). They determine how well each formulation meets the performance criteria. Teams begin to create a presentation about their designs, which they will communicate to the class. Students complete a math assignment about mixing formulations.

Lesson 6: Communicate and Critique. The class hosts a design review in which all teams present their formulations. Students evaluate each team's designs and look for ideas that might inform redesign.

Lesson 7: Redesign and Test Your Formulation. Teams make changes to their formulations and test them to see if there are any improvements. Teams create a summary report of their project including the process, their experience, and final results.

Lesson 8: Career Connections and Assessment. Students watch a brief video about real-life engineers and discuss the problems they solve using biotechnologies. Students complete a summative assessment.

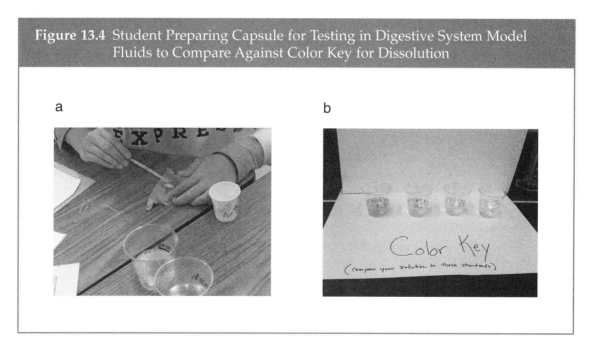

Figure 13.4 Student Preparing Capsule for Testing in Digestive System Model Fluids to Compare Against Color Key for Dissolution

Images by Lorraine Grosslight. Courtesy of the Museum of Science, Boston.

Instructional Model

The Importance of Teamwork. Each unit is designed so that there are six teams in a classroom. Four students per team are optimal with a class size of 24. But the activities can also be done with teams of five or even six students per team. Students are given specific guidelines for successful teamwork during the first lesson, and reminders are displayed prominently on a Teamwork Expectations Wall (see Figure 13.5). Students and teachers can add ideas to the wall as needed during the unit.

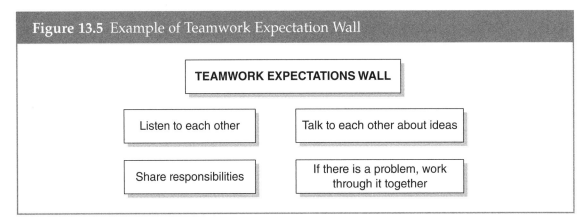

Figure 13.5 Example of Teamwork Expectation Wall

TEAMWORK EXPECTATIONS WALL

Listen to each other

Talk to each other about ideas

Share responsibilities

If there is a problem, work through it together

Image courtesy of the Museum of Science, Boston.

It is important to note that the design challenges are not competitions. Student teams need to meet criteria and constraints to solve a problem. The teams need to report their solutions and critique each other. They can then improve their designs based on the other teams' work as long as they cite their sources for changes. Yet, it is natural for students to have some competition in the classroom. So these design challenges can loosely be called "coopetition," where the teams help each other but also look forward to having a top-notch design solution.

Where does this course fit in the curriculum? Engineering Now is not intended to replace the science curriculum, but rather to complement it. Consequently, the units can be used in any sequence. Since the NGSS do not have grade-specific standards in the middle grades, the order in which science subjects are taught varies from state to state or even school to school. Suggestions are given for how best to pair an Engineering Now unit with a science unit. For example, the Cable Cars unit fits with a force and motion unit in science. Guidelines for coordinating Engineering Now units with the most common middle school science curricula are available. The curriculum is not grade specific, and teachers can adjust the content level for their class.

How can these units fit within the time available for science? One of the most important contributions of the NGSS is to eliminate some traditional science concepts so that more time can be spent enabling students to study topics in greater depth. To meet the new standards, teachers will be expected to eliminate certain topics in their curriculum that are not included in the new standards, making room for Engineering Now to provide the experiences that will enable their students to learn the remaining core concepts in greater depth.

Who should teach these units? Science teachers can use these units to supplement their science program to meet the engineering practices in the NGSS. These units can also be taught by technology teachers, or by a team of science and technology teachers working together. In some middle schools, where all of the teachers share the same student body, it is possible to use these units to coordinate the school curriculum so that each teacher can expand the unit within his or her own discipline. For example, a social studies teacher could complement the Cable Car unit by having students research the development of public transportation in San Francisco, while English teachers could have their students write essays about how San Francisco's cable cars changed daily living and business in the city at the end of the 19th century.

Connections to the NGSS and CCSS Standards

The curriculum was developed using a backward design process that begins with standards, enduring questions, and evidence of student achievement, followed by development and testing of focused student experiences (Wiggins & McTighe, 1998). Lessons were designed with the 5E instructional model (Bybee, 1997; Bybee & Landes, 1990).

Connections to NGSS. Although the curriculum has been under development for nearly five years, we have closely watched the release of Common Core State Standards in Mathematics and English Language Arts (NGA and CCSSO, 2010) and the *Framework for K–12 Science Education* (NRC, 2012), so that we have been able to adjust the curriculum to meet these standards before the first release of Engineering Now. Table 13.1 lists the connections between the first eight units to be released and performance expectations in the NGSS. In addition, Engineering Now provides examples of all of the crosscutting concepts in the NGSS.

Table 13.1 Connections Between Engineering Now and NGSS Performance Expectations

Performance Expectations From the NGSS	Resilient Shelters	Pump Production	Cable Cars	Active Ingredient	Sunflowers	Blimps	Waterwheels	Biomechanics
MS-ETS1–1. Define the criteria and constraints of a design problem with sufficient precision to ensure a successful solution, taking into account relevant scientific principles and potential impacts on people and the natural environment that may limit possible solutions.	✓	✓	✓	✓	✓	✓	✓	✓

(Continued)

Table 13.1 (Continued)

Performance Expectations From the NGSS	Resilient Shelters	Pump Production	Cable Cars	Active Ingredient	Sunflowers	Blimps	Waterwheels	Biomechanics
MS-ETS1–2. Evaluate competing design solutions using a systematic process to determine how well they meet the criteria and constraints of the problem.	✓	✓	✓	✓	✓	✓	✓	✓
MS-ETS1–3. Analyze data from tests to determine similarities and differences among several design solutions to identify the best characteristics of each that can be combined into a new solution to better meet the criteria for success.	✓	✓	✓	✓	✓	✓	✓	✓
MS-ETS1–4. Develop a model to generate data for iterative testing and modification of a proposed object, tool, or process such that an optimal design can be achieved.	✓	✓	✓	✓	✓	✓	✓	✓
MS-ESS3–2. Analyze and interpret data on natural hazards to forecast future catastrophic events and inform the development of technologies to mitigate their effects.	✓							
MS-ESS3–3. Apply scientific principles to design a method for monitoring and minimizing a human impact on the environment.		✓				✓		
MS-PS1–3. Gather and make sense of information to describe that synthetic materials come from natural resources and impact society.		✓						
MS-PS1–6. Undertake a design project to construct, test, and modify a device that either releases or absorbs thermal energy by chemical processes.					✓			
MS-PS2–1. Apply Newton's Third Law to design a solution to a problem involving the motion of two colliding objects.			✓					
MS-PS2–2. Plan an investigation to provide evidence that the change in an object's motion depends on the sum of the forces on the object and the mass of the object.		✓	✓			✓		✓

Performance Expectations From the NGSS	Resilient Shelters	Pump Production	Cable Cars	Active Ingredient	Sunflowers	Blimps	Waterwheels	Biomechanics
MS-PS3–1. Construct and interpret graphical displays of data to describe the relationships of kinetic energy to the mass of an object and to the speed of an object.			✓					
MS-PS3–3. Apply scientific principles to design, construct, and test a device that either minimizes or maximizes thermal energy transfer.					✓			
MS-PS3–5. Construct, use, and present arguments to support the claim that when the kinetic energy of an object changes, energy is transferred to or from the object.			✓				✓	
MS-LS1–3. Use argument supported by evidence for how the body is a system of interacting subsystems composed of groups of cells.				✓				✓
MS-LS4–4. Construct an explanation based on evidence that describes how genetic variations of traits in a population increase some individuals' probability of surviving and reproducing in a specific environment.				✓				

Connections to CCSS Mathematics Standards. Each unit also has explicit connections to common core mathematics standards at the sixth-grade level, and provides optional materials that engage students in using mathematics from the CCSSM at the seventh- and eighth-grade levels. For example, the Cable Cars unit engages students in developing the following mathematics skills.

CCSS.M.6.RP.A.3.d. Use ratio reasoning to convert measurement units; manipulate and transform units appropriately when multiplying or dividing quantities.

CCSS.M.6.EE.A.2.c. Evaluate expressions at specific values of their variables. Include expressions that arise from formulas used in real-world problems. Perform arithmetic operations, including those involving whole-number exponents, in the conventional order when there are no parentheses to specify a particular order (Order of Operations).

CCSS.M.7.RP.A.1. Compute unit rates associated with ratios of fractions, including ratios of lengths, areas, and other quantities measured in like or different units.

CCSS.M.7.G.A.1. Solve problems involving scale drawings of geometric figures, including computing actual lengths and areas from a scale drawing and reproducing a scale drawing at a different scale.

CCSS.M.8.EE.C.8. Analyze and solve pairs of simultaneous linear equations.

Connections to CCSS English Language Arts Standards. Engineering Now engages students in developing their English-language skills. The following Common Core State Standards in English Language Arts are emphasized in *every unit.*

CCSS.ELA.RST.6–8.3. Follow precisely a multistep procedure when carrying out experiments, taking measurements, or performing technical tasks.

CCSS.ELA.WHST.6–8.1. Write arguments to support claims with clear reasons and relevant evidence.

CCSS.ELA.SL.6–8.1. Engage effectively in a range of collaborative discussions (one-on-one, in groups, teacher-led) with diverse partners on grade topics, texts, and issues, building on others' ideas and expressing their own clearly.

CCSS.ELA.SL.7.4. Present claims and findings, emphasizing salient points in a focused, coherent manner with pertinent descriptions, facts, details, and examples; use appropriate eye contact, adequate volume, and clear pronunciation.

CCSS.ELA.SL.7.5. Include multimedia components and visual displays in presentations to clarify claims and findings and emphasize salient points.

Assessment

Formative Assessment. A number of tools are embedded in the instructional materials to help teachers assess student progress and adjust their instruction accordingly. Formative assessment tools include the following:

- Wrap-Up is a short series of questions that the teacher can use at the end of each lesson as a daily check on students' progress and to plan the next day's activities.
- A Team Design Rubric is given to the students in the first lesson to help them focus on the criteria, constraints of the task, and guidelines for effective teamwork and other skills so that students understand how their work is being evaluated.
- Student Activity Sheets ask students to sketch, read, calculate, and design, both to guide student work and to enable the teacher to view his or her students' thinking.
- Quiz Show is an activity included about halfway through the unit to assess students' mastery of the unit vocabulary.
- Self-Assessment is an opportunity for the students to reflect on their own progress. Students receive a copy of the Team Design Rubric in Lesson 1 so they can reflect on the extent to which they are accomplishing the expected learning.

Summative Assessment. Teachers can use the summative assessment tools provided during the last two lessons to measure their students' accomplishments of the unit goals. These include the following:

- Video Analysis in Lesson 7 provides an opportunity for the students to record the performance of their final design, enabling teams to review each other's designs, and providing evidence of learning from the teacher's perspective.
- Unit Test in Lesson 8 provides an indication of each student's mastery of the unit content. The questions in the test also provide students an opportunity to practice their writing skills. (Teachers may also use the unit test at the beginning of a unit for diagnostics, or to measure student learning with a pre-post comparison.)
- Technical Report in Lesson 8 is a written report by each student of his or her team's findings, including how well his or her team's design responded to the criteria and constraints of the challenge, as well as design improvements and possible impacts. This can help to assess student performance in English Language Arts writing across the curriculum.

Conclusion

The Next Generation Science Standards are being widely embraced for the vision that they project of students engaged in using science and mathematics to solve problems and meet human needs. But an exciting vision alone is not sufficient to transform what happens in the classroom. As teachers modify their curriculum plan for the year by eliminating certain topics no longer considered to be "core," they will be expected to add units to enable students to learn the science in greater depth, while providing practice in appropriate mathematics and language arts skills. Engineering Now units can help teachers meet that need.

Design Squad videos used to launch each Engineering Now unit provide an engaging context to get students excited about the activities to come. The well-designed and classroom-tested hands-on activities and ancillary digital materials provide the experiences that students need to learn to apply what they just learned in science, and to develop important teamwork skills that they will need as successful students and citizens. The materials also provide a number of tools for teachers to assess student learning throughout the unit that are embedded in the lessons, so that students are not overwhelmed with tests.

Most important, however, is what students will gain from these units. The design challenges are thoroughly engaging, so that there is no clear line between practicing concepts and skills and fun, creative team activities. And as a unit comes to a close, after experiencing the enjoyment of engineering activities and gaining confidence in their capabilities as designers, the students have opportunities to expand their horizons about possible careers that could provide a lifetime of satisfying and creative work in service to society.

References

Bybee, R. W. (1997). *Achieving scientific literacy: From purposes to practices.* Portsmouth, NH: Heinemann.

Bybee, R. W., & Landes, N. M. (1990). Science for life & living: An elementary school science program from Biological Sciences Curriculum Study. *American Biology Teacher, 52*(2), 92–98.

National Governors Association Center for Best Practices and Council of Chief State School Officers (NGA and CCSSO). (2010). *Common core state standards.* Washington, DC: Author.

National Research Council (NRC). (2012). *A framework for K–12 science education: Practices, crosscutting concepts, and core ideas*. Committee on a Conceptual Framework for New K–12 Science Education Standards. Board on Science Education, Division of Behavioral and Social Sciences and Education, National Research Council (NRC). Washington, DC: National Academies Press.

NGSS Lead States. (2013a). *Next generation science standards: For states, by states. Volume 1: The standards*. Washington, DC: National Academies Press.

NGSS Lead States. (2013b). *Next generation science standards: For states, by states. Volume 2: Appendices*. Washington, DC: National Academies Press.

Wiggins, G., & McTighe, J. (1998). *Understanding by design*. Alexandria, VA: ASCD.

14

Engineering by Design

An Integrative STEM Approach to Middle School

Barry N. Burke, Director
STEM Center for Teaching and Learning
International Technology and Engineering Educators Association
Gaithersburg, Maryland

Figure 14.1 EbD™ Students Analyzing Design Versus Constraints

Image by Aaron Gray, courtesy of ITEEA.

Imagine students walking through your door with an enthusiasm that soaks up every ounce of teaching you can provide. They are eager to learn every bit of information from you that will give them "the edge." They are inspired to innovate because they have connected to material they have learned in mathematics, science, English language arts, and their geography classes. Now they are applying those concepts in their engineering and technology class in a program called Engineering byDesign™. Opportunity is what these students see. Not just in this class, but by connecting the dots from all their classes, they are excited about school. They can see themselves in the future.

Chaos! That might be what some would call this classroom, while for others, it would be music to their ears. As the principal stops by to see what all the commotion is about, you find yourself smiling at the fact that the students in your classes are engaged in multiple activities simultaneously. Some are entering the day's engineering accomplishments and challenges into their Engineering Design Journal. Others are using software applications to design intricate solutions to today's problem, while still others are using research and data tools to find that special design that will make their team's solution stand out above the rest.

"The Engineering byDesign™ curriculum is built on the belief that the ingenuity of children is an untapped, unrealized potential that, when properly motivated, will lead to the next generation of engineers, designers, innovators, and technologists" (ITEEA, 2013). So what is this program? How can it work in my school? How much will it cost? Where can I get training? How can I measure student achievement and growth? Who else is using this program? Where can I find out more? The purpose of this chapter is to answer these questions.

Engineering byDesign™

The STEM±Center for Teaching and Learning™ (STEM±CTL)—the curriculum and professional development arm of the International Technology and Engineering Educators Association (ITEEA)—has developed EbD™ as a truly integrative and comprehensive standards-based STEM curriculum for Grades K–12 to enable all students to achieve engineering and technology literacy. EbD™ is built on the Common Core State Standards and the Standards for Technological Literacy (ITEEA). And as we'll show later in the chapter, it also has close connections with the Next Generation Science Standards (NGSS Lead States, 2013a, 2013b).

In EbD™, students learn concepts and principles in an authentic, problem-based, and project-based environment designed with a constructivist educational philosophy. Through an integrative STEM environment, EbD™ uses standards and benchmarks from science, mathematics, technology, and engineering and English language arts to help students understand the complexities of tomorrow.

Mission

We live in a technological world that requires much more from every individual than a basic ability to read, write, and perform simple arithmetic. Technology and engineering affect every aspect of our lives, from enabling citizens to perform routine tasks to requiring that they be able to make responsible, informed decisions that affect individuals, our society, and the environment. Understanding how technology can improve or endanger the natural world, and how engineering our world can make it better or worse, is a key attribute for responsible citizens of the 21st century.

> Technology is the modification of the natural environment in order to satisfy perceived human needs and wants. (ITEA, 2000, p. 7)

While students have been using technology since they were old enough to eat or walk, many are not aware of what technology really is and how technology and engineering modify the natural world to make life better (or worse). Consequently, the EbD™ middle school program was developed with the idea that students need to understand technology in order to make informed decisions about their use, and to learn how to analyze technologies and create and modify technologies to solve problems they consider to be relevant to their lives.

Vision

Students who complete the EbD™ courses will have the knowledge and abilities to help them become informed, successful citizens; be able to make sense of the world in which they live; and be wise consumers, advocates, and change agents of the technological resources in their own community. Those who are inspired to pursue engineering and technology as a career will be prepared to engage and succeed in advanced technological study in the high school years and beyond.

Organizing Principles

The program is organized around the following 10 principles:

1. Engineering through design improves life.
2. Technology and engineering have affected and continue to affect everyday life.
3. Technology drives invention and innovation and is a thinking and doing process.
4. Technologies are combined to make technological systems.
5. Technology creates issues and impacts that change the way people live and interact.
6. Engineering and technology are the basis for improving on the past and creating the future.
7. Technology solves problems.
8. Technology and engineering use inquiry, design, and systems thinking to produce solutions.
9. Technological and engineering design is a process used to develop solutions for human wants and needs.
10. Technological applications create the designed world.

The Engineering byDesign™ K–12 Core Sequence

The EbD™ core sequence begins at kindergarten and is articulated through Grade 12 with a capstone course (Engineering Design).

Through its work with postsecondary institutions, the STEM±CTL/EbD™ has articulated for credit with engineering programs in Maryland. Work is currently underway to articulate the program with engineering programs in other states during 2014–2015. The core program is shown in Table 14.1.

Table 14.1 The EbD™ K–12 Core Sequence

Elementary Materials		
K–2	*EbD*-TEEMS™	1 to 6 weeks
3–6	*EbD*-TEEMS™ and I³	1 to 6 weeks
Middle School Courses		
6	Exploring Technology	18 weeks
7	Invention and Innovation	18 weeks
8	Technological Systems	18 weeks
High School Courses		
9	Foundations of Technology	36 weeks
10–12	Technology and Society	36 weeks
10–12	Technological Design	36 weeks
11–12	Advanced Design Applications	36 weeks
11–12	Advanced Technological Applications	36 weeks
11–12	Engineering Design (Capstone Course)	36 weeks

Information about the EbD™ is available at www.engineeringbydesign.org. Schools in EbD™ Consortium states can become a part of the EbD-Network™ to access the full benefits of the entire EbD™ program and learning community. Further information on the Consortium is included later in the chapter.

The Middle School Course Sequence

The middle school program takes students from an understanding of what technology "is" to how engineers and innovators create systems to make life better. Key enduring understandings and big ideas in the middle school center around exploration, innovation, and systems.

Grade 6: Exploring Technology (18 Weeks)

Exploring Technology builds on K–5 experiences and develops a student's understanding of the scope of technology and its impacts on society. Students learn about the core concepts of technology, including the universal systems model, and about the various approaches to solving problems, including engineering design and experimentation.

Students participate in engineering design activities in which they learn about the iterative nature of technological design and problem-solving processes. They have firsthand experience in how criteria, constraints, and processes affect designs (see Figure 14.1). They learn about brainstorming, visualizing, modeling, constructing, testing, experimenting, and refining designs (see Figure 14.2). Students also develop skills in researching information, recording their work in an Engineering Design Journal, and communicating design information and recording their ideas and results. Students learn how technology, innovation, design, and engineering interrelate and are interdependent.

Figure 14.2 Students Constructing a Redesign of a Robotic Device

Image courtesy of ITEEA.

Grade 7: Invention and Innovation (18 weeks)

In seventh grade, students investigate the history of invention and innovation and how changes in technology have shaped the world—in many cases for good, but in other cases "not so good." A central theme is to identify human wants and needs and how to modify existing technologies to create spin-offs that better meet these wants and needs. Emphasis is placed on design processes and the core concepts of technology and engineering, including engineering design and experimentation. Key ideas include why innovation is important, how the natural world influences inventions, and why that is important. Students learn how technology, innovation, design, and engineering interrelate and are interdependent.

Students apply their creativity in the invention and innovation of new products, processes, or systems, noting how criteria, constraints, and processes affect designs. Students engage in brainstorming, visualizing, modeling, constructing, testing, experimenting, and refining designs at a more sophisticated level than in sixth grade. Students also further develop their skills in searching for information and maintaining Engineering Design Journals, emulating the way inventors and innovators use design journals.

Grade 8: Technological Systems (18 Weeks)

In the Technological Systems course, students learn how systems work together to solve problems and capture opportunities. A system can be as small as two components working together (a technical system at the device level) or can contain millions of interacting devices (a user system at the network level). We often break down macro systems into less complicated micro systems in order to understand the entire system better. Technology is becoming more integrated, and systems are becoming more and more dependent upon each other. Electronic systems are interacting with biological systems as humans use more and more monitoring devices for medical reasons. Electrical systems are interacting with mechanical and fluid power systems as manufacturing establishments become more automated. This course gives students a general background on the different types of systems but concentrates primarily on the connections between these systems and their impacts as viewed through the lenses of culture, society, economics, and the environment.

Students also engage in engineering design with emphasis on developing a rationale for a given design that takes into account the pros and cons of a design and community acceptance for new technologies. Students research and use data tools to evaluate technology systems with respect to their impacts on the environment, human wants and needs, and global demand and acceptance (see Figure 14.3). Engineering Design Journals play an important role in the development of a student's knowledge and understanding of how core technologies evolve to become technology systems.

As a capstone middle school course, Technological Systems provides the foundation for future studies in a high school technology education sequence.

Curriculum Development

Engineering byDesign™ was created in 2004 as a standards-based instructional model for use by technology and engineering educators. The courses were developed using a backwards design process (Wiggins & McTighe, 1998) that begins with standards and the evidence that students would need to demonstrate to show that the standards are met, followed by the development of activities that provide the experiences students need to achieve the standards.

We distinguish this standards-based approach versus a standards-reflective method. Standards-reflective refers to materials that are already developed and then are crosswalked after the standards and benchmarks are identified—making the activity fit the standards rather than starting with the standards and developing the activity to ensure that students can meet them. To be standards-based, teams of technology and engineering, science, and mathematics authors were engaged to develop the materials, and were charged with considering the standards first.

The process followed by the development team, using backwards design and taking into account the mission, vision, and organizing principles, is shown in Figure 14.4.

Figure 14.3 Student presents research on a curling iron system

Image by Aaron Gray. Courtesy of ITEEA.

Since 2004, the STEM Center for Teaching and Learning™ has evolved from a focus on science and technology to one that focuses on integrative STEM. New materials being developed for EbD™ courses, including course modifications, will continue to follow a backwards design process, using the current standards, including the Next Generation Science Standards (NGSS Lead States, 2013a) and the Common Core State Standards (NGA and CCSSO, 2010) as well as the Standards for Technological Literacy (ITEA, 2000, 2007).

Teacher Guides

All of the EbD™ middle school courses are structured to have units of instruction and several lessons within each unit. Each lesson is written in the format of a modified 5-E Instructional Model (Bybee, 1997; Bybee & Landes, 1990). As described in the teacher guides, each unit consists of the following:

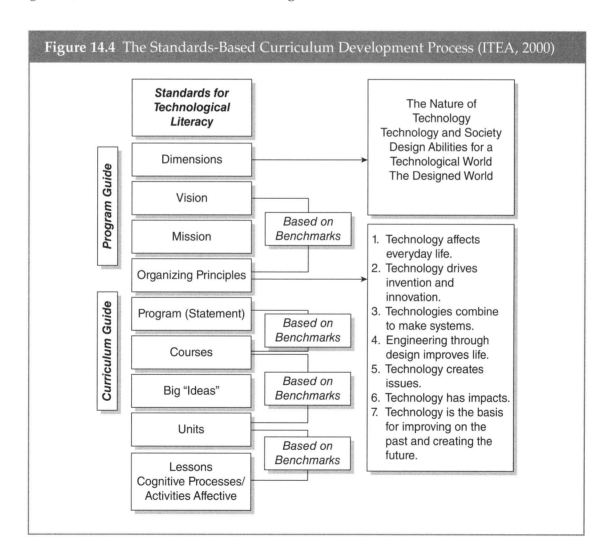

Figure 14.4 The Standards-Based Curriculum Development Process (ITEA, 2000)

1. Unit Overview
2. Lesson Overview
   a. Big Idea
   b. Purpose of Lesson
   c. Lesson Duration
   d. Required Knowledge/Skills
   e. Snapshot of What the Lesson Will Accomplish
   f. Standards and Benchmarks
   g. Objectives
   h. Formative Assessment
   i. Resources
   j. 5E Lesson Plan
   k. Lesson Prep
   l. Supporting Files

Engineering Design Journals as Tools

STEM Engineering Design Journals (EDJs) are notebooks maintained by the students that can help them develop, practice, and refine their understanding of STEM concepts, while also enhancing students' reading, writing, mathematics, science, and communication skills. As teachers involve students in inquiry-based science and engineering design investigations, the need to communicate learning and understanding has never been more important. If students are encouraged to communicate their understanding of concepts through EDJ writings, these journals can be an effective strategy to help students learn the integrative nature of the content. Research has shown that STEM writing may also be a way for students to strengthen their language skills as they develop an understanding of the world around them (Hargrove & Nesbit, 2003).

The students are encouraged to use their EDJs as scientists and engineers would: before, during, and after all investigations. The EDJs are a place where students formulate and record questions; make predictions; record data, procedures, and results; compose reflections; and communicate their findings. Most importantly, EDJs provide both a place for students to record new concepts they have learned and a valuable service for both teachers and students (Sea Grant Alaska, 2012).

From the teacher's point of view, Engineering Design Journals do the following:

1. Provide feedback to the teacher regarding the lessons/activities in which the students are engaging, yielding formative assessment information to help guide instruction

2. Provide insights into students' thinking and misconceptions, and their procedural and conceptual understanding

3. Support differentiated instruction, so the teacher can structure the class so that students can work at their own level

4. Provide evidence of learning

5. Provide a record of growth over time

6. Engage students in meaningful, purposeful, and authentic tasks

7. Offer a convenient forum for teachers to provide feedback to students to help them improve their performance or develop deeper understanding

From the student's point of view, Engineering Design Journals do the following:

1. Provide a thinking tool

2. Assist in organization

3. Enhance literacy skills

4. Help make sense of observations and investigations

5. Provide a place to keep vocabulary words

6. Illustrate how scientists, engineers, and technicians in the field organize and document information and observations

7. Help develop writing skills

8. Increase communication skills

9. Help develop understanding of scientific (inquiry) and engineering (design) processes

Professional Development

Teachers are encouraged (but not required) to participate in summer institutes. These professional development opportunities are available each summer in states around the country for a minimal fee. Institutes are typically five days in length and prepare teachers to return to their classrooms and implement the curriculum. Additionally, teachers are provided with strategies for working with colleagues in their school to fully discover the power of the EbD-STEM initiative. For more information about the most recent summer professional development opportunities, visit www.iteea.org/EbD/PD/.

Pre- and post-surveys are given at each workshop, and participant comments provide insight into various aspects of the program. Some of the quotes deal with the interactive nature of the curriculum—"EbD curriculum put the E in Engaging"—while others focus on the implementation model— "EbD places STEM at the fingertips of America's students."

Connections to NGSS

Why are connections to standards important? Many times as educators, we think about the coolest, most innovative teaching strategy and we build our content around it. That is great if you are teaching in the Julie Andrews School of "My Favorite Stuff." (I'll teach a few of my favorite activities this year!) But you are not! You are teaching to standards, and your students are expected to meet these standards before they leave your class. Your students are expected to achieve gains from the time they enter your door until the day they leave. Using standards to create curriculum takes the "teaching to standards" out of play. Because the standards are used to develop the curricula from the outset, what you get as a teacher is tried-and-true units and lessons that help children to construct learning based on their prior knowledge. What they "do" helps to solidify understanding. That is why EbD™ uses the backwards design process when developing its materials (Wiggins & McTighe, 1998).

In April 2013, when the NGSS were released, many rushed to align their work with the new standards. The STEM Center for Teaching and Learning™ took a different approach to ensure the standards-based theme follows with NGSS as it has with the Common Core State Standards and the Standards for Technological Literacy (STL). The Center's approach is to do a careful and considered review of the new standards and modify or develop new instructional materials that are fully aligned with the new standards.

During this transition period, while materials are being modified and new materials developed that are fully aligned with the NGSS, as illustrated in Table 14.2, the current materials can be used since they are consistent with several of the core ideas, science and engineering practices, and crosscutting concepts in the NGSS.

Table 14.2 Connections of Engineering byDesign™ to the NGSS

Next Generation Science Standards (NGSS) Performance expectations are quotes from NGSS Lead States (2013a), and appendices are from NGSS Lead States (2013b).	Exploring Technology	Invention and Innovation	Technological Systems
MS-LS2–3. Develop a model to describe the cycling of matter and flow of energy among living and nonliving parts of an ecosystem.	✓	✓	
MS-LS2–4. Construct an argument supported by empirical evidence that changes to physical or biological components of an ecosystem affect populations.	✓	✓	✓
MS-LS2–2. Construct an explanation that predicts patterns of interactions among organisms across multiple ecosystems.	✓	✓	
MS-LS2–5. Evaluate competing design solutions for maintaining biodiversity and ecosystem services.	✓	✓	
MS-ESS1–1. Develop and use a model of the Earth-sun-moon system to describe the cyclic pattern of lunar phases, eclipses of the sun and moon, and seasons.	✓	✓	
MS-ESS1–3. Analyze and interpret data to determine scale properties of objects in the solar system.	✓	✓	
MS-ESS3–2. Analyze and interpret data on natural hazards to forecast future catastrophic events and inform the development of technologies to mitigate their efforts.	✓	✓	
MS-ESS3–3. Apply scientific principles to design a method for monitoring and minimizing a human impact on the environment.	✓	✓	✓

Next Generation Science Standards (NGSS) Performance expectations are quotes from NGSS Lead States (2013a), and appendices are from NGSS Lead States (2013b).	Exploring Technology	Invention and Innovation	Technological Systems
MS-ESS3–4. Construct an argument supported by evidence for how increases in human populations and per-capita consumption of natural resources impact Earth's systems.	✓	✓	
MS-ETS1–1. Define the criteria and constraints of a design problem with sufficient precision to ensure a successful solution, taking into account relevant scientific principles and potential impacts on people and the natural environment that may limit possible solutions.	✓	✓	✓
MS-ETS1–2. Evaluate competing design solutions using a systematic process to determine how well they meet the criteria and constraints of the problem.	✓	✓	✓
MS-ETS1–3. Analyze data from tests to determine similarities and differences among several design solutions to identify the best characteristics of each that can be combined into a new solution to better meet the criteria for success.	✓	✓	✓
MS-ETS1–4. Develop a model to generate data for iterative testing and modification of a proposed object, tool, or process such that an optimal design can be achieved.	✓	✓	✓
Science and Engineering Practices (from Appendix F) 1. Asking questions (for science) and defining problems (for engineering) 2. Developing and using models 3. Planning and carrying out investigations 4. Analyzing and interpreting data 5. Using mathematics and computational thinking 6. Constructing explanations (for science) and designing solutions (for engineering) 7. Engaging in argument from evidence 8. Obtaining, evaluating, and communicating information	✓	✓	✓
Crosscutting Concepts (from Appendix G) *Systems and system models:* Defining the system under study—specifying its boundaries and making explicit a model of that system—provides tools for understanding and testing ideas that apply to science and engineering.		✓	✓
Influence of Science, Engineering and Technology on Society and the Natural World (from Appendix J): Scientific discoveries and technological decisions affect human society and the natural environment. Also, people make decisions that guide the work of scientists and engineers.		✓	✓

Access to Engineering byDesign™

The EbD™ curriculum materials are available through the International Technology and Engineering Education Association (www.iteea.org). However, schools can become a part of the EbD™ school network to access the full benefits of the entire EbD™ program and learning community. These benefits include the following:

- Online access to the curriculum and the latest updates
- Exclusive access to ebDonline™ to converse with online facilitators and teachers around the country who are also implementing the same courses
- Online assessments for the students in their classes—access to real-time student performance data

To become an EbD-Network™ school, you can download and complete a network agreement at www.iteea.org. Additionally, EbD™ has created a consortium of states to serve as leaders in collaborating for higher quality education. Any schools within a consortium state are provided with free access to the EbD™ program. The leaders in these states work together to create consistency in the advancement of STEM education. The state leaders implement the EbD™ curriculum in their school systems and together evaluate student achievement to make informed decisions in enhancing technological and engineering literacy for all through an integrative STEM study. These state members develop the necessary professional growth opportunities for teachers and propose any

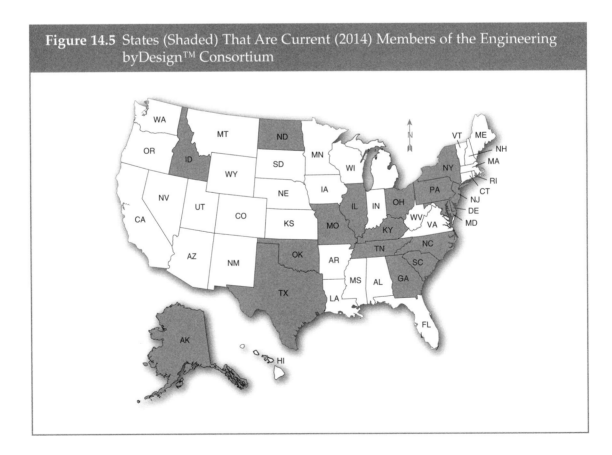

Figure 14.5 States (Shaded) That Are Current (2014) Members of the Engineering byDesign™ Consortium

needed changes to the curricula. With the increase of states in the consortium, state decisions can become a powerful tool in shaping the future of education and furthering students' technological and engineering literacy. Figure 14.5 illustrates the current consortium of states for EbD™.

Online Curriculum and Assessment Tools

As a teacher, one is always in search of the "perfect" curriculum tool that has the assessments built in. There are many models for this, and EbD™ has made its entry into the fray with a MediaRichEdition (MRe™) and the StandardEdition (SE™). These two platforms provide teachers with a level of content and support depending on the needs of the school. The MRe™ is an integral part of the EbD-Portal™ and includes a dynamically updated web-based curriculum guide as well as the online assessment tools (pre- and posttests) and the online learning community known as EbDonline™. Only EbD-Network™ schools are eligible for this level.

The Network schools are able to use the online assessment tools and receive instantaneous feedback in order to made decisions about content that will need to be covered to ensure student understanding of the concepts in each course. Information about the Network can be found at http://www.iteea.org/EbD/Resources/EbDresources.htm.

The SE™ version of the EbD™ guides provides all the same standards-based materials on a CD for use on standalone computers that do not have Internet access. They do not contain the online assessments nor the online learning community.

The EbD-Network™ schools and consortium states have access to the curriculum through the EbD-Portal™. The EbD-Portal™ is a cloud-based solution for providing curriculum, assessment, and professional development. Through the portal, teachers can access the dynamic course curriculum and EbDonline™ for ongoing professional development. Additionally, teachers can assign and mange student assessments through the portal to make data-driven decisions about their instruction.

Conclusion

At the time of this writing (May 2014), there are more than 600 EbD-Network™ schools, 1500 teachers, and more than 53,000 students taking pre- and postassessments as part of the program. EbD™ has grown at an average of 35% per year since 2008. With the introduction of the elementary EbD-TEEMS™, and as more states sign on, these numbers are expected to grow.

For those of us who have taught middle school, we know that content is just one thing in a middle schooler's life. They are struggling to gain acceptance into adulthood and can either identify with what a teacher has to offer or be turned off entirely. The EbD™ middle school program helps students bridge the gap by learning about the world around them, so that learning is relevant to the students' personal interests. The quote below, from a sixth-grade student whose comments were published in a local newspaper, sums up what many middle school students experience when their teachers implement the EbD™ curriculum:

The next thing we learned about was the engineering design process of input (the problem), process (how you get to your solution), output (the solution), and feedback (how well it works). We also learned about journaling and scale drawings as part of this lesson. Then, to put it all together, we had to create a solution to make a pencil that we couldn't lose. Now we are learning about transportation subsystems and working on a project to create a vehicle that can be propelled by wind across ice. This helps us apply our knowledge of control, guidance, structure, support, suspension, and propulsion as well as our knowledge of the Engineering Design Process. Tech Ed is one of my favorite subjects. If you're going to take it, look forward to it!

— sent to us by Ruth Akers, EbD™, Teacher, MD

References

Bybee, R. W. (1997). *Achieving scientific literacy: From purposes to practices.* Portsmouth, NH: Heinemann.

Bybee, R. W., & Landes, N. M. (1990). Science for life & living: An elementary school science program from Biological Sciences Curriculum Study. *American Biology Teacher, 52*(2), 92–98.

Hargrove, T., & Nesbit, C. (2003). What are science notebooks? Retrieved December 12, 2011, from ERIC Clearinghouse for Science Mathematics and Environmental Education.

International Technology Education Association (ITEA). (1996). *Technology for all Americans: A rationale and structure for the study of technology.* Reston, VA: Author.

International Technology Education Association (ITEA). (2000, 2005, 2007). *Standards for technological literacy: Content for the study of technology.* Reston, VA: Author.

International Technology Education Association (ITEA). (2003). *Advancing excellence in technological literacy: Student assessment, professional development, and program standards.* Reston, VA: Author.

International Technology and Engineering Educators Association. (2013). *Engineering byDesign: A national standards-based solution for the delivery and implementation of science, technology, engineering & mathematics* [Program flyer]. Retrieved September 19, 2013, from www.engineeringbydesign.org.

National Governors Association Center for Best Practices and Council of Chief State School Officers (NGA and CCSSO). (2010). *Common core state standards.* Washington, DC: Author.

National Research Council (NRC). (2012). *A framework for K–12 science education: Practices, crosscutting concepts, and core ideas.* Washington, DC: National Academies Press.

NGSS Lead States. (2013a). *Next generation science standards: For states, by states. Volume 1: The standards.* Washington, DC: National Academies Press.

NGSS Lead States. (2013b). *Next generation science standards: For states, by states. Volume 2: Appendices.* Washington, DC: National Academies Press.

Sea Grant Alaska. (2012). Science notebooks. Alaska Seas and Rivers Curriculum. Retrieved December 16, 2012, from http://seagrant.uaf.edu/marine-ed/curriculum/science-notebooks.html.

Wiggins, G., & McTighe, J. (1998). *Understanding by design.* Alexandria, VA: ASCD.

Index

A SAGE Company

Corwin is committed to improving education for all learners by publishing books and other professional development resources for those serving the field of PreK–12 education. By providing practical, hands-on materials, Corwin continues to carry out the promise of its motto: **"Helping Educators Do Their Work Better."**